Best Knock-Knock Book Ever

Charles Keller

Illustrated by Jeff Sinclair

Sterling Publishing Co., Inc.

New York

To Gabriel and Bowen

I would like to acknowledge the help of Stephen Blance, Marcus Bocchino, Rhoda Crispell, and Brenda Gordon

10   9   8   7   6   5   4   3   2   1

Published by Sterling Publishing Company, Inc.
387 Park Avenue South, New York, N.Y. 10016
© 2000 by Charles Keller
Distributed in Canada by Sterling Publishing
$^{c}/_{0}$ Canadian Manda Group, One Atlantic Avenue, Suite 105
Toronto, Ontario, Canada M6K 3E7
Distributed in Great Britain and Europe by Chris Lloyd
463 Ashley Road, Parkstone, Poole, Dorset, BH14 0AX, England
Distributed in Australia by Capricorn Link (Australia) Pty Ltd.
P.O. Box 6651, Baulkham Hills, Business Centre, NSW 2153, Australia
Manufactured in the United States of America

ISBN 0-8069-7174-6

Contents

Knock-knock.
Who's there?
Aaron.
Aaron who?
Aaron all the way home.

Knock-knock.
Who's there?
Abbot.
Abbot who?
Abbot time we eat, isn't it?

Knock-knock.
Who's there?
Abe Lincoln.
Abe Lincoln who?
Abe Lincoln break in the strongest chain.

Knock-knock.
  Who's there?
A.C.
  A.C. who?
A.C. come and A.C. go.

Knock-knock.
  Who's there?
Acme.
  Acme who?
If you acme I'll tell you.

Knock-knock.
  Who's there?
Adam.
  Adam who?
Adam up and give me the bill.

Knock-knock.
  Who's there?
Adore.
  Adore who?
Adore is between us.

Knock-knock.
  Who's there?
A.E.
  A.E. who?
A.E. I owe you.

Knock-knock.
Who's there?
Aikido.
Aikido who?
Aikido you not.

Knock-knock.
Who's there?
Alaska.
Alaska who?
Alaska and you ask him.

Knock-knock.
Who's there?
Alex.
Alex who?
Alex plain later.

Knock-knock.
Who's there?
Alfreda.
Alfreda who?
Alfreda the dark.

Knock-knock.
Who's there?
Amarillo.
Amarillo who?
Amarillo-fashioned girl.

Knock-knock.
Who's there?
Amen.
Amen who?
Amen hot water again.

Knock-knock.
Who's there?
Amnesia.
Amnesia who?
Oh, you got it too.

Knock-knock.
Who's there?
Andy.
Andy who?
Andy all lived happily ever after.

Knock-knock.
Who's there?
Andy.
Andy who?
Andy music goes on and on.

Knock-knock.
Who's there?
Anita.
Anita who?
Anita you like Anita hole in the head.

Knock-knock.
Who's there?
Anita.
Anita who?
Anita ride into town.

Knock-knock.
Who's there?
Anvil.
Anvil who?
Anvil you be coming too?

Knock-knock.
Who's there?
Apricot.
Apricot who?
Apricot my key, open up.

Knock-knock.
Who's there?
A quorum.
A quorum who?
A quorum is where I keep my fish.

Knock-knock.
Who's there?
Arizona.
Arizona who?
Arizona room for one of us in this town.

Knock-knock.
Who's there?
Arm.
Arm who?
Arm always chasing rainbows.

Knock-knock.
Who's there?
Armstrong.
Armstrong who?
Armstrong as an ox.

Knock-knock.
Who's there?
Ash.
Ash who?
Bless you.

Knock-knock.
Who's there?
Asparagus.
Asparagus who?
Asparagus the argument, we don't want to hear it.

Knock-knock.
Who's there?
Astor.
Astor who?
Astor what her name is.

Knock-knock.
Who's there?
Atlas.
Atlas who?
Atlas I'm here.

Knock-knock.
Who's there?
Avenue.
Avenue who?
Avenue heard this joke before?

Knock-knock.
Who's there?
Babylon.
Babylon who?
Babylon if you must.

Knock-knock.
Who's there?
Bella.
Bella who?
Bella the ball.

Knock-knock.
Who's there?
Ben and Don.
Ben and Don who?
Ben there, Don that.

Knock-knock.
Who's there?
Bernie D.
Bernie D who?
Bernie D candles at both ends.

Knock-knock.
Who's there?
Bertha.
Bertha who?
Bertha the blues.

Knock-knock.
Who's there:
Bette.
Bette who?
Bette you can't guess my name.

Knock-knock.
Who's there?
Blank.
Blank who?
You're welcome.

Knock-knock.
Who's there?
Blast.
Blast who?
Blast, but not least.

Knock-knock.
Who's there?
Bolivia.
Bolivia who?
Bolivia me!

Knock-knock.
Who's there?
Booty.
Booty who?
Booty is only skin deep.

Knock-knock.
Who's there?
Button.
Button who?
Button into what's not your business.

Knock-knock.
Who's there?
Cameron.
Cameron who?
Cameron over here.

Knock-knock.
Who's there?
Candace.
Candace who.
Candace door be opened?

Knock-knock.
Who's there?
Canoe.
Canoe who?
Canoe help me with my homework?

Knock-knock.
Who's there?
Carlo.
Carlo who?
Carlo on gas.

Knock-knock.
Who's there?
Casino.
Casino who?
Casino evil.

Knock-knock.
Who's there?
Castanet.
Castanet who?
Castanet in the water to catch fish.

Knock-knock.
Who's there?
C.D.
C.D. who?
C.D. forest for the trees.

Knock-knock.
Who's there?
Censure.
Censure who?
Censure letters by first class mail.

Knock-knock.
Who's there?
Cereal.
Cereal who?
Cereal McCoy.

Knock-knock.
Who's there?
Chantelle.
Chantelle who?
Chantelle you anything.

Knock-knock.
Who's there?
Checker.
Checker who?
Checker out.

Knock-knock.
Who's there?
Cheese.
Cheese who?
Cheese funny that way.

Knock-knock.
Who's there?
Cindy.
Cindy who?
Cindy movie, read the book.

Knock-knock.
   Who's there?
Clancy.
   Clancy who?
Clancy where I'm going.

Knock-knock.
   Who's there?
Coma.
   Coma who?
Coma your hair.

Knock-knock.
   Who's there?
Conan.
   Conan who?
Conan the cob.

Knock-knock.
Who's there?
Conscience stricken.
Conscience stricken who?
Don't conscience stricken before they hatch.

Knock-knock.
Who's there?
Cows.
Cows who?
No, cows moo.

Knock-knock.
Who's there?
Crate.
Crate who?
Crate to be here.

Knock-knock.
Who's there?
Crepes.
Crepes who?
Crepes of Wrath.

Knock-knock.
Who's there?
Crimea.
Crimea who?
"Crimea River."

Knock-knock.
Who's there?
Cybil.
Cybil who?
Cybil War.

Knock-knock.
Who's there?
Cypress.
Cypress who?
Cypress your suit.

Knock-knock.
Who's there?
Czar.
Czar who?
Czar she blows!

Knock-knock.
Who's there?
Dakota.
Dakota who?
Dakota fits fine, the pants are too long.

Knock-knock.
Who's there?
Darby.
Darby who?
Darby stung me.

Knock-knock.
Who's there?
Darrel.
Darrel who?
Darrel never be another you.

Knock-knock.
Who's there?
Darwin.
Darwin who?
Darwin young man on the flying trapeze.

Knock-knock.
Who's there?
Dawn.
Dawn who?
Dawn bite off more than you can chew.

Knock-knock.
Who's there?
Debt.
Debt who?
Debt men tell no tales.

Knock-knock.
Who's there?
Dee.
Dee who?
Dee joke's on me.

Knock-knock.
Who's there?
Defense.
Defense who?
Defense keeps the dog in.

Knock-knock.
  Who's there?
Demure.
  Demure who?
Demure you get, Demure you want.

Knock-knock.
  Who's there?
Demure.
  Demure who?
Demure the merrier.

Knock-knock.
  Who's there?
Dennis.
  Dennis who?
Dennis this rain going to stop?

Knock-knock.
  Who's there?
Denver.
  Denver who?
Denver in the world are we?

Knock-knock.
  Who's there?
Depend.
  Depend who?
Depend is mightier than the sword.

Knock-knock.
Who's there?
Derby.
Derby who?
Derby ghosts in that haunted house.

Knock-knock.
Who's there?
Diesel.
Diesel who?
Diesel be your last chance.

Knock-knock.
Who's there?
Dina.
Dina who?
Dina at eight.

Knock-knock.
  Who's there?
Dinosaur.
  Dinosaur who?
Dinosaur at you—you burnt the toast.

Knock-knock.
  Who's there?
Divide.
  Divide who?
Divide world of sports.

Knock-knock.
  Who's there?
Dobie.
  Dobie who?
Dobie cruel to animals.

Knock-knock.
Who's there?
Dole.
Dole who?
Dole truth and nothing but the truth.

Knock-knock.
Who's there?
Don and Greta.
Don and Greta who?
Don and Greta round much any more.

Knock-knock.
Who's there?
Don.
Don who?
Don want to tell you my name.

Knock-knock.
Who's there?
Doughnut.
Doughnut who?
Doughnut thing till you hear from me.

Knock-knock.
Who's there?
Duane.
Duane who?
Duane the bathtub, rubber ducky drowning.

Knock-knock.
  Who's there?
Duncan.
  Duncan who?
Duncan your doughnut again?

Knock-knock.
  Who's there?
Dustin.
  Dustin who?
Dustin furniture with polish.

Knock-knock.
  Who's there?
Dwight.
  Dwight who?
Dwight as rain.

Knock-knock.
Who's there?
Eamon.
Eamon who?
Eamon the mood for love.

Knock-knock.
Who's there?
Eben.
Eben who?
Eben a good girl.

Knock-knock.
Who's there?
Eddy.
Eddy who?
Eddy body got a tissue? I've got a cold.

Knock-knock.
Who's there?
Effie.
Effie who?
"Effie Thing's Coming Up Roses."

Knock-knock.
Who's there?
Eggs.
Eggs who?
Eggs marks the spot.

Knock-knock.
Who's there?
Egos.
Egos who?
Egos wherever he wants to.

Knock-knock.
Who's there?
Eisenhower.
Eisenhower who?
Eisenhower late for school.

Knock-knock.
Who's there?
Elise.
Elise who?
Elise signed by a tenant.

Knock-knock.
Who's there?
Eliza.
Eliza who?
Eliza lot, so watch your step.

Knock-knock.
Who's there?
Ella Vance.
Ella Vance who?
Ella Vance never forget.

Knock-knock.
Who's there?
Erie.
Erie who?
Erie is, right on time.

Knock-knock.
Who's there?
Eschew.
Eschew who?
Eschew goes on your foot.

Knock-knock.
Who's there?
Estelle.
Estelle who?
Estelle waiting for you to open the door.

Knock-knock.
Who's there?
Etch.
Etch who?
Bless you.

Knock-knock.
Who's there?
Ethan.
Ethan who?
Ethan everything in sight.

Knock-knock.
Who's there?
Eugenes.
Eugenes who?
Eugenes need washing.

Knock-knock.
Who's there?
Europa.
Europa who?
Europa steer and I'll watch.

Knock-knock.
Who's there?
Ewer.
Ewer who?
Ewer getting sleepy.

Knock-knock.
Who's there?
Eyelet.
Eyelet who?
Eyelet you in.

Knock-knock.
Who's there?
Falsetto.
Falsetto who?
Falsetto teeth.

Knock-knock.
Who's there?
Fender.
Fender who?
Fender moon comes over the mountain.

Knock-knock.
Who's there?
Ferdinand.
Ferdinand who?
Ferdinand is worth two in the bush.

Knock-knock.
Who's there?
Flea.
Flea who?
"Flea, fie, foh, fum."

Knock-knock.
Who's there?
Florist.
Florist who?
Florist the opposite of ceiling.

Knock-knock.
Who's there?
Flossie.
Flossie who?
Flossie your teeth.

Knock-knock.
Who's there?
Forest.
Forest who?
Forest the eye can see.

Knock-knock.
Who's there?
Fortification.
Fortification who?
Fortification I go to the seashore.

Knock-knock.
  Who's there?
Francine.
  Francine who?
Francine it all.

Knock-knock.
  Who's there?
Frieda.
  Frieda who?
"Who's a Frieda the Big Bad Wolf?"

Knock-knock.
  Who's there?
Fritz.
  Fritz who?
"Fritz a Wonderful Life."

Knock-knock.
  Who's there?
Garter.
  Garter who?
Garter date with an angel.

Knock-knock.
  Who's there?
Gary.
  Gary who?
Gary the package for me.

Knock-knock.
  Who's there?
Gas.
  Gas who?
"Gas Who's Coming to Dinner."

Knock-knock.
Who's there?
G.I.
G.I. who?
G.I. don't know.

Knock-knock.
Who's there?
Gladwin.
Gladwin who?
Gladwin you're leaving.

Knock-knock.
Who's there?
Glove.
Glove who?
"Glove is a Many-Splendored Thing."

Knock-knock.
Who's there?
Goatee.
Goatee who?
Goatee off—the other golfers are waiting.

Knock-knock.
Who's there?
Goosie.
Goosie who?
Goosie who's at the door.

Knock-knock.
Who's there?
Gouda.
Gouda who?
Gouda see you again.

Knock-knock.
Who's there?
Gruesome.
Gruesome who?
Gruesome tomatoes in my garden.

Knock-knock.
Who's there?
Gwen.
Gwen who?
Gwen will I see you again?

Knock-knock.
  Who's there?
Hair combs.
  Hair combs who?
Hair combs the bride.

Knock-knock.
  Who's there?
Half.
  Half who?
Half I got a girl for you.

Knock-knock.
  Who's there?
Hall.
  Hall who?
"Hall the king's horses and hall the king's men."

Knock-knock.
Who's there?
Hallow.
Hallow who?
Hallow down there.

Knock-knock.
Who's there?
Hannibal.
Hannibal who?
Hannibal in a china shop.

Knock-knock.
Who's there?
Hans.
Hans who?
Hans off my computer.

Knock-knock.
Who's there?
Harpy.
Harpy who?
Harpy to see you again.

Knock-knock.
Who's there?
Harris.
Harris who?
"Harris looking at you, kid."

Knock-knock.
Who's there?
Harry.
Harry who?
Harry up, I'm starving.

Knock-knock.
Who's there?
Harvey.
Harvey who?
Harvey going to stop meeting like this?

Knock-knock.
Who's there?
Harvey Gotti.
Harvey Gotti who?
Harvey Gotti wait here all night?

Knock-knock.
Who's there?
Heaven.
Heaven who?
Heaven you heard enough knock-knock jokes?

Knock-knock.
Who's there?
Hector.
Hector who?
"Hector halls with boughs of holly."

Knock-knock.
  Who's there?
Hedda.
  Hedda who?
Hedda off at the pass.

Knock-knock.
  Who's there?
Highway cop.
  Highway cop who?
Highway cop at seven every morning.

Knock-knock.
  Who's there?
Hippie.
  Hippie who?
Hippie birthday to you.

Knock-knock.
Who's there?
Honor.
Honor who?
"Honor clear day you can see forever."

Knock-knock.
Who's there?
Hoover.
Hoover who?
Hoover you expecting?

Knock-knock.
Who's there?
Horace.
Horace who?
Horace and buggy.

Knock-knock.
Who's there?
House.
House who?
House business?

Knock-knock.
Who's there?
Hugh.
Hugh who?
Hugh who yourself.

Knock-knock.
Who's there?
Humphrey.
Humphrey who?
Humphrey ever blowing bubbles.

Knock-knock.
Who's there?
Hunger.
Hunger who?
Hunger wash out to dry.

Knock-knock.
Who's there?
Huron.
Huron who?
Huron time for once.

Knock-knock.
Who's there?
Ice water.
Ice water who?
Ice water fly with my fly swatter.

Knock-knock.
Who's there?
Ida.
Ida who?
Ida who potato.

Knock-knock.
Who's there?
Imus.
Imus who?
Imus get in out of the rain.

Knock-knock.
Who's there?
India.
India who?
India cool, cool of the evening.

Knock-knock.
Who's there?
Indy.
Indy who?
Indy mood.

Knock-knock.
Who's there?
Iraq.
Iraq who?
Iraq my brain but couldn't get the answer.

Knock-knock.
Who's there?
Irish.
Irish who?
Irish upon a star.

Knock-knock.
　Who's there?
Irma.
　Irma who?
Irma going to sit right down and write myself a
　letter.

Knock-knock.
　Who's there?
Iron.
　Iron who?
Iron joy being a girl.

Knock-knock.
　Who's there?
Isidore.
　Isidore who?
Isidore unlocked?

Knock-knock.
Who's there?
Israel.
Israel who?
Israel or fake?

Knock-knock.
Who's there?
Issue.
Issue who?
Issue ready to go?

Knock-knock.
Who's there?
Itzhak.
Itzhak who?
"Itzhak small world after all."

Knock-knock.
Who's there?
Ivan.
Ivan who?
Ivan, you lose.

Knock-knock.
Who's there?
Jackson.
Jackson who?
Jackson the box.

Knock-knock.
Who's there?
Jaws.
Jaws who?
Jaws till the well runs dry.

Knock-knock.
Who's there?
Jenny.
Jenny who?
Jenny a hearing aid? I've been knocking for five
minutes.

Knock-knock.
Who's there?
Jenny.
Jenny who?
Jenny body home?

Knock-knock.
Who's there?
Jess.
Jess who?
Jess in time.

Knock-knock.
Who's there?
Jewel.
Jewel who?
Jewel be sorry.

Knock-knock.
Who's there?
Jimmy.
Jimmy who?
Jimmy liberty or Jimmy death.

Knock-knock.
Who's there?
Josie.
Josie who?
Josie who's at the door.

Knock-knock.
Who's there?
Jules.
Jules who?
Jules are in the safe.

Knock-knock.
Who's there?
Juliet.
Juliet who?
Juliet the cat out of the bag.

Knock-knock.
Who's there?
Junior.
Junior who?
Junior flowers will come up.

Knock-knock.
  Who's there?
Juno.
  Juno who?
I don't know, Juno?

Knock-knock.
  Who's there?
Jupiter.
  Jupiter who?
Jupiter note on my door?

Knock-knock.
  Who's there?
Justice.
  Justice who?
Justice I got home the phone rang.

Knock-knock.
  Who's there?
Justin.
  Justin who?
"Justin time, I found you Justin time."

Knock-knock.
Who's there?
Karaoke.
Karaoke who?
Karaoke or not okay?

Knock-knock.
Who's there?
Katmandu.
Katmandu who?
Katmandu what Catwoman wants.

Knock-knock.
Who's there?
Kermit.
Kermit who?
Kermit me to introduce myself.

Knock-knock.
Who's there?
Ketchup.
Ketchup who?
Ketchup with her before she gets away.

Knock-knock.
Who's there?
Kip.
Kip who?
Kip your sunny side up.

Knock-knock.
Who's there?
Knoxville.
Knoxville who?
Knoxville get you an answer if you wait long enough.

Knock-knock.
Who's there?
Koala-T.
Koala-T who?
Koala-T knock-knocks are hard to find.

Knock-knock.
Who's there?
Kokomo.
Kokomo who?
Kokomo food—I'm hungry.

Knock-knock.
Who's there?
Land.
Land who?
It's "land-ho," not "land who."

Knock-knock.
Who's there?
Levin.
Levin who?
"Levin on a jet plane."

Knock-knock.
Who's there?
Leopold.
Leopold who?
Leopold the class and everyone wants a new teacher.

Knock-knock.
Who's there?
Letter.
Letter who?
Letter smile be your umbrella.

Knock-knock.
Who's there?
Lice.
Lice who?
Lice out by ten o'clock.

Knock-knock.
Who's there?
Lilac.
Lilac who?
Lilac that and you'll get punished.

Knock-knock.
Who's there?
Liv.
Liv who?
Liv no stone unturned.

Knock-knock.
Who's there?
Liver.
Liver who?
Liver round here?

Knock-knock.
Who's there?
Macon.
Macon who?
"Macon a list, checking it twice."

Knock-knock.
Who's there?
Macon.
Macon who?
Macon whoopie.

Knock-knock.
Who's there?
Major.
Major who?
Major bed, now lie in it.

Knock-knock.
Who's there?
Mandalay.
Mandalay who?
Mandalay the kitchen tiles.

Knock-knock.
Who's there?
Massachusetts.
Massachusetts who?
Massachusetts is what you hear when a train blows
its whistle.

Knock-knock.
Who's there?
Mayonnaise.
Mayonnaise who?
"Mayonnaise be merry and bright..."

Knock-knock.
Who's there?
Melissa.
Melissa who?
Melissa longer than your list.

Knock-knock.
Who's there?
Me.
Me who?
Meow.

Knock-knock.
Who's there?
Menu.
Menu who?
Menu stay here, women over there.

Knock-knock.
Who's there?
Michigan.
Michigan who?
"Michigan," said the batter after the third strike.

Knock-knock.
Who's there?
Midas.
Midas who?
Midas well open up, I'm not going away.

Knock-knock.
Who's there?
Mira.
Mira who?
Mira, Mira, on the wall.

Knock-knock.
Who's there?
Monet.
Monet who?
Monet burns a hole in my pocket.

Knock-knock.
Who's there?
Moose.
Moose who?
Moose beautiful girl in the world.

Knock-knock.
Who's there?
Mustard.
Mustard who?
Mustard been a beautiful baby.

Knock-knock.
Who's there?
Nathan.
Nathan who?
Nathan to lose.

Knock-knock.
Who's there?
Nestor.
Nestor who?
Nestor lives my neighbor.

Knock-knock.
Who's there?
Newark.
Newark who?
Newark for Noah.

Knock-knock.
Who's there?
Newark.
Newark who?
Newark keeps piling up.

Knock-knock.
Who's there?
Noggin.
Noggin who?
Noggin at your door.

Knock-knock.
Who's there?
Notify.
Notify who?
Notify can help it.

Knock-knock.
Who's there?
Nova.
Nova who?
Nova look back.

Knock-knock.
Who's there?
O. A.
O. A. who?
"O. A. down South in Dixie."

Knock-knock.
Who's there?
Occult.
Occult who?
Occult in my nose.

Knock-knock.
Who's there?
Ocelot.
Ocelot who?
Ocelot of money for that.

Knock-knock.
Who's there?
Ohio.
Ohio who?
Ohio than the highest mountain.

Knock-knock.
Who's there?
Oil well.
Oil well who?
Oil well that ends well.

Knock-knock.
Who's there?
Oklahoma.
Oklahoma who?
Oklahoma and wash your face.

Knock-knock.
Who's there?
Olaf.
Olaf who?
"Olaf My Heart in San Francisco."

Knock-knock.
Who's there?
One door.
One door who?
One door where you are tonight.

Knock-knock.
Who's there?
Opel.
Opel who?
Opel of mine.

Knock-knock.
Who's there?
Orange shoe.
Orange shoe who?
Orange shoe going to let me in?

Knock-knock.
Who's there?
Oregon.
Oregon who?
Oregon and I'm not coming back.

Knock-knock.
Who's there?
Orson.
Orson who?
Orson buggy—want a ride?

Knock-knock.
Who's there?
Osborne.
Osborne who?
Osborne in the hospital.

Knock-knock.
Who's there?
Osgood.
Osgood who?
Osgood as it gets.

Knock-knock.
Who's there?
Oslo.
Oslo who?
Oslo down, you're going too fast.

Knock-knock.
Who's there?
Oswego.
Oswego who?
"Oswego into the wild blue yonder."

Knock-knock.
Who's there?
Otter.
Otter who?
Otter apologize for these bad jokes.

Knock-knock.
Who's there?
O. Verdi.
O. Verdi who?
"O. Verdi Rainbow."

Knock-knock.
Who's there?
Owls.
Owls who?
You got it right this time.

Knock-knock.
Who's there?
Paddy.
Paddy who?
Paddy your own canoe.

Knock-knock.
Who's there?
Pakistan.
Pakistan who?
Pakistan lunch. He's working late.

Knock-knock.
Who's there?
Pasadena.
Pasadena who?
Stop when you Pasadena—I'm hungry.

Knock-knock.
Who's there?
Pasteurize.
Pasteurize who?
Pasteurize and over the gums, look out stomach,
here it comes.

Knock-knock.
Who's there?
Patella.
Patella who?
Patella story before bedtime.

Knock-knock.
Who's there?
Paula.
Paula who?
Paula few strings for me.

Knock-knock.
Who's there?
Pawtucket.
Pawtucket who?
I had a dollar, but Pawtucket.

Knock-knock.
Who's there?
Pay cents.
Pay cents who?
Pay cents is a virtue.

Knock-knock.
Who's there?
Peekaboo.
Peekaboo who?
Peekaboo live in glass houses shouldn't throw stones.

Knock-knock.
Who's there?
Peking.
Peking who?
Peking is not allowed.

Knock-knock.
Who's there?
Pembroke.
Pembroke who?
Pembroke, can I use yours?

Knock-knock.
Who's there?
Picture.
Picture who?
Picture favorite flowers.

Knock-knock.
Who's there?
Plate.
Plate who?
"Plate again, Sam."

Knock-knock.
Who's there?
Poker.
Poker who?
Poker Hontas.

Knock-knock.
Who's there?
Poland.
Poland who?
Poland or rich country?

Knock-knock.
Who's there?
Quaint.
Quaint who?
"Quaint nothing but a hound dog."

Knock-knock.
Who's there?
Quake.
Quake who?
Quake up, you sleepyhead.

Knock-knock.
Who's there?
Que Sarah.
Que Sarah who?
"Que Sarah, Sarah; whatever will be, will be."

Knock-knock.
Who's there?
Radio.
Radio who?
Radio not, here I come.

Knock-knock.
Who's there?
Randy and Vanna.
Randy and Vanna who?
Randy race and Vanna medal.

Knock-knock.
Who's there?
Raptor.
Raptor who?
Raptor presents before Christmas.

Knock-knock.
Who's there?
Rhoda.
Rhoda who?
Rhoda dendron.

Knock-knock.
Who's there?
Rich.
Rich who?
Rich way did he go?

Knock-knock.
Who's there?
Robin.
Robin who?
Robin you! Hand over your money!

Knock-knock.
Who's there?
Roger.
Roger who?
Roger. Over and out.

Knock-knock.
Who's there?
Rubber.
Rubber who?
Rubber the wrong way and she'll smack you.

THISSSSSSS KNOCK-KNOCK BOOK ISSSS SSOMETHING SSSPECIAL!!

Knock-knock.
Who's there?
Safari.
Safari who?
Safari so good.

Knock-knock.
Who's there?
Salome.
Salome who?
Salome on rye with mustard.

Knock-knock.
Who's there?
Sarah.
Sarah who?
Sarah doorbell around here? I'm tired of knocking.

Knock-knock.
Who's there?
Sarasota.
Sarasota who?
Sarasota in the fridge? I'm thirsty.

Knock-knock.
Who's there?
Sari.
Sari who?
Sari, wrong number.

Knock-knock.
Who's there?
Sauna.
Sauna who?
"Sauna clear day you can see forever."

Knock-knock.
Who's there?
Schenectady.
Schenectady who?
Schenectady plug to the socket.

Knock-knock.
Who's there?
Scissors.
Scissors who?
Scissors lovely way to spend the evening.

Knock-knock.
  Who's there?
Sedimentary.
  Sedimentary who?
Sedimentary, my dear Watson.

Knock-knock.
  Who's there?
Serbia.
  Serbia who?
Serbia yourself.

Knock-knock.
  Who's there?
Sew.
  Sew who?
Sew what else is new?

Knock-knock.
  Who's there?
Shirley.
  Shirley who?
Shirley you know my name.

Knock-knock.
  Who's there?
Simmer.
  Simmer who?
"Simmer time and the living is easy."

Knock-knock.
Who's there?
Singapore.
Singapore who?
Singapore song or a rich song.

Knock-knock.
Who's there?
Sizzle.
Sizzle who?
Sizzle be my shining hour.

Knock-knock.
Who's there?
Slater.
Slater who?
Slater than you think.

Knock-knock.

Who's there?

Snow.

Snow who?

Snow use using the doorbell, it's broken.

Knock-knock.

Who's there?

Stan.

Stan who?

Stan up and be counted.

Knock-knock.

Who's there?

Stark.

Stark who?

Stark in here, turn on the light.

Knock-knock.
Who's there?
Statue.
Statue who?
Statue in there?

Knock-knock.
Who's there?
Stephen.
Stephen who?
Stephen out with my baby.

Knock-knock.
Who's there?
Stephen.
Stephen who?
Stephen the gas.

Knock-knock.
Who's there?
Stu.
Stu who?
Stu darn hot.

Knock-knock.
Who's there?
Stu.
Stu who?
Stu late now.

Knock-knock.
Who's there?
Tanya.
Tanya who?
Tanya come out and play?

Knock-knock.
Who's there?
Tara.
Tara who?
"Tara-ra-boom-ti-ay."

Knock-knock.
Who's there?
Tarragon.
Tarragon who?
Tarragon with the wind.

Knock-knock.
Who's there?
Tarzan.
Tarzan who?
Tarzan feather 'em.

Knock-knock.
Who's there?
Taylor.
Taylor who?
Taylor I can't make it.

Knock-knock.
Who's there?
Thayer.
Thayer who?
Thayer sorry or I'm leaving.

Knock-knock.
Who's there?
Thee.
Thee who?
Thee old gray mare.

Knock-knock.
Who's there?
Theresa.
Theresa who?
Theresa crowd.

Knock-knock.
    Who's there?
Thistle.
    Thistle who?
Thistle teach you not to ask silly questions.

Knock-knock.
    Who's there?
Tissue.
    Tissue who?
Tissue were here.

Knock-knock.
    Who's there?
Titus.
    Titus who?
Titus a drum.

Knock-knock.
Who's there?
Tobacco.
Tobacco who?
Tobacco your car you have to put it in reverse.

Knock-knock.
Who's there?
Toby.
Toby who?
Toby continued.

Knock-knock.
Who's there?
Tobias.
Tobias who?
Tobias you need a lot of money.

Knock-knock.
Who's there?
Toothache.
Toothache who?
Toothache the high road and I'll take the low road.

Knock-knock.
Who's there?
T. Rex.
T. Rex who?
T. Rex your appetite more than coffee.

Knock-knock.
  Who's there?
Turnip.
  Turnip who?
Turnip the volume. I can't hear.

Knock-knock.
  Who's there?
Twain.
  Twain who?
Twain on track nine.

Knock-knock.
  Who's there?
Typhoid.
  Typhoid who?
Typhoid you were looking for me.

Knock-knock.
Who's there?
Uma.
Uma who?
"Uma Darling Clementine."

Knock-knock.
Who's there?
Upton.
Upton who?
Upton Sesame.

Knock-knock.
Who's there?
U-turn.
U-turn who?
U-turn my legs to jelly.

Knock-knock.
Who's there?
Vanna.
Vanna who?
Vanna go to the movies?

Knock-knock.
Who's there?
Verdi.
Verdi who?
Verdi wave goes, so goes the surfer.

Knock-knock.
Who's there?
Vi.
Vi who?
"Vi do fools fall in love?"

Knock-knock.
Who's there?
Waiter.
Waiter who?
"Waiter till the sun shines, Nellie."

Knock-knock.
Who's there?
Waiver.
Waiver who?
Waiver hands in the air.

Knock-knock.
Who's there?
Wanda.
Wanda who?
Wanda tell me the password? It's cold out here.

Knock-knock.
Who's there?
Wanda Witch.
Wanda Witch who?
Wanda Witch you a Merry Christmas.

Knock-knock.
Who's there?
Weevil.
Weevil who?
Weevil meet again.

Knock-knock.
Who's there?
Wiener.
Wiener who?
Wiener and still champion.

Knock-knock.
Who's there?
West Point.
West Point who?
West Point are you trying to make?

Knock-knock.
Who's there?
Wok.
Wok who?
Wok, don't run.

Knock-knock.
Who's there?
Woody.
Woody who?
Woody want me to say?

Knock-knock.
Who's there?
Woolly.
Woolly who?
Woolly win the race?

Knock-knock.
Who's there?
Wyatt.
Wyatt who?
Wyatt always pours when it rains?

Knock-knock.
Who's there?
Xena.
Xena who?
Xena picture in the paper.

Knock-knock.
Who's there?
Yale.
Yale who?
"Yale, Caesar."

Knock-knock.
Who's there?
Yawl.
Yawl who?
Yawl come back, you hear.

Knock-knock.
Who's there?
Yoda.
Yoda who?
Yoda smart one, you tell me.

Knock-knock.
Who's there?
Yoga.
Yoga who?
Yoga your way, I'll go mine.

Knock-knock.
Who's there?
Your sister.
Your sister who?
You mean you don't know me?

Knock-knock.
Who's there?
Yukon.
Yukon who?
Yukon win 'em all.

Knock-knock.
Who's there?
Zachery.
Zachery who?
Zachery what I want for Christmas.

Knock-knock.
Who's there?
Zeal.
Zeal who?
Zeal it with a kiss.

Knock-knock.
Who's there?
Zest.
Zest who?
Zest things in life are free.

Knock-knock.
Who's there?
Zinc.
Zinc who?
Zinc like the Titanic.

Knock-knock.
Who's there?
Zoophyte.
Zoophyte who?
Zoophyte anyone who bothers the animals.

Knock-knock.
Who's there?
Zymosis.
Zymosis who?
Zymosis come back with the Ten Commandments?

Knock-knock.
Who's there?
Zone.
Zone who?
Zone worst enemy.

Index

THE CHILDREN
OF DIVORCE

Youth, Family, and Culture Series

Chap Clark, series editor

The Youth, Family, and Culture series examines the broad categories involved in studying and caring for the needs of the young and is dedicated to the preparation and vocational strengthening of those who are committed to the spiritual development of adolescents.

THE CHILDREN
OF DIVORCE

THE LOSS
OF FAMILY
AS THE LOSS
OF BEING

ANDREW ROOT

Baker Academic

a division of Baker Publishing Group
Grand Rapids, Michigan

In memory of my teacher Ray S. Anderson,
who taught me how to think

© 2010 by Andrew Root

Published by Baker Academic
a division of Baker Publishing Group
P.O. Box 6287, Grand Rapids, MI 49516-6287
www.bakeracademic.com

Printed in the United States of America

Library of Congress Cataloging-in-Publication Data
Root, Andrew, 1974–
     The children of divorce : the loss of family as the loss of being / Andrew Root.
         p.   cm.
     Includes bibliographical references (p.   ) and index.
     ISBN 978-0-8010-3914-0 (pbk.)
     1. Divorce—Religious aspects—Christianity. 2. Divorce. 3. Loss (Psychology) in children—Religious aspects—Christianity. 4. Children of divorced parents—Psychology. I. Title.
     BT707.R66 2010
     261.8'3589—dc22   2010000043

Scripture is taken from the Revised Standard Version of the Bible, copyright 1952 [2nd edition, 1971] by the Division of Christian Education of the National Council of the Churches of Christ in the United States of America. Used by permission. All rights reserved.

10   11   12   13   14   15   16   7   6   5   4   3   2   1

In keeping with biblical principles of creation stewardship, Baker Publishing Group advocates the responsible use of our natural resources. As a member of the Green Press Initiative, our company uses recycled paper when possible. The text paper of this book is comprised of 30% post-consumer waste.

green
press
INITIATIVE

Contents

Series Preface

In many ways, youth ministry has come of age. No longer seen as "a stepping-stone to real ministry in the church," especially in North America, youth ministry is now seen as a viable career option. Over the last few decades a wide range of professional resources, conferences, periodicals, and books have been developed on this topic. Most Christian colleges and seminaries now offer a variety of courses—if not degree programs—in youth ministry. Youth ministry has all it needs to continue to push the church to care about and serve the needs of the young in God's name, except for one thing: we have a long way to go to develop a rich, broad, and diverse conversation that frames, defines, and grounds our missional call.

There is good news, of course. There is a professional organization, Association of Youth Ministry Educators, that sponsors an annual conference and publishes a solid emerging journal. Several thoughtful books have helped to shape the discipline's future. There are also now two major publishers who have academic lines dedicated to furthering the field of youth ministry. We have made great progress, but we must all work together to continue deepening our understanding of what youth ministry should be.

The purpose of Baker Academic's Youth, Family, and Culture series is to raise the level of dialogue concerning how we think about, teach, and live out youth ministry. As a branch of practical theology, academic youth ministry must move beyond a primarily skills-based focus to a theologically driven expression of a contextualized commitment

of the local church to a targeted population. James Fowler defines practical theology as "theological reflection and construction arising out of and giving guidance to a community of faith in the *praxis* of its mission. Practical theology is critical and constructive reflection leading to ongoing modification and development of the ways the church shapes its life to be in partnership with God's work in the world."[1] And as Scott Cormode reminds us, we must not shirk our calling, but "must strive to nurture leaders that are faithful. . . . Schools must prepare leaders to translate this faithfulness into effective action."[2] This is precisely what those of us who are called to engage the church in theological reflection of contemporary youth and family issues must do—develop a practical theology that takes seriously the reality of the context we are in, regardless of how and where it takes us. This is the future of youth and family ministry in the church.

Andrew Root's *The Children of Divorce* is the fourth book in the Youth, Family, and Culture series. In this deeply intimate, honest, and academically solid work, Dr. Root forces those who minister to kids to carefully examine the lifelong effects divorce has on children of all ages and backgrounds. As a practical theologian, he weaves together multiple strands of thought, theory, and practice into a tapestry that reminds us how serious our calling is, and how fragile those we serve actually are, especially with those young people whose lives have been ripped apart by the brokenness of human frailty. Like the other books in this series, *The Children of Divorce* provides a vital and accessible tool for youthworkers that will be a significant resource for years to come.

Chap Clark
Fuller Theological Seminary
January 2010

Preface

I could see the pain spilling from his eyes; his disposition was heavy, and his sentences slow as he discussed his children. He would be my first friend with kids to go through a divorce. I have had countless friends whose parents had divorced, who were the children of divorce (and in every way this book is for them), but he would be the first of my friends to go through divorce as a parent. As he talked of his children his words poured out from the gash in his broken heart. This whole experience was more painful than he could bear. As I sat next to him, listening intently, his pain drawing me to his person, every cell in me wanted to say it; every fiber wanted to say the same phrase every divorcing parent and his or her friends say to mitigate their severe heartbreak. I could feel the words coming to my lips; I could feel my lips curving to release the words. I wanted so badly, sitting in the heavy shadow of his pain, to say, "Your kids will be fine. Kids are resilient; as long as you stay around and tell them you love them, they will be fine. Don't worry about it."

These words tend to be the mantra we give parents, and I now understood why. Divorce is deeply painful and no one wants to face the fact that this event, this event that in so many ways you are responsible for, is hurting, and will continue to hurt, the children you so deeply love. *But it does!* This book you are holding in your hands makes an argument that some will find difficult; it argues that divorce leaves an indelible mark on children, and such a mark that it strikes those who experience it (myself included) at an ontological level, at the level of

their being. This book forces us to wrestle with the deepest, rawest, most unsettling questions of those experiencing the divorce of their parents, the question so deep it is often cognitively oppressed: Can a person *be* at all, now that those who are responsible in their union for creating that person are no longer together? If I am the product of these two people, what does it mean for my very being if these two people have severed and voided their union to each other?

I do understand that those, like my friend, who are facing a future with a broken marriage in it may find themselves threatened by this book. I wish not—I'll say it again—*I wish not* to further grieve or beat up anyone (my own parents included). But I do think we are missing something essential in our national (and ecclesial) discussion on family and divorce. Therefore, I offer you this book in fear and trembling. And I can promise you that within its pages, I do not rely on anecdotal feelings, but rather have done the hard work of placing multiple disciplines and perspectives into conversation. I have included my own experience, but never without delving deeply into disciplines of thought. What is unique about this project is not only that it provides another, new, angle with which to look at the phenomenon of divorce, but that it does so by placing social theory, psychology, and theology in conversation, blending them all with the real experience of children of divorce.

I owe thanks to many people for the appearance of this project. Rodney Clapp has been a superb editor to work with. It is comforting to an author to know that his or her editor not only believes in the project but also has the intelligence, expertise, and compassion to keep you from making grave mistakes and overstatement. I feel blessed to have Rodney overseeing this thesis.

I also owe great thanks to Luther Seminary for valuing the needed space to work on this project, as well as others. The final work on this manuscript was done on a generous writing leave given by the seminary. This book, alongside my first two books, in many ways fulfills the title of the position I was called to at Luther: assistant professor of youth and family ministry. This book is, at its core, about family and the painful reality of divorce.

Luther Seminary provided not only the time to do this work, but also wonderful colleagues and students who were so willing to engage

it. I owe a great thanks to my two dear friends and colleagues Theresa Latini and Amy Marga, for reading and commenting on the whole manuscript. Their insight was invaluable. One of my very gifted students, Megan Koepnick, was also kind enough to read the full manuscript, providing helpful feedback on its contents and ways to make it more readable.

My greatest thanks and love go to my family: first to Owen and Maisy, my two greatest treasures, and finally to my wife, Kara, whose story also shows up in these pages. Our marriage began in the hell of the death of both of our parents' marriages, but in that hell, as a witness to our Lord, we have made a life of great beauty and wonder. Here is to many, many more decades . . .

Introduction

I was sitting in a window seat of a Northwest flight from Los Angeles to Minneapolis, my anxiety higher than the plane's altitude. As we flew over the deserts of Nevada, my eyes focusing on the mountains set against the backdrop of a pink-hued sky, I thought to myself, "I hope this plane goes down." The thought of the plane hurtling toward the desert floor and crashing into a ball of fire was more appealing than what awaited me in Minneapolis.

The plane didn't crash. But as I trudged toward the baggage claim, fear gripped me. I found myself noticing emergency exits, wondering what would happen if I ran through one, contemplating how I could sneak onto a flight to Beijing. I got on the escalator down to baggage claim, knowing it would deliver me to my nightmare. As the escalator dropped me on the baggage claim floor and I walked closer, I could feel every muscle in my neck and back tighten. My heart started to race, my legs felt heavy, my mouth went dry. And then my nightmare piped out, "Welcome home! We're so glad to see you." It was my parents.

The nightmare had actually started six months earlier.

The last time that I had been in Minneapolis had been Christmas. During the two weeks home, my girlfriend and I, two graduate students, decided that we would get married. We excitedly told both of our families, then received words of encouragement and good wishes. Flying back to Los Angeles, passing over the same mountains I would cross with dread months later, I eagerly anticipated my future. When the automatic exit doors slid open at the LAX terminal, and the warm Southern California air hit my body, I felt whole, happy, and hopeful.

But on a cold, rainy LA night this all changed. I returned home from a late class and found a frantic voicemail from my fiancée. I raced to her apartment, where she was curled on her bed, sobbing. Her mother had caught her father, who had been her hero, with inappropriate and illicit material on his computer, including love letters to and from another woman. Just as our own was months from starting, her parents' marriage was over.

The grief consumed our lives. The loss of her parents' marriage seemed to be affecting my fiancée from the inside out. At twenty-three, Kara found herself questioning who she was and where she belonged. These were not simply questions of social location—"Where will we spend Christmas? What about the house we grew up in?"—although those thoughts were painful in their own right. Her more distressing questions were existential; they seemed to come from the core of her being. In the middle of many nights she would call me, awakened from a deep sleep in a state of terror. Kara felt as if the split in her parents' marriage had become a split in her own being. "I have to start all over again. I mean seriously, who am I?" she stated repeatedly.

It was Memorial Day when her questions became my own. We had returned from Kansas City, where Kara's sister had just gotten married. It was the first time that Kara had seen her father since her parents' break-up. Thoughts of seeing him paralyzed her for weeks. But as painful as it was, we had survived. I sat down to work on a paper when the phone rang. It was my father. Since it was a holiday, I wasn't surprised to hear from him. He began by asking how I was, and I thought we were easing into a routine conversation. With this in mind I rehearsed recent small events, then returned his softball question with one of my own: "And what's going on there?"

"A lot, actually," he said. For the next twenty minutes my father explained that my mother was having an affair and that he'd had his own in the years of their marriage. He explained that they didn't know what was next, but they wanted me to be aware. In phone calls over the following days, both my parents assured me that they were going to work through this, that they were going to try to save their marriage. I doubted them from the start. I had never been privy to many specifics, but I had known for many years that their marriage was anything but solid. Now, hearing of their infidelity, I, like Kara,

felt as if I were being sucked into a dark pit. In a real sense I started to wonder who I was, to question whether my very existence rested on anything solid at all. I couldn't help but feel that their actions attacked me, the core of my person. After all, I was the product, quite literally, of their love and commitment. I came into being out of their union, their mutual desire that created a community called "parents" to love and care for me. I existed because of their choice, and now they were choosing to destroy the very communion that made me. Their disunion threatened me nothing less than ontologically, which is to say that it shook my very being and existence.

That was why, during the flight to Minneapolis, I wanted anything to interrupt my first encounter with my parents since their confession, even if it was a plane crash. Kara and I were returning to Minneapolis to finalize our wedding plans. We were struck by the irony that in the brief six-month course of our engagement, both of our parents' marriages of more than twenty-five years had fallen apart.

Kara and I were married a few months later. Her parents divided into different pews, sitting on different sides of the room at our reception. My parents were arm-in-arm, pretending that all was OK, only to return home to sleep in different rooms. After a while the tension became too much, and separation was inevitable. As it approached, my mother especially tried to discuss it with me. She tried to explain that they had married young and that she had been unhappy for many years. She explained that if she were able, she might go back and not have married my father. I could see how painful this had been for her. It was clear that their separation would be a relief, a liberation, for her. But as she talked I could feel that her liberation would mean my oppression.

While she discussed the relief and pain of admitting the defeat of her marriage, I could only feel the defeat of the community that was the source of my very existence. Hearing her quiet, earnest explanation, I could almost feel myself sliding back into nonbeing. I felt numb, cut loose, unbound. My family had never been perfect, but it had been my family. Now that it was falling apart, it seemed as if I had nowhere to stand. It was like the scene late in the movie *Back to the Future*, where Marty begins to become transparent as it looks like he will fail to bring his teenaged parents together. It seemed as if I were fading into nothingness.

Divorce as the Experience of a Generation

Since the 1970s divorce has become a common cultural reality. With the creation of "no-fault" divorce, many were freed from unhappy and unfulfilling marriages. For a generation of young people born in the late sixties and after, divorce is as familiar as Froot Loops and cable television. Parents have been told that if done right, their divorce can be only a minimal disturbance to their children, on a par with changing schools or moving to a new neighborhood. But lately the young people who have lived through and with the divorce of their parents have questioned this assertion. In biographical books like Stephanie Staal's *The Love They Lost*, screenplays like Noah Baumbach's *The Squid and the Whale*, and popular music like Blink 182's "Stay Together for the Kids," Papa Roach's "Broken Home," or Pink's "Family Portrait," the initial and continual pain of their parents' divorce has been expressed palpably. It may be, as Staal asserts, that divorce is *the* defining generational mark of those raised after 1970, as the Kennedy assassination was for our parents, and the bombing of Pearl Harbor for our grandparents.

This book looks at divorce from the child's perspective, examining its impact from the view of the children (whether young or older). I will make *no* direct assertions about whether divorce is ethical or not, nor do I deny that in some cases divorce is necessary to end abuse and dehumanization. I acknowledge that from the perspective of a parent, divorce may feel like a desperately needed liberation. But, again, the focus of this project is not on the parent's perspective, only the child's. Even in instances when divorce was a great gift to one or both parents, it was a silent nightmare to a child. What I am asserting is that divorce—all divorces—leaves major marks on children, marks that reach all the way to the core of their being. (While this book's direct focus is on divorce, my argument may also resonate with those who have never lived through the divorce of their parents, but have not lived with or known both of their biological parents.)

It is my belief that our humanity (and very being) is upheld in community. For each one of us, the most significant and core of these communities is the one made up of a biological mother and father. Without their community, there would be no child. So when that community is

destroyed, it is a threat to the child's being. Divorce, therefore, should be seen as not just the split of a social unit, but the break of the community in which the child's identity rests. Divorce is much more than a psychological or sociological reality. It is about something deeper than economic advantage, psychological stability, or social capital. Divorce is a threat to a child's very ontology, to his or her very being. It is this very threat that Kara and I felt; it is this threat that is powerfully sung about in popular songs and illustrated in popular movies. When the community that created a child dissolves, the child is left exposed not only psychologically and socially, but ontologically.[1]

I am taking my cue from philosophers like Martin Heidegger, social theorists like Anthony Giddens, and theologians like Karl Barth, all of whom assert that being can be being only in relation to others. To *be* is to be *here* or *there* (this has been called *Dasein*, "being there"). The child *is* because of the union of his or her biological parents. Without them, he or she *is not*. When divorce, separation, or extended absence occurs the biological parents say, possibly with words but definitely with actions, that they desire for their union to no longer be. But the child *is* the result of their union; the child has his or her primary being in relation to the community called family.

Examining questions of divorce has often been the territory of psychologists and sociologists. Because this is a societal issue and results from decision making and personal affect, these two disciplines have seemed to be the most relevant. But it may be, as I am arguing, that there is something deeper and therefore more existential going on with those who experience the divorce of their parents. Accordingly, this project is energized not only by the work of social theorists such as Anthony Giddens, but also by the philosophy of being and the theological perspective of Karl Barth. Barth's theological anthropology will help us see how community is central to our humanity.

However, this project is not simply an examination of divorce through theology. Rather, this project is a practical theological examination of the issue. What that means is that though theology (God's action) is given central attention, this project will also seek to use multiple other perspectives and disciplines to understand our experience (human action). Therefore, sociology, psychology, history, and philosophy will be brought into conversation with theology, all

with the objective of examining deeply the impact and significance of divorce on children.

My overall thesis is that divorce is an ontological issue, one that impacts our very being-in-the-world. To this end, chapter 1 examines the history of the Western family, looking at how childhood and marriage itself has been understood. Divorce has been with us as long as marriage has, but as we will see, in the past divorce was nothing like it is today. Both marriage and divorce were rarely choices motivated by love and personal fulfillment, but were rather for economic or political gain. When it is love or its absence that motivates marriage and divorce, we are discussing a different animal. We will see how this transition has affected young people touched by divorce.

In chapter 2 we will examine how the cultural transitions of late modernity have caused divorce to become an all-too-common cultural reality. Drawing on the social theory of Anthony Giddens, we will explore how late modernity affects us, changing the way we construct identity through intimacy, and how this impacts our being and acting in the world. Continuing to follow Giddens, in chapter 3 we will see how social life is meant to create ontological security, and how divorce therefore strikes at our very being.

In chapter 4 we will turn directly to theology, looking specifically at the work of Karl Barth. This theologian asserts that our very humanity is bound in relational communion of action, just as God's own being as triune is relational and acts with and for us. We will discover what ramifications this relational theological perspective has for our understanding of divorce's impact on young people.

The *imago Dei* (image of God) is the focus of chapter 5. Here Barth's theological assertions come to bear on his anthropology (the study of what it means to be human in relation to God). To speak directly to the situation of divorce, I place Barth's thought in conversation with object relations psychology.

Throughout these chapters we will be looking deeply at these multidisciplinary theories, but never without delving into the experience of young people affected by divorce. Issues like the myth of the good divorce, living between two worlds, stepparents/stepfamilies, the difference between divorce and the death of a parent, and the commonplace fears that many young people feel toward their own

search for love and commitment will be taken up throughout these chapters. By placing these issues alongside multiple theories, I hope to show that we can see divorce as much more than a problem of thinking correctly (e.g., "the divorce was not your fault") or maintaining social solidarity (what social theorists have called "social capital"). Rather, we will begin to see divorce as a deeply ontological reality that impacts our very being-in-the-world.

Then, in the final chapter (chapter 6), I direct my attention toward articulating what congregations, parents, church leaders, and grandparents might do to help those suffering through the loss of their primary familial community.

A Disclaimer and the Conclusion to My Story

Before moving into our discussion, I should elaborate on an important issue that may otherwise distract readers. That issue can best be posed in the form of a question: am I opposed to families other than the biological family? I have already indicated that it is possible that some intact families are so filled with hate and neglect that though the parents are together, the family is only a shell and has no inner life of community in which being may rest. Therefore, these families can be considered de facto divorced families. Here let me add that blended families, stepparents, foster families, families of adopted children, or children raised by homosexual parents may be healthy and vital families. I wish not to disparage these families. But as is seen often with adopted children, the yearning for connection to one's biological parents is intense. Often, while thankful and content in their present family, the adopted children desire some kind of connection to their biological parents. We might say that their being longs for connection to its origin. Therefore, while family can be defined outside of biological connection (something I affirm), there remains nonetheless a longing for biology to connect its being with the being of those responsible for bringing one into the world.

That said, this book should not be read as a call for a return to a so-called traditional (nuclear) family of male patriarchy. Rather, the focus here is on the experience of children. I do believe there is something

mysterious about the communion of biological father, mother, and child(ren). But this mysterious interaction of being leaves it vulnerable to abuse; therefore, divorce and separation are always possible. What this book hopes to show is that more than psychological and social issues must be taken into consideration when helping children deal with the divorce, separation, or absence of a biological parent. Issues of ontology must also be considered. Actions must be taken not only to secure emotional and economic stability, but also (and I will argue, primarily) to secure the child's being in a community of suffering love.

Perhaps I can best summarize my attitudes on these complicated matters by returning briefly to my own story. My parents' marriage held on almost two years after my father's phone call initially alerted me that the marriage was in deep trouble. Over that time my wife and I made a home for ourselves, traveled around the world together, and shared with each other our deepest hopes and fears. It was late one night when my mother called, sadness soaking her voice. "I just wanted you to know that our divorce finally went through. It's over, and I'm sad; I never wanted this, but it's over," she said. I empathized with her, but something was different with me. My father's phone call two years before had thrown me into a crisis of identity, a frantic search for solid ground beneath my being. Hearing my mother's news now, I was much calmer. Why? It may have been that this news was less shocking than my father's initial call, but I had known for a long time before his call that their marriage was troubled. It could have been that I was older, though from twenty-four to twenty-six does not seem like that much of a difference.

As my mother continued talking, my eyes focused on Kara. Listening to this bad news, my gaze sought hers, and I knew that I belonged to her, that my person and being had a place alongside her own. I had a new community, a place to stand; my being was secure alongside hers. The scars and regret of my parents' divorce remain, but I no longer feel transparent or cut free. Rather, I have found a new community for my being, one created from love and shared suffering. It is my hope as a theologian that communities of faith can be such communities of love and suffering, created around the love and suffering of God in Jesus Christ.

1

A History of the Family,
a History of the Self

You will be only the second family to have ever lived there!" we were told when we bought our house. This is not a remarkable fact in a world of suburban housing developments. But in a city neighborhood, with a house built in 1912, it *was* remarkable. In its nearly one hundred years of existence, this old house had known only the Joneses, and now the Roots, roaming its rooms.

As winter approached, our first year in our new old house, I decided that I would reinsulate the tuck-under garage. I started with the disgusting job of tearing out all the old insulation, standing on a stepladder and pulling out worn mats and dusty newspapers from each rafter. As I moved to the area above the garage door and reached in to pull out another wad of insulation, I heard a strange thud on the floor below me. Peering down through my fogged goggles, I saw what looked like a pack of envelopes. At first thinking that old Mr. Jones must simply have used anything to insulate his garage, I gathered the bunch of letters (there were about thirty of them) and set them aside. At a break I examined them. They were odd; all were addressed to Mr. Jones, but none to the home address. All were postmarked between

1939 and 1945 and written in the same handwriting. Each letter was from the same person, a young woman, requesting the same thing: money. Many mentioned a small child. It appeared that Mr. Jones had quite a secret: a young former or current lover, with his child, living in another state. I could imagine Mr. Jones receiving these letters at work and for some reason taking them home, perhaps for fear that someone at work would find them, or perhaps because he was conflicted and had deep feelings for this young, desperate woman. Whatever the reason was that he brought these letters home, he clearly didn't want them read; he sneaked out to the garage, grabbed a stool and pushed them deep into the rafters. His secret, kept for almost seventy years, had now spilled onto my garage floor.

As I sat and read these letters, I felt drawn into another world, as if I had been dropped into a 1940s movie. The trees in my yard shrank to their size seventy years ago, my vinyl siding turned to clapboard, and out on the street hybrid Toyota Camrys transformed into loud, gas-guzzling early-model Fords. I could picture Mr. Jones coming home from work, bustling through the door in suit and tie with briefcase trailing him. In the briefcase were the letters that held his secret. Mrs. Jones met him at the door with a kiss and a scotch. I wondered if she knew of his secret, if she knew but refused to admit it, realizing that there was little she could do. I wondered if he really loved her or if my twenty-first-century ideas of love and family would even make sense to Mr. Jones and his wife. I thought about how much our conception of the family has changed in just the last half century and, more radically, how it has changed in the last five hundred to six hundred years.

After reading through the letters, I wondered what to do with them. Mr. and Mrs. Jones had died long ago. Their son, who had lived in the house just before us, was gone as well. As far as we knew, only Posey, the daughter of Mr. and Mrs. Jones, was still living. I wondered if I should tell her what I had discovered. I wondered how she would feel reading this pile of dusty old letters. Maybe she already knew her father's secret. Or maybe, when reading them, this nearly eighty-year-old woman would feel much as I did when my dad revealed that there were deep secrets in my own parents' marriage, like my own being was thrown into question. I thought about the young child

mentioned repeatedly in the letters, now himself in his seventies. I thought about what scars must exist within him, not having known his father, his very being the secret of an indiscretion. I wondered if Posey, even at eighty, would feel her being shaken upon realizing her father's affair, when a deep deceptive stream that ran hidden under the history of her existence sprang to the surface. I wondered if discovering that her father's love and fidelity was divided would feel like a division within her. I decided that I wouldn't find her, knowing that if it were me, I wouldn't want to know.

The old letters in my hand were historical. They weren't bound for exhibition at a museum or an hour-long *Dateline* special. But they possessed a historical reality in two very significant ways. First, they possessed the history of these people's being; each member of Mr. Jones's family constructed his or her concept of self and world from within the familial social unit Mr. (and Mrs.) Jones had created. This social unit was primary and fundamental. Its history was their own; their individual lives were wrapped around its social life. Even more, their existence was a product of it: they most basically could not be without it. The family is the fundamental community of the self, for it is (to use a biblical phrase) "bone of my bone and flesh of my flesh." Children are the mysterious by-products of the community of man and woman. The self of the child is dependent on this community for its existence and place in the world. The traditions and rhythms, but also eye color, stature, and chin line, bind the family members into an ontological community with a history. ("You have a temper like your father's." "Your nose looks just like Grandpa Hank's." "We Roots open one present each on Christmas Eve.") The secret in the rafters of my garage threatened to puncture this history (thus the reason they were a secret) by making such traits nothing more than a function of biological occurrence. They risked smashing a community of belonging and its traditions on the rocky shores of a hidden history.

Second, these letters were historical in the sense that they pointed to a unique period in the development of the modern understanding of the family. In reading them I felt drawn back to a world that seemed long dead, a world where women seemed powerless and the sense of duty loomed large. But the letters also foreshadowed a world that

seemed much more understandable. Written just before the dawn of the 1950s, when the family was seen as a demigod, these letters expressed the fractures in the hidden foundation of the midcentury idea of the family. The fractures would become radically obvious in the mid-1960s and 1970s.

Prelude to a History

Much of the political discourse of the last several decades seems to suggest that "the family" fell straight out of heaven. This view ignores the reality that the family, like all other sectors of culture, is a social construction that is shaped by the flows of history.[1] There was, for instance, a time when the cultural construction of marriage and family made it unlikely and unusual that divorce would occur. It is much more than just insipid forgetfulness or nefarious deception that has led us away from a world where divorce is rare. Rather, changes (some very good ones) in our understanding of self and world have brought new understandings and actions within family, even if it makes us more vulnerable to divorce. Family is a social construction and has never been a monolithic, unchanging concept. In many ways the evolution of the family is a journey through the benefits and backlash of modernity (as we will see more clearly in chapter 2).

The history of the family has followed a broad progression in the last six hundred years: its objective has shifted from property and power mergers, to labor, and then to love. These changes follow the evolution of cultural currents impacted by the Enlightenment, currents that changed us from premodern to modern to late-modern people. Divorce, then, is the tragic underbelly of the liberation of marriage and family from being centered on land or labor to being centered on love. But now, standing in late modernity, we find ourselves with a problem, a problem much like the effects of modernity on scientific discovery or technological advance. It is the problem of risk. Scientifically and technologically, this means we can split the atom, but in doing so can destroy the world. We can construct effective power plants, but they pollute the planet. Similarly, marriage

and family are free from the bondage of a harsh earlier world, but free for what? Making family about love heightened the significance of the person (the self), but it left us with a dangerous risk. When marriage is about love between persons, and nothing more, what remains when love is doubted or destroyed? And what about those who are young and dependent on the social structure built only on love; what are they to do if the marriage and family on which they depend disappear along with their parents' love for each other? And if these dependents, these children, are the product only of love (not part of a political merger or valued as a helping hand), then who are they once the love that created them and their primary community is gone? The remainder of this chapter seeks to sketch the history of marriage's and family's progression and confront more fully these questions.

History, it is important to note, is much messier than any account can show. A historical period is never clearly or totally one thing or another. It is often tempting to treat history like TV programming, where one show begins after another ends, and the two never connect. But the movements of history are much more like having multiple Web pages open on the desktop of your computer, reading one while glancing occasionally at another, than they are like the program guide on your cable system. For instance, below I make the argument that the purpose and function of marriage in Western society have moved from mergers to labor to love. While this is broadly true, it is not to say, for instance, that even in the medieval period labor or love were not significant reasons for some people to marry. That said, we turn to a sketch of the family's history that moves through four broad periods: pre-sixteenth century, sixteenth through eighteenth centuries, nineteenth to twentieth centuries, and late twentieth century. As I mentioned above, this history seeks to examine the effect of the Enlightenment on the conceptions and operations of the family. Therefore, I have taken the liberty to label everything before the arrival of the Enlightenment (and even the Reformation and humanism) pre-sixteenth century. This is not to say there were not familial distinctions and nuances in those thousands of years of history (that would be absurd), but the more comprehensive look is not the story to be told for the argument of this project.

Pre-sixteenth Century: Passing on Property, Power, and Tradition

What Is Marriage For? Mergers

As a teenager I was always confused, and to be honest, repulsed, by the biblical texts that discussed the need for a man to marry his deceased brother's wife (Matt. 22:23–28; see also Deut. 25:7–10). It seemed so odd to ears that had been raised on pop love ballads and romantic comedies. It seemed wrong to me, violating my understanding of love and marriage, and even my understanding of God. Of course this cultural practice, which was so important to this society that it became law, was not concerned with love but with lineage. It was beyond tragic for an older brother's *name* to disappear from the earth, so the younger brother would marry the widow and provide an heir for his dead brother. Since marriage in that setting had little to do with love, but everything to do with lineage, this law maintained the sanctity of marriage—even if it seemed the opposite to a late-modern teenager.

For most of human history marriage and family has been about securing fortune, land, or line. Stephanie Coontz says, "The system of marrying for political and economic advancement was practically universal across the globe for many millennia."[2] In almost all cultures prior to the sixteenth century, marriage was never the choice of the individuals being married but was arranged by parents to benefit the kin unit as a whole. It mattered little whether the couple had affection for, or even knew, each other. What mattered was how the matrimony would benefit the larger group. "Marriage allowed families to pool . . . resources or to establish some kind of partnership between two different kin groups."[3] Especially in Europe where family groups began to assert a permanent right to land and assets, "marriage exchanges became a way of consolidating resources."[4] This was true of rich aristocrats and rulers, but also of peasants.

Marriage was a way of making strangers into friends, and enemies into partners; it was a way to hold on to a group's status and property and maybe even increase it.[5] For some, marriage was all about business; for others, it was all about survival. But it is clear that in both cases marriage had a functional operation bound in economic

and status categories.[6] Where today beauty makes one's future marriage prospects hopeful, in the sixteenth century and prior, dowry attracted marriage attention. Just as today's parents begin saving for college tuition the day a child is born, in the past it was the dowry of a daughter that received attention from her birth. The idea was, much as with college, that with the right amount of saved money you could secure a promising future for your child and your family as a whole. With a larger dowry came suitors that promised a marriage that would benefit the kin unit as a whole. E. J. Graff explains, "The marriage ceremony itself was usually when money (or its stand-in, the ring) actually changed hands."[7]

Romance and affection had little to do with marriage and family in this setting.[8] They were not completely absent or undesired, but romance and affection were neither the justification for marriage nor the glue that held the family together.[9] Marriage was a contract, no doubt to link destinies and identities, but also to link these through a conglomeration of resources and status—not through the romance of individuals.

Childhood

It has been well documented that "childhood" as an idyllic stage of treasured innocence did not exist through early Western history.[10] Instead, children themselves were seen as the seal of an economic and status merger. This is not to say that some parents didn't adore their children or see them as valuable. However, their value was not measured primarily through individual feelings of adoration, love, and pleasure, but rather by their benefit to the kin unit.[11] The job of parents was not to raise children that would love them, but to raise children that could provide continuation of the family name, property, or esteem. To meet this end, fathers and mothers often needed to take a heavy hand in parenting. The existence of the kin unit was dependent on children; the mergers made in marriage were fleeting if children could not continue the economic advantage and possible societal esteem the marriage union offered. Today we often judge a good parent by her or his ability to raise independently thinking and behaving *individuals* who can seek self-fulfillment. But in the

pre-sixteenth-century view, buttressed by the Augustinian theology of original sin, parenting was about breaking a child's *sinful will*, a will that could easily threaten the stability, survival, or reputation of the *kin unit*.[12] Good parenting was not about forging independence in the child, but about securing his or her commitment and contribution to the kin unit. Therefore, once the child was old enough to work (around six or seven), he or she was thrust into the adult world alongside others in the kin unit. There seemed to be simply no such thing as the idea that children were too innocent and too vulnerable to participate in the adult activities necessary to survive in this period. According to Phillippe Ariès, infants and toddlers were often shown little direct affection until they matured. Some have believed this was because of the risk of heartbreak linked to high infant mortality rates and childhood diseases, but it no doubt also had something to do with the perception of a child's commitment to the kin unit.[13] If the child was seen as a sinful creature, then intense affection and care would not be offered until the child had shown commitment that reassured parents (and others) of his or her benefit to the family's future. This may sound harsh to our ears, but that is because it *was* harsh. At least according to Ariès, parents at this time did not see the need to protect children from the harsh realities of the world. Rather, they needed their children in order to survive in the world and maintain any advantage in it. Of course, this was not possible for infants or toddlers, so they were often treated with suspicion. It has been well documented that children in this period were often called "poor-sighted animals."[14] What was then regarded as important was not individual development, but instead, having a place, being part of a unit that provided one not with love but with the resources to survive.

While we must be careful to not overstate the severity of parents toward children in this period, we must also not underestimate the severity of the premodern world, wracked by disease, violence, and poverty. The family in this period was much like the buildings that still exist from that period. While few people actually lived in castles, the family itself (as kin unit) functioned like a castle, even for poor agrarian peasants living on dirt floors. That is, if the family was cold and rigid, it was also a solid structure that provided protection, order,

and shelter within its walls. It ultimately promised survival in an unshakable environment.

But a castle is a rigid, unmovable structure, and wasn't the family an ever-changing unit, due to high mortality rates and the common practice of children leaving home and kin to work for others? This argument has often been used to support the belief that the high divorce rate of our time is no more a disturbance to families and their children than have been upheavals at other periods in history. It was commonly asserted that children in this period would be shipped out of the family at age nine or ten to go work for wealthier families, or on land far from the place of the biological kin unit. But some recent historians have argued, Colin Heywood most directly, that this has been overstated.[15] No doubt children left home for work or (for young girls) marriage, but it was much more common for the departing child to be between fifteen and twenty years old rather than the often-assumed seven or eight. So the kin unit was much more stable than many have imagined. Children lived with and worked alongside parents, uncles, and cousins for many years before leaving the family on their own accord (which was rare) or because of the family's need (which was more common).

But what about the intrusions and divisions of death? It is true that many children lived through the death of a parent in their early years and that for most spouses, even those marrying very young, the years spent in marriage were much fewer than today's, since life expectancy has almost doubled. Therefore, wasn't the family just as vulnerable to breakups then as it is today? This argument too easily equates our feelings of the family with those of the past. It also ignores the historical journey of modernization and its effect on our conception of the self (which we will examine below). In the pre-sixteenth century world, the death of a biological parent was no doubt tragic and threatened the family greatly, but the effects were more devastating economically than emotionally. Because the family was built not on emotional connection (love), but mergers of kin units, when a parent died the children still found themselves securely cemented (whether for good or bad) within a narrative, tradition, and place that could not be easily shaken. One major benefit that marriage and family provided was a social safety net supplied in the connection (belonging)

within a larger kin unit.[16] Therefore, while the pre-sixteenth-century family was overall a cold, and at times harsh, social unit, in which women and children were completely dependent on men and men were completely dependent on other men, it did offer a place in which one unquestionably belonged, with its own anchoring tradition and narrative.[17] When marriage and family are built on mergers, they are susceptible to (and perhaps encourage) sexism and rigidity, but they also provide an entrenched location, good or bad, in which children are secure. And it is a belonging that connects not only to a place but a place with biological correlation. Hence, even if the father dies, one is connected to the kin unit of which one is biologically a member. Living close to uncles and cousins on farms or in villages, and immersion in stories of common ancestors, cements one in a tradition and place.

In this period, achieving a "self," to claim one's individuality and search the depths of one's person for meaning and identity, was not a common pursuit. Surely some had embarked on a journey of discovering the self as differentiated from his or her social location (one thinks of Augustine's *Confessions*, for instance), but this was rare. For most people the self could not be divided or teased out from the fabric of the encompassing social places and units in which they belonged. Not only could it not be teased out, rarely did one contemplate that the self was anything other than what the social unit determined. A person's identity was almost completely determined by his or her kin. So, the common formula of identifications: "I am the son of ___ from ___."

These framing realities made divorce very rare. Because marriage was a merger based on economics, divorce might have occurred when wealthier families could not meet the agreed-upon dowry or when a husband negotiated a better merger with another family.[18] Then the wife would be sent away with a legal document articulating that the business arrangement had ended, and that the husband had found a new merger with another wife that was more beneficial to his larger kin unit. It could be quite painful for children to watch this occur, and there is documentation of sons plotting to kill fathers who left mothers for "better" wives and families. This is understandable, for when place is completely shaken, so too is the self, potentially leading

to a state of vengeful rage. But for most people, especially the majority who were not of noble birth or economic advantage, once a merger occurred it lasted, fortifying a kin structure and enveloping children in a place of belonging that could not be doubted or avoided.

Sixteenth through Eighteenth Centuries: Maintaining Tradition in a World of Needed Labor

The overall shape of the pre-sixteenth-century family would hold through the seventeenth and eighteenth centuries and into the nineteenth century. But a number of cultural transformations were bringing change. The cultural winds would take years to radically alter the landscape of the family, but gusts like the Reformation, the Enlightenment, the American and French revolutions, and the early arrival of the industrial/urban economy would greatly change the family.[19] For many, the family shifted from mergers of larger kin units to smaller units of people who mostly married for the benefit of mutual labor.

With the rise of a money-based economy, fewer people were dependent on parents and kin units to kick-start their married life. This also allowed for more choice; no longer were children completely dependent on their parents for economic needs. For many, especially those in the working class, marriage was happening later in life, as people spent ten to fifteen years in the service of more wealthy families to earn the money to afford a business or buy a piece of land. This kind of indentured servanthood pushed back the age of marriage in Europe and accordingly reduced the size of most families.[20]

People found themselves with more freedom to choose a marriage partner, but this often had very little to do with love. Instead, marriage was about who could provide the spouse with an adequate labor-mate. People were often drawn to men and women who would be ideal partners for their small businesses or farming. Graff states, "If your life's income was based on your marriage, you wouldn't be so foolish as to marry only because you 'fell in love,' any more than you'd hire a business partner based only on sexual infatuation. . . . Rather, you'd look more for a stable, reliable, companionable workmate, someone

you could get along with, someone you might well grow to care for by sharing your work."[21]

While this allowed for some release from the earlier strictures of marriage solely as mergers, it did not mean, as it would in the twentieth century, that people were completely independent of kin units or tradition-based village communities. People remained dependent on them, at the very least to find their marriage partners. So in this period individual choice in marrying increased, but the choice was based on labor needs and made within the limited community of the wider kin unit and village.[22]

The transition to marriage centered on labor seemed to allow for more mutuality between husband and wife. The wife was no longer simply the embodiment of a merger contract, but a vital partner in the earnings and therefore the survival of the family. Accordingly, as one historian puts it, "The most common words for wives in seventeenth- and eighteenth-century colonial America were 'yoke-mates' or 'meet-helps,' labels that indicated women's economic partnership with men. Until the early nineteenth century, men and women worked together on farms or in small household businesses, alongside other family members. Responsibility for family life and responsibility for breadwinning were not two different, specialized jobs."[23] A partner was chosen because of what his or her partnership could accomplish. Carl Degler agrees: "Prior to the opening of the 19th century the vast majority of people in the world lived on farms or in peasant villages. And for almost all of them the family was a cooperative economic unit, with children and mother working along with husband. . . . This was true whether production was for subsistence or for sale. Even those relatively few families which lived and worked in towns acted as cooperative enterprises in their shops, inns, and other businesses. Home and work were close together, and wife and husband participated in both."[24] Yet, while it was impossible for those other than aristocrats to survive without the trusted and vital work of their wives, the earlier hierarchical ideology of sexual order prevailed. Following the American and French revolutions, the family was understood as its own "little commonwealth,"[25] with all (children and women) playing an essential role, but the husband and father still possessed the power of ultimate leadership and decision

making. The male head of such a family didn't expect affection so much as duty from his wife and children.

If family life could be perceived as harsh in the pre-sixteenth century, the sixteenth through the eighteenth centuries saw little change in that regard. Children were seen earlier as the seal of mergers and promises of the continuation of the merger advantages of a marriage. But in the sixteenth through the eighteenth centuries, with the family becoming smaller and the economy now money-based, children became essential employees in the labor of the family unit. Children often felt like employees, in the sense that they were expected to work and could not expect intimate, affectionate relationships with their parent employers. Child–parent relationships tended to be punitive, or at least cold, in this period.[26] On farms children were often conceived for their provision of cheap labor. In villages a child worked the land or in the small merchant business very early in his or her life.[27] As work became more complicated and individual skills were needed more and more in villages, children were often sent away for apprenticeships. This was not a way of achieving independence from the family, as leaving for college training is today. Instead, the child learned new skills to return home and contribute to the diversification of the family portfolio.[28]

The need for particular skills would have further impact as the economy continued to change and technology (such as the printing press) began to reshape life.[29] It became more and more common for children to receive education. This was not only the impact of the changing economy and developing technologies, but was also due to the Reformation emphasis on the catechization of children. The Reformation and then the Enlightenment and Romantic thought broke with the perception of childhood sinfulness and the necessity of breaking the child's will. Mintz and Kellogg explain, "Although few . . . would go so far as the English poet William Wordsworth or the French philosopher Jean-Jacques Rousseau in celebrating children's innocence, by the late eighteenth century there is clear evidence of a decline in the belief in childhood depravity."[30] This understanding would be an antecedent of what would become full-blown in the next period: childhood as a stage of play and innocence. While these ideas were evolving, most families simply didn't have the luxury of

anything other than bearing and rearing children for the performance of essential labor.[31] They might now sit at their father's knee and read the Scripture in the evening, or go to church to read the catechism with the village pastor, but they were still expected to labor for and alongside the family.

With the Reformation and the rise of Protestantism, new ideas were impacting not only families but also the way people understood themselves. The dawn of the Enlightenment saw the possibility that the individual, the self, could be thought of and reflected upon outside the communal reality of kin unit, village, or tradition. Now that people could read the Bible for themselves, and individually were justified, and with the Enlightenment's concern for individual knowing, the self became something to reflect on.[32] "I" and "mine" began to be understood as a reality separate from kin, clan, or village.[33]

Viewed through our own present-day lens of marriage and parenting for love, the pre-sixteenth-century family may seem harsh and distant, though we can see that it provided its members a solid place to belong. Similarly, in the sixteenth through eighteenth centuries the family continued to provide a solid place of belonging, though now with later marriage, smaller households, and more apprenticeships. The family may have felt less insulated and impermeable, less like an impregnable fortress, than it did earlier. But with the transition from mergers to labor, the family provided young people another compensation: unquestioned purpose and meaning.

Children were essential to the survival of the family; without their labor the family would cease to exist. Therefore, unlike today, where each individual in a family is under the cultural obligation to carve out a meaningful life and future for himself or herself, the family as a unit provided meaning and purpose in this period. While the idea of the self as independent from the kin unit was evolving, ultimately the idea of self was still held securely within the family unit, which provided unquestioned purpose and meaning to life. You were an essential cog in your family's labors. In sum, while the Reformation and Enlightenment raised issues of the individual self, functionally the self remained embedded in the family unit that provided belonging, but even more, offered purpose and meaning.

This nascent awakening of the self had little impact on divorce. In fact, in this period divorce became even less common than it had been in the pre-sixteenth century.[34] As long as the labor union was working, why would one break the bond? The husband and the wife needed the other to keep the business running or the land productive. The impact of the Enlightenment and the new reflection on the self may have led some to admit their personal unhappiness, but this would be no reason to divorce. After all, marriage was for labor, not for individual feelings of the self (at least not yet). Some children too may have been unhappy in families, but the family had little to do with self-fulfillment; what was valued was the family's stability. And then stability itself provided purpose and meaning for the self.

Nineteenth to Mid-Twentieth Century: For Intimacy

The world changed dramatically and rapidly in the nineteenth and twentieth centuries. With the arrival of a full-blown industrial economy, the extension of the power of the nation-state, and a society-wide embrace of Enlightenment perspectives, the world changed in countless ways. Not the least of these transitions was the conception of marriage and family. As the Enlightenment perspective began to soak into the soil of society, people awakened from the all-encompassing slumber of labor and lineage to give attention to their individual selves. Journals, novels, and love letters began to permeate the culture. Whereas in our earlier two periods marriage and family were the central location and outworking of the economy, in the Victorian age they were decentered. Instead of one's survival being dependent on kin unit or familial labor, one's survival became dependent on oneself. With mechanization, nascent bureaucracy, and budding urbanization, the individual could go out, alone, into a money economy and find an individualized job. The division between home and work became distinct and widened significantly through the mid-twentieth century. People became more and more detached from their labor, because of mechanization and bureaucratic organization, and began to give more and more attention to the self (a unique person with internal desires and dreams beyond labor and lineage). From the dawn of the

Victorian age onward, the purpose of marriage shifted from labor to love. Coontz states, "For the first time in five thousand years, marriage came to be seen as a private relationship between two individuals rather than one link in a larger system of political and economic alliances."[35] Making marriage about love freed the individual or the self. As Degler observes, "Love as the basis for marrying was the purest form of individualism; it subordinated all familial, social, or group considerations to personal preference."[36]

No longer did parents choose a child's spouse (though they no doubt continued to influence the decision), nor were people choosing spouses for their ability to work. Rather, marriage was now based solely on the couple's individual feelings of attraction and desire. The question became, Do you love him? not, What does his family offer us? or, What does he offer you? "The older conception of the family as a 'little commonwealth,' a microcosm of the larger society, had receded and been replaced by a new image of the family as a 'haven in a heartless world,' a bastion of morality and tender feelings and a refuge from the aggressive and selfish world of commerce."[37] The criteria of marriage *transitioned from concrete operations to subjective feelings*; marriage was now something chosen by the individual, not something constructed by kin units and village communities.[38] As Coontz summarizes it, "These economic changes, interacting with Enlightenment ideology, shifted the basis of marriage from sharing tasks to sharing feelings. The older view that wives and husbands were work mates gave way to the idea that they were soul mates."[39] Earlier, marriage was held together by the steel of kin mergers and, later, the stone of a labor agreement; in this period marriage was held together by the tissue of love. While the love-based union was clearly softer and warmer, it lacked the strength and resilience of earlier structures.

The transition to marriages based on the love between two individuals would lead to the unique Victorian family form of the separate spheres for the sexes.[40] Because marriage was no longer the sharing of labor, and labor was something done outside the home, the home became a haven, a place to escape the pressure of labor to the loving embrace of spouse and children. When men returned from the competitive world of economic competition, they expected a sanctuary

of comfort. It became the wife's job, now that she was no longer a partner in labor, to provide just such an environment. "Before the 19th century the rearing of children and the maintenance of the home had never been a full-time job; there had always been too many other things expected and demanded of the wife and mother," Degler notes.[41] Now it was her job, alone, to create a clean, comfortable environment brimming with love and affection.[42] And she was to do this *not* because of kin pressure or economic necessity, but because she loved her husband and children.

This Victorian idea of the family, based on love and separate spheres, stretched all the way forward to the mid-twentieth century, to what we *imagine* as the golden days of the American family, the 1950s. No doubt, the love-based, separate-spheres perspective showed some wear before the 1950s, most especially in the early decades of the twentieth century. Women began to demand more freedom in sexual expression and participation in the modernized work environment, and then with a depression and a Second World War they were needed in the workforce. But the economic boom generated (at least in part) by governmental intervention in housing costs and GI Bills helped to bolster the crumbling two-sphere structure and set the stage for the golden moment in the love-based marriage, the *Leave It to Beaver* family.[43]

The zenith, however, was also its culmination, as the weak underbelly of love-based marriage began to appear in the mid-1960s. The self had been cut loose to live in a world of freedom won by Enlightenment ideas, Victorian culture, and a modernized economy. But one was freed from the merger of kin units and the labor of village life for what? In the shadow of a globalized world of frantic consumer choice, the solely love-based marriage became an unsteady vessel for the free individual self. One was free but had nowhere to stand other than the subjective feeling of love, which itself seemed to become more and more tenuous in our complicated world.[44] For over 150 years marriage and family based on love had promised complete *self*-fulfillment. Liberated from mergers and labor, the self was free to choose whom to love in order to fulfill his or her individual happiness. But by the 1950s, fissures began to appear in this picture or model of ideal happiness. In marriages chosen in love, many—especially women—began

to realize that they were not happy (self-fulfilled), and thus began questioning whether they loved their spouses at all. But if there was no love, there was no reason (especially as the workforce opened to women) to remain in union. Divorce consequently became far more prevalent. Such a reality allowed for freedom and the possibility of equality (and helpfully freed many from abusive and miserable marriages). Yet while the love-based marriage assumed that individual selves had freely chosen the union, and therefore were free to choose against it, this freedom of choice was not transferable to their children. Divorce may have brought freedom for parents, by their own choice. But children did not participate in that choice, however much they suffered its consequences.

In the love-based marriage, children were seen not only as a product of the parents' love union, but as objects of love themselves. No longer the seal of a merger or a tool for labor, a child's worth in the nineteenth and the first half of the twentieth century was elevated to the level of transcendence. Once "poor-sighted animals" who had not learned to control their sinful wills, children were now sweet angels meant to be coddled.[45] Children moved from being seen as sinful to being regarded as innocent, and therefore it became the job of parents to protect them from an evil world. This was yet another way in which the family became a haven of love and affection. "By the beginning of the nineteenth century, a radically new definition of the family had emerged. Instead of being viewed as an integral component of the network of public institutions, the family was beginning to be seen as a private retreat," write Mintz and Kellogg.[46] Child labor was first frowned upon and then outlawed, and education became widely available even for non-middle-class families. Children were now seen as precious individuals to treasure, as nothing more than innocent, adorable offspring.[47] No longer an essential partner in labor, the mother became responsible for loving and nurturing children. The family, then, as a separate sphere, took on its own specialization.[48] Or, as Graff puts it, "Affection replaced duty at both ends of the bond: just as children were with parents not to obey but to be loved, so also parents were to have children not out of duty but love."[49]

Corporations, schools, and shops had begun to specialize in particular tasks or goods, and so did the family. No longer was the family

primarily the place where kinship was established and passed down through history. Nor was it the locus of labor that supplied for all members of the family their basic needs (such as food, clothing, and education). In a modernized world other institutions took on such responsibilities as making clothes, growing food, and teaching children. The family was left with the specialization of tending to the emotional needs of the selves of children and the love of spouse.[50] It was the family's job, through love and nurture, to help the young person become an individual, a self. Degler explains, "By the early years of the 19th century children were seen in a way quite different from that of previous centuries. Increasingly, children were viewed as individuals, as persons in their own right. The new attitude is reflected, for example, in the decline in the practice of naming children after parents."[51] No longer a harsh place of political mergers or economic labor, the family became *the* place for one to become a self.[52] In the bright lights of modernization, the tradition of the kin, which offered unquestioned belonging, and the meaning of the laboring family melted away; now belonging and meaning became disjointed from communal realities and rested squarely within the four walls of a mother, father, and siblings, a love-based family.[53]

The love-based family, like the love-based marriage, had its golden age in the 1950s. Childhood became a time of play and leisure mixed with education. Children were free from all adult responsibilities to live idyllically in the perceived paradise of suburbia. The nuclear family seemed ideal; because of its size it was flexible and mobile in the currents of a modernized society. And through its love unions it continued to provide children with belonging and meaning of a kinder and gentler sort. The sharp teeth of kin-unit mergers and family labor were dulled on contractual, individually chosen love bonds. A child's belonging no longer rested in the history of a lineage, but in the affection of individuals. Meaning no longer was it formed in the heat and sweat of labor for survival, but in the affection of loving and being loved within the union of father and mother.

While the family based on love tamed the harsh realities of life and elevated the child as an individual self in the family unit, it came with its own risks. Because the family was based solely on the affection of individuals, it was a cozier place but also a more tenuous and fragile

place. Because love was based on the free decisions of the self, the mother/wife and father/husband now possessed not only the power to create the family, but also the freedom to destroy it. The child was protected from the harsh politics of the merger-family and the severities of the labor-based family unit, but he or she could not be protected from the *parent's choice*. Now that the family and one's belonging and meaning within it was based solely in the affection of love, whenever father or mother decided that love no longer existed, then neither did the union that provided the self of the child with his or her essential belonging and meaning. In a modern world of impersonal corporations and bureaucracy, rather than community and tradition, the endings of the love unions became a great threat to children. It meant the end of their primary and essential community, the one responsible for their very existence, with no other institutions ready to step in as replacements.

It was not the love-based union that created divorce, but it was the love-based union that democratized it.[54] As we have seen, divorce stretched back into ancient societies, as a legal option to allow for a more advantageous political or power merger. It was never the announcement of dead love made by the self in need of freedom. In the nineteenth and twentieth centuries it was assumed that once love died so too did the marriage, and with it the family.[55] In the early days of the Victorian age, American divorce rates began to increase. There are a number of stories of individuals leaving spouses to be with lovers, many traveling to the state of Indiana, where one could file for divorce without the presence of the soon-to-be ex-spouse. If couples chose to skip a trip to Indiana, they could simply—if not officially—separate.[56] Cott notes that the love-based marriage led to higher numbers of divorces than were found among marriages centered on mergers or labor. "Although the frequency of divorce was minuscule (not even two divorces per thousand marriages, in 1870) compared to the divorce rate in the late twentieth century, at the time it was noticeably higher in the United States than anywhere in Europe—and the seemingly relentless upward trend caused panic. By 1900 there were four divorces per thousand marriages."[57] Cultural critics warned that the love-based family/marriage was dangerous, weakening the family. They stated, according to Coontz, that "basing

marriage on love and companionship represented a break with thousands of years of tradition. Many . . . immediately recognized the dangers this entailed. They worried that the unprecedented idea of basing marriage on love would produce rampant individualism."[58] While their doomsday assertions were not proven in their own period, they nevertheless pointed to a sleeper cell that rested in the heart of the love-based marriage, waiting for just the right time to break out. That moment came in the mid-1960s, when love and hyperindividualism were blended with a consumer society.

So what kept divorce from escalating from the nineteenth to the mid-twentieth century? What kept the tenuous love-based marriage from dissolving into serial divorce earlier? Coontz explains that the lingering realities of male headship, the social shame of divorce and illegitimate pregnancy, and misogyny in the workforce kept many unions of lost love together.[59] As the late twentieth century sought to right these wrongs, the love-based marriage began to show fissures that had already made marriage and family more fragile.

Becoming a self became the child's vocation, and the family his or her location to do so. The child was dependent, then, on the belonging and meaning provided by the tenuous family, which when sunk by divorce left the self of the child without a place or purpose to grow. Divorce in a modernized world, then, attacks the self, because the self is formed within the belonging and meaning provided by the family. When it is destroyed, the threat of lost place and lost purpose becomes a reality. Without place or purpose, one becomes a lost self.

Late Twentieth Century: Marriage for _____?

It is often assumed that the mid-twentieth-century family form is the ideal, leading to political and religious nostalgia; yet it must be admitted that the 1950s family was an aberration.[60] Coontz says it like this, "Even as people became convinced they had at last created the perfect balance between individual desires and social stability . . . it was on the verge of collapse. When people remarked on the stability of marriage in the 1950s and early 1960s, they were actually standing in the eye of a hurricane."[61] In the mid-twentieth century

the vulnerabilities of the love-based marriage were mitigated by other forces. For instance, because of government-provided economic opportunities and the cultural desire for a quite conservative existence after a depression and WWII, and in the midst of a cold war, all the weak points of love-based marriage appeared to be bolstered and protected by strong pillars. Yet in the dawn of the mid-1960s these supposed strong pillars showed they were not weight-bearing, and they collapsed. As women gradually entered the workforce, and outright sexism and racism were confronted, the love-based marriage was loosed from older ideological perspectives to evolve toward the promise of its name.[62] Coontz states this well: "Men and women initially tried to find fulfillment at home. But when marriage did not meet their heightened expectations, their discontent grew proportionately. The more people hoped to achieve personal happiness within marriage, the more critical they became of 'empty' or unsatisfying relationships."[63] As a consumer culture mixed with a hypermodernization (call it globalization) and the mobility and freedom from tradition it provided, people understood themselves to be responsible to one thing above all, their selves. While this no doubt had strong overtones of narcissism (see Christopher Lasch's *The Culture of Narcissism*), it was believed that concern for your happiness allowed you to truly and fully love others, especially spouse and children. Therefore, to fulfill the obligation of the love-based marriage, individuals would have to first give allegiance to their subjective self-fulfillment. If you were happy or self-fulfilled, then you could fulfill your marital obligation. But if you were not happy, if you did not feel blissful (or something just short of it), then the marriage was thrown into question. An unsatisfying marriage lacked the very foundations upon which marriage was understood to rest, the self's feeling of love. Accordingly, when love was interpreted to be absent, there was de facto no marriage and no family, and tragically (from the perspective of late modernity) the self was denigrated.[64]

The step out of marriage into divorce was then increasingly inevitable. Love was freed to be a subjective, individual reality. It is nearly impossible or even criminal to punish people for their subjective feelings. So the basis for divorce switched from the need to show fault to the agreement that no one was at fault. Instead, the subjective feelings

of love had simply disappeared or had become attached to someone else. Barbara Dafoe Whitehead comments, "Divorce had long been identified with legal freedoms, but in the last decades of the twentieth century it became associated with psychological liberation as well."[65] This is an emancipating reality (painful but freeing) and one that finally released women from oppressive, cold, mean, or even abusive husbands. More open to making a living for themselves and no longer primarily responsible to serve the happiness of others, women were free to love themselves by leaving loveless marriages.[66]

These are laudable developments, but they come with a problem that we have yet to solve, one that with the rise of no-fault divorces has affected millions of people.[67] When the two selves are allowed to depart the union when there is no longer love, the product of this love, the children, who need the family in order to understand themselves, are left without it. The family is an environment created in either actual or perceived love that the child needs in order to know himself or herself, and his or her world. He or she is no longer the seal of a merger or a necessary laborer but is the tangible realization and monument of the love of the father and mother. Within earlier forms of marriage and family, the child's existence and being was cemented in tradition or function. So for the child to feel thrust into a place of belonging-less-ness and meaninglessness, the centuries-long tradition of his kin unit would need to be destroyed, or the viability of the family's labor would need to disappear. Only major historical and economic changes would shake the typical family and the security it provided for children. But for the children of the late-twentieth-century love union, all it took to destroy a marriage was a change in Mom and Dad's individual, subjective feelings. Here, then, is the conflict that we have yet to solve: what do you do when the self-fulfillment of mother and father requires the dissolving of a marriage, but the security and self-fulfillment of the child depends upon its continuation?

In a culture where the communal realities have largely migrated under the purview of bureaucratic institutions, the family serves as one of the last organic communal realities of belonging and corporate purpose that allow children to discover their selves. In the security of the love of the marriage union that shared the child's very biological

material, they are blanketed and safe to develop and understand their selves.[68] What is there for the self (or is there even a self?) when there is no place to belong, when a family narrative is shattered, and purpose is disconnected from the community of one's being?[69]

There have been great changes in the way we have understood intimacy, sexuality, and love in the last sixty years, changes that set up this double bind of divorce: what may offer humanizing freedom for parents may be a dehumanizing void for children.

2

Marriage and Divorce
in Late Modernity

Being and Action in Giddens's Social Theory

Introduction

An old barn was transformed into a reception hall for the wedding of my wife's childhood friend and college roommate. Lana was in her mid-thirties and had been tenaciously seeking love since she and my wife met in college. It had been a long journey, and now Lana stood glorious in her wedding dress as flashbulbs fired and bridesmaids and friends chased toddlers and preschoolers, balancing both champagne glasses and sippy cups.

As we wrangled our own preschooler into his seat for dinner, the maid of honor took the microphone and announced to the crowd, "I would like to introduce to you for the first time . . ." She paused. She muffled the microphone and turned to someone behind her for consultation. In a moment she continued, "I would like to introduce Mr. and Mrs. Arrabella!"

At our table we exchanged confused glances, wondering who were Mr. and Mrs. Arrabella, even as we clapped politely. Lana and her

husband bustled to their places at the head table. As the applause faded, I asked, "Is Arrabella his last name?" No one had any idea where this name had come from, and as we nibbled vegetable appetizers we hypothesized about the mystery. "Maybe it's his mom's maiden name," someone suggested. "Maybe it's some kind of combination of both of their last names, but I guess that doesn't work," added another. Finally, someone from another table put an end to our speculation. "Arrabella" was, loosely, Italian for "answered prayer." Lana and her groom had decided to create an altogether new name for themselves. The fulfillment of their love, they believed, burst the old wineskins and required a whole new category outside of past, tradition, and the lineage preserved by family names.

Hearing this, I could only smile, because it summed up Lana's endearing quirkiness, but also because their creation of the Arrabellas spoke volumes about living and loving in late modernity. Marriage is so completely no longer about lineage, land, and labor that a couple can choose an entirely new name for themselves. Love has become so central to the fulfillment of the self, and the self so significant, that tradition has simply melted away, leaving individuals so free that they can literally choose to be with each other outside of anything but their own choice. *Arrabella*, answered prayer, was perfect, for it signaled both the need for the self to find love and the self's individual journey to discover it. This severance from the past and social bonds was heightened by the setting of the reception. The old barn was no longer an actual barn but had instead been transformed into a kitschy relic of a past world, dripping with vines and dotted with suspended glowing tea lights. It was clear in that moment that however traditional the wedding might otherwise have appeared, it was occurring in a new and different world, a world where the self was cut loose from many of the traditions that had governed the lives of those who had used this barn as a barn, to house livestock.[1]

As the night continued we heard more about this name choice. We heard that the families of the bride and groom had no idea that this new name had been chosen. It was as much a surprise to them as it was to everyone else. Later we heard that the groom's father was not happy, perhaps feeling as though in choosing this new name his son and daughter-in-law were rejecting him and his name, maybe

grieving what this would mean for his future grandchildren, and what it meant to the family members gathered around the couple. It was clear that these two individuals did not see the marriage as the linking of the history of one family line with another; for them it was an episode beginning an all-new union that could not be weighed down by past, expectation, or obligation. Mr. and Mrs. Arrabella were free, so free that they could choose their own surname. And it was not just a name different from forebears'. It was an altogether new, invented name. The name had meaning only to them and arose from their personal corporate self, the union of their individual selves. It revealed the radical freedom that we all possess in our time. But it also revealed something very risky, something that might make the radical freedom feel more disorienting than pleasurable.

In chapter 1 we placed the family on center stage, examining it through history and considering the self only as it related to the history of the family. In this chapter we will reverse field, placing the self at center stage. We will examine changes the self undergoes in late modernity, using Anthony Giddens's theory of modernity. We will note how changes in the self have impacted our understanding of marriage. Specifically, we will see the impact of these changes on the being (ontology) and acting (agency) of children of divorce. Finally, we will characterize these changes in marriage and family as the emergence of "pure relationships," again focusing especially on their impact on children of divorce.

Marriage and Modernity

Modernity is often seen as the growth of the technological economy (industrialization) and the radical evolution in epistemology (how we know things) after the Enlightenment.[2] While modernity does affect our economic structures and conception of reality, it does more. Modernity transforms how we understand and create intimacy and identity by shaping how we understand our very selves in the world. So it is about more than epistemology. It is also about ontology. It is about more than economic structures. It is about agency as well. Or to say it in another way, modernity shapes how we "are in the

world" and how we "act in the world." If we are to understand the self in relation to the family and how divorce impacts this self, then we will have to understand the self within the shifts brought by modernity.

Focus on the Future

What is it about modernity that changes the way people understand themselves and their actions? According to Giddens, modernity alters the way we think about time and space. Modernity changes our vision of humanity. Instead of seeking to correlate yourself and your actions to a known past—to rituals, elders, and custom—modernity creates selves that seek to colonize the unknown future. Modernity is future-oriented, and as such it places the self in center view, for only the self, the individual cut free from all past constraints, can colonize an unknown future. We saw in chapter 1 that marriage was once seen as submission to the lineage, to the good of the kinship. Marriage was about correlation to the past. But modernity turns toward the future, to what might be. Likewise, the love-based marriage is marriage no longer bound to the past, but free to seek the future. Thus Lana and her husband are free to create a surname for themselves—they are looking forward rather than back.

Mobile and Portable

But modernity does more than lead to transitions in conceptions of time. It also alters conceptions of space. If we turn our attention to the future, then our orientation to location must change. When the self is central, so too is mobility, for individuals are free, at the very least in their own minds, to think of themselves beyond the space they inhabit. They are free to imagine themselves, by peering into the future, in multiple locales across time. They are free to live one place as a child, another as a college student, and yet others with every subsequent job change. With modern communication technologies, they may even live in one place while simultaneously working in many others. The love-based marriage itself reinforces mobility of space. Because love is between two individuals moving into the future, it need not locate itself squarely in any location. Love can move anywhere the two individuals

might go. The marriage is based on love, on each other's subjective feelings, which are not bound by space, but only by the mutual belief that such feelings will live on into the future.

The transitions in time and space are born most fully in what Giddens calls "the end of tradition in modernity."[3] When correlation to the past gives way to colonization of the future, and space becomes easy to navigate, the hold of tradition gives way.[4] People no longer need to look to the past to answer basic questions about who they are and how to act. Ontology and agency are free from tradition. In reference to Giddens's perspective Kenneth Tucker says, "More and more people realize that their identities and moral systems can no longer rely on taken-for-granted traditions, but must be actively created by themselves."[5] In terms of marriage and family, this means that couples are free to choose a love partner outside of the desire, need, or expectations of a community of generations.

THE CHANGE IN "TRADITION"

In the early dawn of modernity, tradition did not die as much as it became lodged in future-oriented structures that promised to transcend concrete space, structures like science, markets, and the nation-state.[6] All three structures provided people a kind of tradition (though without a community of the past) that helped them understand who they were and how to act. But because these so-called traditions of early modernity were directed toward the future and then were ultimately binding only so far as the individual self gave them power, they were vulnerable to doubt.[7] When being (ontology) and acting (agency) are bound in correlation to the past, doubt is *not* central, for your objective is to follow the paths of others who have already blazed a trail. But when the future is given prominence and the trail has never been walked, all traditions of authority (even those future-directed ones like markets, science, and nation-state) can be, and in late modernity are, open to doubt. Giddens says, "Modernity turns out to be enigmatic at its core, and there seems to be no way in which this enigma can be 'overcome.' We are left with questions where once there appeared to be answers."[8]

In early modernity marriage becomes about love, about walking into the unknown future. Residues of old traditions remain with it,

even after marriage freed itself from correlation to the past in lineage and labor. Patriarchy and sexual mores remain and new realities like the separate spheres are born. But soon these perspectives cannot bear the weight of the selves' unconstrained journey into the unknown future that modernity promises; these perspectives cannot tolerate the pressure of the necessary doubt of everything that may hinder the selves' being and acting on the horizon of the future. Divorce then becomes a maneuver done always for the future: for future happiness, for future health, for the possibility of future love. It is a maneuver undertaken for the self, so that the self might have a future worth being and acting in. In Giddens's words, "Ideals of romantic love . . . inserted themselves directly into the emergent ties between freedom and self-realisation."[9]

But of course here again is our rub: the child too lives in modernity, the child too is free from the constraints of tradition and must seek to be a self that blazes his or her own trail into the future. While divorce can liberate parents to seek a new, meaningful future, for the child divorce likely hinders self-development, as we will see below.

Risk and Trust

In modernity, custom, elders, and obligatory communal structures no longer determine people's identities. Tradition can no longer determine the structure of society and how people know things (epistemology), but tradition can also no longer determine how people are in the world (ontology) and how they act (agency). John Thompson explains that in such a world "individuals are obliged increasingly to fall back on their own resources to construct a coherent identity for themselves. Whereas traditions once provided . . . a relatively stable framework for the self and for the process of self-formation, today individuals must chart their own course through a world of bewildering complexity."[10] In a world beyond tradition, where the individual self is unconstrained, we move into an unknown future disconnected from the past. Consequently, our being and acting in the world are governed not by tradition but by risk and trust.

Modernity itself is a Pandora's box. It promises liberation from attention to the past by freeing individual selves to seek the future. But

this future is not known; if blazing your own trail can be freeing, it is always risky.[11] Markets, scientific advancement, and nation-state policies are supposed to assure a future horizon for the individual self. They do this by mitigating risk. For instance, markets open up industries such as insurance, science provides medicine, and government creates policies for unemployment and regulation for safe workplaces. All of these, and many others, do not orient us back to the strictures of community, custom, and ritual. What they do instead is provide procedures and policies that act as safety nets for a more secure high-wire walk into an unknown future. Then the individual self can be and act for this future without being paralyzed by an overwhelming threat of future risk.

No-fault divorce, as a government policy (as law) stands in this same stream of logic. If marriage is about the fulfillment of two individual selves through love, then what about the possibility of love dissolving or departing? How could you possibly face the risk of the degradation of self and narrowing of the future if you could not escape a loveless marriage? Giddens asserts, "In a world where one can no longer simply rely on tradition to establish what to do in a given range of contexts, people have to take a more active and risk-infused orientation to their relationships and involvements."[12] No-fault divorce addresses the risk of the self loving another in a future-oriented modernity. It is the safety net thrown across the chasm that yawns beneath love-based marriage.

Giddens has explained that there was nothing like risk in premodernity.[13] By this he does not mean that a premodern world was not dangerous; as a matter of fact, it was much more hazardous than our own modern world. Disease, violence, and oppression were everywhere. But risk is different from danger. Risk imagines vulnerability, but vulnerability that can be avoided with the right maneuvering of the individual. In contrast, avoiding danger is not contingent on the individual. If danger was avoided in the premodern world, it was not because of the maneuvering of the individual self, but because of fate, intervention of the ancestors, or the hand of God. Danger is faced communally; risk is an individual concern.[14]

When marriage was about lineage and labor, it was surely dangerous. The ordeals of childbearing, along with the capriciousness of kin

betrayal (rather than cooperation) and volatile political arrangements, could make it quite treacherous. But marriage itself does not become risky until it consists of individual selves seeking love, until it is possible for the marriage to die when love does. Marriage becomes risky when the self and the future can be darkened by the betrayal, neglect, or decision of the lovers themselves. Marriage becomes risky when either partner can decide that present or future happiness is not congruent with the continuation of the marriage. And this can happen at any moment, for it is ultimately based (solely) on the subjective feelings of the self. Giddens puts it this way: "Now [marriage] is a much more open system with new forms of risk. Everyone who gets married is conscious of the fact that divorce rates are high, that women demand greater equality than in the past. The very decision to get married is constitutively different from before. There has never been a high-divorce, high-remarriage society before. No one knows, for example, what its consequences are for the future of the family or for the health of children."[15]

THE RISKY FAMILY

Because the family is constantly vulnerable to the individual choice of father and mother as they move into the future, the family is intrinsically risky in late modernity. Elizabeth Marquardt states, "One major national study has turned up an important finding. . . . The researchers found that one-third of divorces end high-conflict marriages, in which the parents report physical abuse or serious and frequent quarreling. . . . However, two-thirds of divorces end low-conflict marriages, in which the parents divorce because they are unhappy or unfulfilled, or have other problems that are not seriously threatening."[16] This reveals that there is absolutely no guarantee that a child's parents' marriage will continue, and that the family will not be radically changed. For some it may be unlikely, but it is never impossible. Today's family is always under the risk of being shattered. The young person must be and act in a world where this risk could become reality.

We witness this riskiness in the experience of fifteen-year-old Carie as she reflects on the announcement that her parents intended separation: "They never fought much at all," she says, "then one night,

it was a family meeting. We had pizza, and then they cleared the table. I don't really remember exactly how they said it, but my older brother started crying. . . . I didn't know that it was coming. When they told us, I ran upstairs to see if it wasn't just a dream and I was still asleep."[17]

Carie's words demonstrate the precariousness of the family in late modernity. She had no idea the announcement of her parents' divorce—and the dissolution of their family—was coming. It is reminiscent of the story of a ten-year-old boy who ran to a family meeting thinking his parents would tell him that he would be given a canoe he had asked for, only to realize the meeting was to inform the children that their dad was moving out.[18] But Carie's quote also powerfully exposes how divorce itself is an ontological reality. After the announcement, Carie reports that she ran upstairs to see if it was just a dream. The idea that her parents would no longer be together, and her family would be radically changed, seems to collide with reality. It must be a dream. How can she *be* without them together?

When parents choose divorce they choose to be in the world in a different way. They choose an action that allows each one's self to move into the future separate from the other. Even if it is painful and unwanted, in divorcing the parents make a maneuver for the future. But children, especially young ones, are left maneuverless. Their being and acting for the future is clouded, for it was from the family that the child discovered who they were in the world (ontology) and how to act in it (agency). The self of the parents chose the union of one to another for the future, but the child made no choice; rather the child is the product of the union and the realization of the parents' chosen future—so long as their future together endures.

The act of divorce asserts that a particular union cannot provide fulfilling self-development for the parents. It cannot support their well-being into the future. Yet the child is dependent upon the future. His or her life is to be lived, his or her identity is to be formed, his or her actions are to be taken, in the future. If the future can no longer sustain his or her parents' marriage, how can it be welcoming to the child? How can the future be anything but disjointed? Stephanie Staal, in her autobiographical book, *The Love They Lost: Living with the Legacy of Our Parents' Divorce*, states this reality powerfully through reflection

on her own experience: "I know splitting up was often a painful process for them—sometimes devastating—but while our parents endured their divorces armed with the resources of age and experience, we were confronted with new and complicated emotions before we were fully capable of understanding them. For those of us who bore witness to the wave of divorce that engulfed our parents, their breakups defined our childhood, leaving imprints that may last a lifetime."[19]

THE FUNCTION OF TRUST

The only way to navigate the ever-present riskiness of modernity is through trust. Trust does not eliminate risk; instead, trust asserts that the self will continue to live for the future despite the risks. As Giddens suggests, trust is inoculation against the risks we face daily. For instance, there is no guarantee that the low-fat snack foods I eat are not filled with preservatives that will give me cancer in the future. There is no guarantee that the bolts on my axle were tightened correctly and with care by the mechanic I have never met. Though I have no personal contact with the company that makes my snack food and no bond with my mechanic, I nevertheless have to trust. Giddens defines trust "as confidence in the reliability of a person or system, regarding a given set of outcomes or events, where that confidence expresses a faith in the probity or love of another, or in the correctness of abstract principles."[20] This trust is risky. There is no community and tradition to link us one to another, for we are free to think of ourselves beyond the pre-given knowledge and actions of community and tradition. Yet the only option other than trust is manic, paralyzing paranoia. The irony of modernity is that it promises certainty in science and bureaucracy, but because of its future orientation beyond tradition, it actually demands trust in confrontation with a plethora of choices, answers, motivations, and perspectives. To be in this world as a self, I have to learn to trust in spite of my awareness of risk; I have to trust that the future will not swallow me. I have to trust that there is an enduring place for my being and acting.

The love-based marriage, especially after opposition to sexism, and rising wages for women, is based almost completely in trust. No communal ritual demands the continuation of marriage, and the

cultural taboo of divorce is minimal at best. Therefore, to enter into marriage in late modernity is to trust that the love that binds will be enough to avoid the many unknown risks that the future holds.[21] Our being and acting in the world are based on trust. When trust is betrayed at the level of love, the self of husband or wife finds little to stand upon, for trust in love has been the foundation of the marriage. When the foundation crumbles, the structure of the family is no longer inhabitable. Mother and father must depart from the structure built on the foundation of trust because that foundation is gone. But, again, children do not belong to the family because they have chosen to trust it. Children do not belong by choice, but by being—by being the very creation of the union of mother and father.[22]

When trust in love is gone, and the foundation crumbles, parents may label the structure uninhabitable and try to move on. They may find it difficult and painful, but they are free even in confusion and hurt to seek the future. The child, on the other hand, is not able to leave, for his or her being and acting in the world are wrapped up in this now condemned structure called family, this union of one biological parent with another. Eighteen-year-old Jewel states, "It's so much harder on the kids than it is on the parents because a relationship can split, and you're like, 'Okay, this guy's a jerk,' or 'This girl is a jerk,' and you can go on with your life. But for the kids, that's their dad or their mother, and it's so much harder for them. The parents often don't consider that aspect of the divorce."[23]

We rarely consider that children *are* through their parents' union, and in their separation children are unable to leave the structure created by their union that they now deem uninhabitable. Now that trust has failed at such a fundamental level, risk grows teeth and trust becomes harder and harder to negotiate in the future.

Identity and Intimacy in Late Modernity

Modernity brings transitions in our orientation to time and space by directing the self toward an unknown future in an unknown place. Tradition no longer regulates or organizes human life in the profound ways it once did. We must negotiate our own futures as individuals,

by balancing risk and trust. This unavoidable and ongoing negotiation transforms how the self formulates identity and finds intimacy. No longer does tradition provide people with predetermined or everlasting identities. No longer does tradition direct how and with whom intimacy will be shared. We have seen that the love-based marriage itself is the elevation of the self seeking its destiny outside of rigidly determined patterns and past practices. The self freely determines who it is and whom it will cherish. I have argued throughout this chapter that identity and intimacy and their transitions in the blur of late modernity reveal how our cultural realities have a deeper impact than simply on epistemology (how we know) and technological economy (structures). They bear also on our being (ontology) and acting (agency) in the world.

This, accordingly, means that the self, not tradition, is responsible for determining who you are and how you should find deep connection.[24] Giddens writes, "Identity is the creation of constancy over time, that very bringing of the past into conjunction with an anticipated future."[25] In a detraditionalized world, the self must maintain and govern identity. Where earlier custom and ritual provided the constancy of identity in relation to past and future, now the self creates its own identity by formulating its own individual story, a story that need not connect with the strictures of some predefined way of life (tradition). This is a great liberation; no longer can ruler, priest, or elder tell you who you are and whom you should love or hate. The possibilities for identity and intimacy are no longer bound by custom, but only by your imagination. Giddens states, "My relationship to modern society—my social identity—has become unglued from the contexts, communities and expectations that once circumscribed my knowledge of who I am and how I live. Today, I am responsible and liable for my own identity."[26] When we are directed toward the future, identity and intimacy must be flexible enough to adapt to the changes the future inevitably brings.

The Flexibility of Identity

While this reality provides a great freedom for the self, it also thrusts upon it great responsibility. In moving into the future, the

self is propelled to keep its identity constantly open. Who you are must enter into what Giddens calls "a process of constant reflexivity."[27] The self must always be reflecting on who it is in relation to the world, because living into the future is about negotiating risk through trust. Identity, then, is bound up in reflexivity. In the process of constant reflection on your world and yourself, you create an identity for yourself. Therefore, my identity is in a constant state of flux as the future dawns and a new future is anticipated.[28] Even more difficult, I must continue to keep my identity open as I move into the future, but in such a way that I find some kind of continuity in my own narrative across time. Giddens explains, "The reflexive project of the self, which consists in the sustaining of coherent, yet continuously revised, biographical narratives, takes place in the context of multiple choices."[29] The self must also sustain this continuity of narrative. Therefore, I must not only continue to adapt my identity as I move into the future but must work to keep my adapting identity in some kind of continuity with my past.[30] Inconsistency with my past narrative may be explained by saying things like, "Well, that was my religious stage," or "I was really into New Wave fashion at that time." Such assertions show that identity can change easily in a future-oriented world without tradition; lifestyle choice becomes a way for me to take on new identities and agencies in the world. It also serves as a way to keep my biographical narrative intact, as a whole. The self acts to take on new, different, or distinct perspectives that connect one phase of my life with another. My perspectives, dress, and consumption may change, but it remains I who act.[31] My ability to construct my own biographical narrative is key. I must create my own story; elders, custom, and ritual are mute.[32]

With identity an open process determined by the constant reflexivity of the self, intimacy becomes democratized. When it is up to the self to determine who it is, then it is also up to the self to determine whom to love and befriend. Identity and intimacy are indelibly linked, and when either identity or intimacy is open to the freedom of the self, so too is the other. Giddens writes, "Self-identity is negotiated through linked processes of self-exploration and the development of intimacy with the other."[33] As we saw in the last chapter, before the Victorian age intimacy in marriage was neither

common nor necessary.[34] Identity was predetermined, and custom and ritual dictated who you were, so intimacy was not something to be sought or something one needed to have an identity. But when the self determines identity, intimacy becomes essential, for it is on the playing field of intimate interactions (agency) that one discovers who one is (ontology).[35]

This means that almost all relationships of intimacy in late modernity are self-chosen, and in that sense they are what Giddens calls "pure relationships."[36] Friendships and sexual partners are not chosen because of the strictures of tradition, but because they provide the intimacy and support needed for carrying out the reflexive project of the self in an unknown future. These relationships are formed on the basis of affection, emotional communication, and the hope for a shared history. They are pure from all predetermined obligations, such as kin, community, and religion.

The pure relationship is pure not because it is free from guilt or dysfunction (it is, in fact, much more open to such realities), but because it is unbound to anything other than the free negotiation of the individuals' selves that choose to find intimacy with each other. The pure relationship, then, can become messy when tradition no longer regulates urges and behaviors that may violate the union that holds the relationship together. It becomes messy because giving in to certain urges, behaviors, or desires may cause tension or the termination of the relationship (and therefore have ramifications). But in themselves the urges and desires are not wrong, for what governs our being and acting in the world is not obedience to custom but the freedom to determine our future by continuing to reformulate ideas of who we are and therefore whom we should love. Giddens states powerfully, "What holds the pure relationship together is the acceptance on the part of each partner, 'until further notice,' that each gains sufficient benefit from the relation to make its continuance worthwhile."[37]

As soon as identity and intimacy are askew, as soon as your intimate relationship does not seem to satisfy your conception of who you are (or want to be), then the relationship's future is darkened, and there is justification to move on. The self, cut free from the obligation of tradition, must seek its own identity through intimacy

with a plethora of possible others. The pure relationship provides the self with the opportunity to attach and detach easily and quickly as you move into the future. Again, this is quite liberating; we are no longer bound to toil in relationships that smother our selves. We are free to seek identity and intimacy outside of "ought," "must," and "have to." Yet this freedom is also very risky, for it is only the wills of individuals that promise the continuation of the bond.

The Pure Relationship: The Impact on Children

Divorce itself, in late modernity, is the product of reflexivity. People divorce because they are free to imagine their identities anew outside marriage. Marriage in late modernity must bow to the fluctuations of the pure relationship. Where earlier marriage bowed to political mergers and labor negotiations, today marriage bows to the reflexive project of self-identity. It seeks intimacy on the horizon of the future. No-fault divorce allows marriage to take on the marks of the pure relationship. No longer are individuals bound to the institution of marriage itself. Rather, no-fault divorce allows the self the freedom to rework its identity as it moves into the future with or without the spouse.[38] This may be good for the selves of husband and wife.[39] But what about their children?

As the self moves into the future, open to transitions in identity and formulating intimacy through the pure relationship, the self is free from obligatory structures. The pure relationship itself is contingent on the *choice* to be together outside of any kind of coercion. But herein again lies the rub: children are bound to their parents not by choice but by biology.[40] While parents can relate to each other through the pure relationship, and the child can relate to many others in its world in such a manner, the relationship of parent to child, or rather family to child, cannot be based on the pure relationship. The very sharing of DNA creates an obligatory bond between children and parents (we will see how this is so in the following chapters).[41] Jen Abbas, in discussing her parents' divorce, reveals how the pure relationship can serve parents well by providing the freedom of a second chance, but in so doing can strike children at a deeply ontological level. "Our perspective on the divorce differs vastly from that of our parents. We

do not perceive divorce as a second chance, and this is part of our pain. Divorce shatters our sense of home. As much as our parents strive to convince us otherwise, we still feel rejected."[42]

For instance, nineteen-year-old Christina says, "Oh, yeah, my dad had failed as a father, but he was my father. He loved me, and it's been very hard for me to try to build a relationship with him. I want to have a relationship with him, because you only get one dad. Even if your mom remarries, to a certain extent you only get one dad."[43] Christina points to the fact that children are bound to their parents by more than the free choice of the pure relationship. Even though her (biological) father failed her, something in her being desires communion with him, her being in relation to his creates an obligatory bond that keeps her yearning for him, and for the union of those responsible for her being.

The Child's Identity and Intimacy

Divorce in late modernity is a two-edged sword. It assumes that the freedom of the pure relationship can set the terms for the marriage, yet such terms cannot support the being of the children this marriage creates.[44] The obligatory bond of biology provides an unalterable chapter in the child's biographical narrative. While he or she can choose to enter and leave multiple relationships to formulate an identity with continuity over time, the child nevertheless must come to some kind of acceptance of the relationship that resulted in his or her being. When there is division in that basic union, the narrative of the self lacks coherence (we will discuss this further below). At some point in defining who you are, you must come to grips with where you come from.

Therefore, the promise of late modernity that identity can be formed and reformed on the terrain of intimacy does not work when it concerns parent and child, for identity (who you are) cannot escape definition, even when intimacy is not present. Even if I do not know my father (thus making intimacy impossible), my very being is drawn to his; his being becomes (even in not knowing it) that by which I define myself, or that by which I fail to be able to define myself because I do not know him.

This is why, in theory, a step- or blended family should be especially suited to facing the winds of a future-oriented modernity, for the step- or blended family is organized by the patterns of the pure relationship and is free from determinative obligation.[45] But in actuality, many step- or blended families confront the tension of the conflict between the obligatory bonds of biology that form a straight line to one's identity ("I'm the daughter of . . .") and the free choice of the pure relationship that constructs identity through intimacy. Often in stepfamilies parents will seek to recast the new family in the same molds as the biological family. They will ask children to act like their new stepfather is their dad, or at least like their new stepsiblings are their brothers and sisters. They are asked or told to choose to see these strange new people in such a way. They are asked to connect to these others through the pure relationship while making it appear that there is biological correlation. Parents can choose to act in such a manner because it is solely through their choice that this new family or marriage comes to be. But children are told to act like these people are family, while having no real choice at all. For the child, the stepfamily lacks both the biological correlation and the free choice to be with and for these people. Jen Robinson discusses these very issues in her own story:

> During the first year of the new marriage, my mother encouraged me to treat my stepbrothers as if we had always been siblings, and asked me to treat my stepfather in a similar manner. She wanted us to be a real family but what is real? What is family? At this distance I can both admire the energy my mother devoted to reconstructing a family and acknowledge that the process was at best uncomfortable for me. With, I suppose, typical teen angst, I felt I was being asked to participate in a lie. I didn't see us as a family; I saw us as a bunch of strangers who lived together.[46]

For children the conflict between obligatory biology and the pure relationship leads to confusion and frustration. They must form identity in a world free of obligation while feeling an intrinsic pull toward the union of their origins. We can hear this in Michelle's experience of her stepfamily. "Dad's first marriage is a skeleton in their Cleaver family closet. After nearly twenty-five years, Joyce [the stepmom] still

seems to struggle with the fact that Dad was married to someone else before he was married to her. And now what has evolved is that my brother and I have no defined identity within his second family. We aren't peers to our half-siblings, nor are we authority figures. We are electrons, forever destined to orbit their family nucleus."[47] Michelle and her brother are painfully stuck between the pure relationship and obligatory biology. Their stepmother has no bond to them other than through her choice to be with their father. They experience themselves as strangers and unable to form identity in this stepfamily. Their half-siblings are bound to the family by biology, but Michelle and her brother are bound by the tenuous pure relationship. Their dad, even with his obligatory bond, can send them back to their mother if the pure relationship upon which his marriage is built demands it.

Stepfamily is so difficult because it is not only a new family, but it creates two new families—one related to the biological mother and another related to the biological father.[48] When the biological obligatory bond is broken, and one world becomes two separate worlds, children are forced to form identity not through the solid place of shared being, but through choice. Children must be two selves in two different families, neither of which firmly hold them in biological correlation. Matt says of his siblings and himself, "[Our stepmother] wondered if we hated her. Really we just hated having two families where we'd had one before. We hated being two different people, where before we could just be our parents' kids."[49] This makes forming an identity difficult and conflicted at best.

It is not uncommon for children of divorce to struggle with forming identity on the playing field of intimacy, even though they have confronted more directly the reality of the pure relationship than their peers. Yet, trapped in a divided connection to their obligatory biology, they often feel as though they cannot articulate a clear sense of their identity, even temporarily, making intimacy ever difficult. As Staal says about her parents' own divorce, "When parents divorce . . . they leave us with fractured narratives and loose ends that we carry with us into adulthood. After viewing the events of our parents' breakup within the limited scope of youth, many of us find that as adults, we lack the facts to see the parts of the past as a meaningful whole."[50] We might add to her rich statement, "We lack the facts to see *ourselves as whole.*"

3

Divorce as an Issue of Being

Ontological Security and the Loss of Self

For some time after our parents divorced, my Kara and I flinched whenever the phone rang. It was always nothing so threatening—a telemarketer, a classmate, a friend. But we had been shell-shocked; the phone calls of our parents' infidelities and pending doom of their marriages had shaken us deeply. Just as fireworks on the Fourth of July draw soldiers back into memories of combat, the ring of the phone reminded us of calls that shook our world. I kept telling myself that this was not as big of a deal as it felt, not as big of a deal as my soldier analogy suggests. No one died. It would be much worse if the voice on the other end of the line informed us that one of our parents was killed or a loved one had cancer. Or would it? I wondered. At least I would know how to feel and react to such horrible news. Maybe it is an overstatement to insinuate that our experience was like battle fatigue, but I felt raw, questioning which way was up and what I could count on as real after this experience.

Kara often awakened in the night to find herself overwhelmed by fear. There was never anything specific to the fear, no fright of something supernatural like a ghost, no worry that an intruder had picked

her apartment lock. It was just blind fear, fear she could articulate only as fear of being alone. I understood this, because I myself was feeling it, sleeping most nights on the couch so that when the fear enveloped me I could try to escape it by turning on the TV. It was an odd kind of fear, for it had no form, no rational categories to talk myself beyond it. It simply felt like I was losing my being, as if in the midst of my sleep I could simply disappear, fade away into nothing. It was the fear that now that the union that created me was dissolving, I might dissolve with it.

In the documentary film *One Divided by Two: Kids and Divorce*, there is an animated scene that relays the haunting dream of a child after the divorce of his parents. The narrator begins:

> When my parents first divorced I was scared that my parents would both start new families and forget about me. Around this time I had a dream. It was Christmas and we were all doing our shopping. I had some money to go and buy my parents and family some gifts. All of a sudden, out of the corner of my eye I see my mother. I was so happy to see her that I decided to run up to her and give her a big hug and then wish her a merry Christmas. My mother was with two other children, and I kept calling her, "Mommy, Mommy." But she didn't even know who I was; she was calling the little children her little children, and they were calling her "Mommy." I felt so strange and awkward, I had seen my mother in a different family, and she didn't even recognize me.[1]

This dream reveals the ontological ramifications of divorce. This child's dream communicates the questions of being he faces as he confronts the loss of a familial community. As he thinks about the divorce of his parents, his deepest fear is that in their division they will start new families. In these families and communities he is a stranger and, as such, worries that his being will be forgotten. If he *is* in the midst of *acting* with and for these people, if he has his being in the midst of this family, what will it mean for him (what will it mean for his *being*) if they depart to start new families? The children born into this new family will be elected through the union of parent and stepparent (they will have biological correlation to both parents), but this boy will be part of this new family only

through choice. He can depart the new family at any time to live with the other parent (or grandparent, etc.). In this back-and-forth of choice, this boy wonders whether between one family and the next he might get lost or, rather, feels, ontologically, like he *is* lost. This new family will be forever tenuous for him, for his being is not the outgrowth of it. He is there only by "choice" (choice of his parent or his own choice).

In this community, this new family, he is ontologically different, for his being is not bound to both parents, but only to one, and this one—in this instance, his mother—has cleaved her being to others that have no direct connection to the boy. Will she remember him and the way they were together? Will she honor their connection? And if she forgets or denies it, then who *is* the boy? How can he *be*? He worries so deeply about this that his unconscious communicates it to him in a dream in which his mommy has other children and forgets, ignores, or, more radically, negates his being. His being, in his dream, has become a stranger to her own. He calls her "Mommy!" from the core of his being, but now with these other children and family all around her, she cannot see him. His plea is a deep ontological cry (as object relations psychology has told us, and as we will see below), but the dream-mother returns his longing for community (for being-with, being connected to the origins of his being) with nothing but confusion, for her being is now connected to others.

This of course is just a dream! Few parents are in danger of forgetting their children. But the dream reveals a fear that is deeper than logic. Too often we have ignored such deep dimensions in examining the phenomenon of divorce. Therefore, in this chapter we will take up this challenge by examining Giddens's articulation of how our social environment must provide us with ontological security. This discussion will then take us into conversation with the work of philosopher Martin Heidegger and his understanding of being.

Ontological Security

It has been often assumed that divorce or single-parenthood is a societal issue. What is meant is that divorce can contribute to realities

such as poverty, delinquency, and poor educational performance for children. It has been assumed that at its core divorce is an issue of social capital, that it cuts off connections between young people and adults that can provide them the personal and relational currency to avoid or overcome pitfalls such as delinquency. Therefore, it is posited that, if we can simply provide young people who experience divorce with enough social capital, the divorce itself will be neither traumatic nor debilitating.[2] We therefore encourage parents to separate without visible conflict, and urge the departing parent to find ways to provide emotionally and economically for his or her children. And if this is not possible, then we must provide societal outlets (after-school or mentoring programs, for instance) to help.

Of course, this is all true, and does positively affect school perfor-mance, for example. But it is not the whole story. We have assumed that if cushioning social structures are in place, the impact of divorce is nullified or at least greatly diminished. But divorce is more than an issue of social capital or simple psychology (like self-esteem), for we are more than our place in the structures and knowledge of society. Even if young people preserve their social capital and un-derstand why their parents split up and what the divorce means, it still leaves a mark that cannot be erased by retained social capital or correct knowledge. And these are marks that last well beyond the age of custody, for divorce is ontological. For instance, Jody says, "It seems like it should be all over and done with after eight years, but it's really not. I guess I feel weird being like 'yeah, but . . .' because I'm twenty."[3] Loretta also confronts the common misconception that with the right support, children should be able to move on and smoothly put their parents' divorce behind them.

> People, especially people whose parents haven't been divorced, think that because it happened when I was nineteen and because I was away at college and because I wasn't there in the home, it shouldn't be a big deal . . . but that doesn't mean it wasn't just as emotional, and it doesn't mean that I don't have my own issues to deal with whether I was there or not. It's still a problem for me, and I get angry when people think, "Oh, well, you should be fine now. It should be no big deal. You weren't even there."[4]

When we assume that divorce is an issue primarily of social capital, we ignore that it may be more fundamentally an issue of identity, which after-school programs and argument-free separations may not solve. Giddens has shown us that social life touches us much deeper than simply structuring our life and framing our epistemology (how we know). Rather, social life impinges on our very ontology and calls us into action; social life impacts identity and intimacy, as we have just seen. Dealing with divorce, then, is about much more than helping young people think rightly about themselves ("the divorce was not your fault") and finding footholds in the structures of society (e.g., child support, tutoring, etc.). We must address the ways divorce shakes us to our core, our ontology—how we most fundamentally are and act in the world.

Ontological Security for Acting—How We Are in the World

Ontological security is a sense of safety. It is confidence and trust that the natural and social worlds are as they appear to be. Giddens explains, "The phrase [ontological security] refers to the confidence that most human beings have in the continuity of their self-identity and in the constancy of the surrounding social and material environments of action. A sense of the reliability of persons and things . . . is basic to feelings of ontological security."[5] You must trust that your social world is as you experience it.[6] And this experiencing is more than simply cognitive knowing; it is more basically about unconscious encountering. An infant does not cognitively know that if she cries, her caregiver will appear to meet her needs, but in multiple encounters with her caregiver (experiences of feeding, embracing, and cooing), she feels her being secure. Ontological security is a deep awareness of reliability, for it is based in being, not simply in knowing. For instance, if the child believes the family is secure (not perfect, but secure), and then she is told that the family as it is presently constituted will no longer exist, then the child is struck not at the level of social capital (not now, at least), but at the level of ontological security. Her world is no longer steady and dependable.[7]

Staal expresses this ontological insecurity as she reflects on what she calls "the night of revelation":

> The night when I learned of my mother's affair . . . in my mind . . . is that night of revelation when my family abruptly came undone, even though my mother didn't actually move out for another year. That night, in the span of minutes, my entire belief system was shattered. And sometimes when the phone rings late at night or someone walks into the room with a stricken look, I feel the same icy tingle I felt so many years ago, as if my body has programmed itself to receive the unexpected jolt. That's how deep the memory lies for me.[8]

The memory is as deep as her being itself, for in hearing the news of her family coming "undone," the dependability on which she *is* (has her being) is thrown into question.

As Giddens states, "Basic trust is established in the child as part of the experiencing of a world that has coherence, continuity and dependability. Where such expectations are violated, the result can be that trust is lost, not only in other persons but in the coherence of the . . . world."[9] Her ontological security is pulled out from under her, for her social world is no longer secure, and she is left with the perplexing question whether it ever was, or could ever be, truly secure.

My wife Kara's idyllic childhood was rooted in the idea of "family first" and grounded in the perceived permanence and security of her strong, cohesive family. When the secrets spilled out and the family crumbled, the foundation dissolved beneath her. She describes her feelings this way: "Suddenly any irrational and horrible thing was possible. There were no guarantees in the world, death could take anyone, accidents could and would happen, God was untrustworthy, the elements in the universe didn't function by any rational order anymore, and everything I had thought made sense in life was up for grabs. There was nowhere secure to anchor myself; I was adrift and terrified."

Ontological security is needed because it protects the human being from constantly having to confront the abyss of death that is present under the thin layer of social life and personal identity. Giddens states, "To be ontologically secure is to possess, on the level of the unconscious and practical consciousness, 'answers' to fundamental

existential questions."[10] Therefore, ontological security is the ability to depend on the self and the social unit enough that we are not thrust at every turn into terror that death, destruction, or derangement may seize us. Ontological security is the ability, to use Ernst Becker's phrase,[11] to deny death, to not be paralyzed by the fact that we are being-toward-death, to use Heidegger's term.[12] It is the ability to unconsciously feel oneself safe enough to be and to act in the world. Therefore, when divorce occurs and the ontological security that the family provided in the dependable (so dependable that its members share biology) social environment is lost, the protection of ontological security is shattered, and the child is left naked to face the existential abyss of non-being.[13]

Working from many of the same sources as Giddens, practical theologian James Loder pushes ideas deeper into the inner life of the human being, showing how negation (the unreal) exists within us. Therefore, when negation occurs in our social world (as in divorce), it can trigger the negation within ourselves, pushing us into ontological insecurity.

Loder explains that the human being's inner constitution exists in four dimensions. The first dimension he calls the "I." This is the dimension of the ego, the ability to claim oneself, to be a self. Loder contends that this ego reality of a unique "I" within the individual is irreducible. It is fundamental to our humanity. We know ourselves in the world through our own eyes. Loder makes this point by discussing the neurological experiments of Willard Penfield. Penfield did open-skull operations on people who were awake and conscious. He discovered that by touching certain places in the brain, he could control a patient's memories and senses. When he touched a location in the brain, the person would hear music or feel a rabbit in his or her hands. But whenever Penfield did this, the patient would respond, "You did that, *I* didn't." As Penfield continued his experiments, he could never discover the cerebral location of this "I." This has led Loder, following Penfield, to assert that the "I" is irreducible. To be is to be a self; it is to be "I."[14]

But this "I" cannot be free-floating. We cannot be an "I," as we have already asserted, without a social world in which to live. The

ability to say, "You did that, I didn't" is possible only because we exist in a social world that forces us to distinguish world from self. Therefore, not only is a social world out there, but it is also within us. We know our distinct "I" as it relates both objectively and internally to a lived world. Or, as Loder would say, the "I" or "the self" needs a lived world or environment in which to exist. Penfield's patients are forced to distinguish between what they do and what he does. Only because another is present doing something to them can they say "I."

When divorce strikes it impacts young people at the level of their lived world. It radically changes their social environment, but more significantly it rearranges their inner concept of the environment of the self. They have known their "I" through the lived world of their mom and dad. The child's very "I" knows itself, but more radically, it *is* at all because the social environment of Mom and Dad provides the "I" of the child a lived world she has taken into herself and made her own. When her social environment implodes, her lived world is shaken, and to such degree that she is forced to even question her "I." Without the social environment, which she used to create a lived world, she is compelled to question her very being. Her being slips from her fingers, for that to which it was rooted has ruptured. Staal says this about herself and her generation: "When we are stripped of the essential sense of acceptance provided by our families, we lose the grounding for our relationships. Any sense of home is torn asunder, and after a childhood of feeling like we don't belong, we can become emotional nomads as adults."[15]

The idea of these dimensions of the "I" and lived world are not unique to Loder. He draws them from psychological sources. What is unique to Loder is his contention that the human being is not only two-dimensional ("I" and lived world), but four-dimensional.[16] These added two dimensions are the void and the holy. This four-dimensional view of the person is what makes Loder's position both distinctly theological and significant for our conversation. Following the work of Kierkegaard, Loder asserts that the inner constitution of the person not only consists of an "I" and the lived world but also holds the reality of negation.[17] This Loder calls "the void."[18] The void is death and all its by-products (depression, isolation, fear, rejection,

etc.).[19] While the person must find a way to construct his "I" in the midst of his lived world, he must do so alongside the very present, but often denied, negation that exists within him.[20] This void "points to the tragic futility and ultimate meaninglessness of existence, which [Kierkegaard] terms 'despair.'"[21] According to Loder there is no way to expunge the void from within us; we all die and must deal with this reality, even before physical death, in experiences of rejection and isolation. Healthy life, then, is not exorcising the void from within, but having the ability to keep the void from monopolizing and therefore threatening to swallow the dimensions of the lived world and "I." What keeps the void from becoming an epidemic that paralyzes most people in existential trepidation is what Loder calls "the holy," the final of his four dimensions.[22]

The holy, at its most basic, is not something intrinsically good within the human; rather, it is the reflex of outrage at the void of negation. There is something within us that is not satisfied (at peace) with death; few of us can accept it easily. Death (the void) is the experience (and result) of broken relationship. Therefore, divorce, as the breaking of the child's primary community of being, has the potential to lead to the triumph of negation. Divorce can overcome the self and lived world by smothering the holy.

When we think of divorce, we often think of it in a two-dimensional way. We see it as affecting the young person's self-concept and rearranging his or her lived world. Therefore, we take action to help young people adopt new concepts of their lived world and think correctly about the value of their own being. But when we do this, we too often ignore the other two dimensions of the void and the holy in the inner constitution of the young person. Again, as I have said throughout, these actions, which we now see as two-dimensional, are often done at the level of epistemology. Not until we recognize that the young person is four-dimensional, not until we confront the void and the holy can we see the impact of divorce at the level of ontology. Action that ignores the void and the holy's ensuing outrage cannot help the young person at the level of ontology. It may be more useful to see divorce not primarily as an issue of the "I" and lived world, but rather as a phenomenon that impacts the person first at the dimension of the void. Only then does it radically affect the two dimensions of

"I" and lived world. The void and holy can be heard in remarks we cited earlier from Amy Conway. After twenty years she is still dealing with how her parents' divorce thrust her into the void. Now married herself, the holy in her seeks for her own children the wholeness she lacked. She hopes from the place of the holy that her child will not know the void in his or her being, as she herself has.

> Twenty years, three stepparents, and countless crying jags later, the story has no ending. I adapted, just as they say kids do. But divorce is more than a crisis to be worked through. No matter how well I weathered the storm when it was at its worst, I still emerged dripping with its effects, and feel a bit waterlogged to this day. Old doubts and questions linger, and mingle with fresh ones that arise as my parents and I get on with our lives. Married myself and seven months pregnant as I write this, I now fervently hope that my husband and I can give our children a life so solid they won't even think to question its foundation, like the one I knew until that afternoon.[23]

Ontological Security of Being—Who We Are in the World

The self's quest for ontological security is at the heart of human action in social life. It defines not just how we are in the world, but our identity—*who* we are in the world. Listen to the deeply ontological statements about identity expressed by Staal as she powerfully speaks for a generation of young adults:

> Divorce strikes at the heart of our identity. No matter how hard we try, we can't escape the fact that we are, according to the rules of biology, the product of both parents. But when the two people who created us then break the vows of love that once held them together, we can't help but feel displaced [ontologically insecure]. The rationale behind our discomfort is not so hard to grasp: If our parents no longer love each other, and on some level we belong to both of them, where does that leave us? We lose our sense of continuity, the comfort of family as anchor, and in its place we are usually left with the disturbing fact that we can't even picture our parents as a couple, let alone believe they were ever in love.[24]

She is shaken because deep in her unconscious self she trusted in the dependable social community of biological father and mother. Because this confusion happens at the ontological level (and the fundamental level of biological mother and father), it is not something that will simply go away after the shock has subsided.[25] Rather, as an ontological reality it becomes an experience that is imprinted on the child's very being.[26] As Helen Lynd puts it, once trust in dependability is lost, "we have become strangers in a world where we thought we were at home. We experience anxiety in becoming aware that we cannot trust our answers to the questions, 'Who am I?' 'Where do I belong?'"[27] Staal articulates this, "When I waved good-bye to my mother on that autumn afternoon thirteen years ago, I knew even then that day would mark the end of my childhood more than my first date or going off to college ever could. I no longer had a mother, at least in the everyday sense of the word, and as a teenage girl, the implications of this loss were staggering. I felt as if I had stepped through a looking glass, and from the other side everything looked wavy, warped, and completely surreal."[28]

"Despite the particulars of our parents' breakup, whether we were two years old or eighteen when it happened, regardless of who had custody or the nature of the subsequent changes, one fact remains constant," Staal states. "Divorce plants a splinter in our minds, and in response, we assemble our identities around it."[29] Or as Elizabeth Marquardt says, "The two people I loved the most and looked to as the rocks on which my own identity was built, my mother and my father, lived completely separate lives a six-hour drive apart."[30]

What floods the child is not exactly fear but anxiety. Upon witnessing the divorce, the child *may* never fear for protection, food, or basic care. But there is a difference between fear and anxiety. Fear is often based in epistemology and structures; for example, I fear snakes, and I fear that the failing housing market will not rebound. But anxiety cleaves onto shaken ontology; it is the chanting of the void; it latches onto something deep within me; it attaches to my very being. Heidegger commenter William Blattner says, "Anxiety . . . is a complete collapse of the . . . meaning in which one lives. In anxiety one does not constitute oneself because one cannot. In a sense, one is unable to exist."[31] Divorce thrusts the child into anxiety because

it strikes the dependability of the social unit that is responsible for his or her being. It thrusts a division within the child's own identity. He is cared for and need not fear for his next meal, for example, but he is anxious, for the very union that is responsible for his existence has regretted and aborted its unity of being. He *is* because *they* are. But now the *they* is not and will never be again. What then is the meaning of his existence when the *they* is now divided? Who is he? And is there not the anxiety of the feeling of division within him? Anxiety nestles deep within him, whispering questions to his very existence. His being and acting in the world lack coherence. Blattner continues, "What I cannot do in anxiety is understand myself. . . . Because we cannot understand ourselves in anxiety, we cannot feel 'at home' in the world."[32]

Loretta experiences the anxiety of non-being palpably when she remembers, "Dad was saying things like 'I never, ever loved your mother. I don't know why I didn't get out of this sooner.' . . . and that was really painful, because it was like he was saying, 'I wish you'd never been born.' That was the implication behind that."[33]

Whether or not children hear words like Loretta did, the divorce communicates such a reality, and this very communication reverberates throughout our being, disorienting us. Non-being floods the cracks of the broken family, and the child is left, not primarily with questions of social capital, but with questions of being. The questions surrounding the child address who the child is and where he or she belongs (and even whether he or she exists at all), and how to "be" and "act" in the world now that the ontological security of the family has become insecure.

When divorce strikes, it is first the void within the constitution of the young person that is opened and gapes wide, for this division of our most primary community thrusts our being into loneliness. With the tearing apart of the community in which we have our being, we find our self lost and our lived world drowning in questions regarding to whom we belong. This ontological loneliness is the tangible experience of death, says Loder, following Harry Stack Sullivan.[34] Marquardt concurs, finding such an actuality in her national survey: "If there is any single experience that unites children of divorce it is

our feelings of loneliness as children. One of the most striking and far-reaching findings of the national survey is that just over a tenth of young people from intact families can identify with the experience 'I was alone a lot as a child,' whereas close to half of us from divorced families can."[35]

When this relational community called family, which gives us our being, dissolves, our lived world is capsized. The void within us becomes unencumbered, for as Loder says, "The void is [present] the moment the lived 'world' is ruptured."[36] We can hear in Staal's words how when divorce sinks the lived world, the void comes rushing in, threatening the destruction of our being. "But as our families are hurtled into an uncertain world, such routines can be difficult to sustain. And the absence of limits, mixed with hurt and loneliness, can set up an inviting backdrop for self-destruction. I remember sitting on the floor of my friend's bedroom shortly after my parents divorced, the late afternoon sun slipping between the slats of drawn blinds, gulping tequila out of the bottle."[37] It sucks our being toward the unreal that exists within and outside of our being. It does this because the community that is responsible for our being is no longer present, thrusting our being into question, into direct exposure to the void.

Divorce first strikes the void within us, shaking our being, throwing us into the nothingness we cannot escape. And then the holy screams "No!" Ethan, reflecting on his parents' divorce when he was eleven, states, "I remember looking up at them, hearing the words, and then letting the news that they were getting divorced flood over me, like a tidal wave drowning out the idyllic life I had dreamed of for all of us. I remember protesting, struggling to fight it all back, imagining that I could change their minds and convince them they could try again and make it work. I remember my sister crying. I remember asking my parents to stay together, and being crushed at how stubborn they were, how determined to ruin our lives they seemed."[38]

Divorce feeds the void within the young person, smothering the holy, making the lived world untrustworthy, and making the "I" feel transparent and thin. Divorce is a death borne within the young person, for it strikes the "these people" that the young person needs to be "this person" in his or her four dimensions.

In sum, the child of a divorce can hear repeatedly that the divorce is not his fault and that school, home, and activities will not be changed. But such assertions address only issues of epistemology and advantage in the structures of society and leave unaddressed the deeper issues, the anxiety of identity, which rests on the now-fractured plates of ontological security. For people to act in the world, they must feel ontologically secure; they must feel that their being is held in an environment of trust and safety. There can be no more secure social environment to provide ontological security than the union of biological mother and father, for the child's very being is the product of their union, the unavoidable foundation their identity must contend with. Consequently, even young people who are given enough social capital to achieve in school and avoid antisocial behavior may still have unanswered questions (anxiety) in their being about the dependability of any social unit—most basically the one called "family" or "marriage."

Ontological Security in Time and Space

When tradition is operative it creates an environment of ontological security, so that even if a parent disappears or dies, the social environment remains stiffly or perfunctorily dependable, and anxiety would be mitigated in tradition operations.[39] In such a traditional setting, grief would certainly be real, but more than likely questions of ontological security would not arise. Existential angst would be silenced in the kin, communal, and religious dependability of the traditional group. Ontological security is the gift that tradition gives to its participants. Your place is secure (even when you may want freedom from it) in the life of the clan, kin unit, or village, with its rituals, customs, and practices.

Of course, ontological security must be renegotiated in a detraditionalized late modernity. When tradition is replaced by late modernity, and space becomes more navigable, issues of ontology come into view. Ontology is most fundamentally about being in time and space. When tradition rules, being is rarely reflected upon, because space is static and time is backward-looking. But freed of the lens

of tradition, space and time change, bringing being (ontology) into view.

Giddens's work draws deeply from German philosopher Martin Heidegger. Heidegger, one of the most important philosophers of the twentieth century, sought to turn philosophical attention back to how human *beings* live in the world. Heidegger wrote in a time of great negation, a time when the void could not be ignored. Living in Germany between the two world wars, Heidegger saw ontological insecurity everywhere and noticed the inability of philosophy to speak of it. Civilization was crumbling and nothingness was around every corner. Therefore, Heidegger's philosophy is not simply abstract but seeks to concretely deal with the nothingness we experience in our being, making him an ideal dialogue partner for our discussion of the feeling of nothingness that haunts children of divorce.

Giddens explains that "ontological security has to do with 'being' or, in the terms of phenomenology, 'being-in-the-world.'"[40] What does Heidegger mean by *being-in-the-world*, and what difference does this make for thinking about young people and divorce?

Heidegger: Being and Divorce

Being-in-the-world rests on a more fundamental category for Heidegger, the category of *Dasein* (literally, *being there*—in German *da* = there, *sein* = being). William Barrett says this in reference to Heidegger's concept: "My Being is not something that takes place inside my skin (or inside an immaterial substance inside that skin); my Being, rather, is spread over a field or region which is the world of its care and concern."[41] To understand being-in-the-world we must understand what Heidegger means by *Dasein*.

Western philosophy since Descartes was obsessed with issues of epistemology (*how* and *what* we know). Heidegger believed that such obsession had led us to ignore the more fundamental category of being. He argued that we are not simply creatures that think and therefore know. More basically, we are beings that *are*, that exist in a place and at a time. As such, our primary issue is not knowing, but rather the

very fact that we are, that we exist. Grasping this, that we are being (that we exist), becomes our problem. So for Heidegger, being comes before knowing, instead of knowing determining existence. We can see clearly how Giddens follows the trail blazed by Heidegger. Giddens asserts that the social world is not only about epistemology and structure, and that attention must be given to the issues of how the social world is formulated through agency, and also how such agency is engendered from the search to stabilize ontological security.

1. My Being Is Mine

There are four closely related traits of *Dasein*.[42] The first is that "Dasein's being is in each case mine."[43] Whereas Western philosophy had constituted existence in the cognitive awareness of the self (epistemology determining existence), Heidegger believes that *Dasein* is more fundamental than simply our ability to cognitively reflect on it.[44] This is why, as I stated above, the issue of divorce is not simply about knowing correctly, for being precedes knowing. Blattner explains that "Heidegger believes that you have an experience of yourself that is more basic than your cognitive awareness that all your experiences are *yours*."[45] This explains why many people, even if their parents divorced or separated before they were cognitively aware of them as together, still feel the burden of their parents' broken union later in their own lives. If it were only a cognitive issue, it could be solved by simple psychology or social opportunity, and you would assume that the ending of marriage before the child's awareness would leave no marks on the child's person. But this seems not to be the case. Instead, as often seen with adopted children, there is a longing deep within the child to find the origins of his or her being. Heidegger's point is that we are connected to our being, or experience it as our own, outside of our ability to cognitively examine and express it. If this is true, then we must begin to understand divorce's impact not only as social/psychological but as ontological as well.

2. I Am How I Live My Life in the World

Second, Heidegger states, "*Dasein* comports itself toward its being."[46] What this odd phrase basically means for Heidegger, here

following Kierkegaard, is that a person as *Dasein* is more than his or her self-consciousness. He or she is more basically how he or she lives his or her life in the world. "[Heidegger] argues that our fundamental experience of the world is one of familiarity. We do not normally experience ourselves as subjects standing over against an object, but rather as at home in a world we already understand." Blattner continues, "We act in a world in which we are immersed. We are not just absorbed in the world, but our sense of identity, of who we are, cannot be disentangled from the world around us."[47] This is what Heidegger means by being-in-the-world.[48] Accordingly, being and agency are closely (and indelibly) related, as we have seen throughout this chapter. And of course, when a divorce occurs what is often most painful for the child is that it radically changes the way he or she lives his or her life. But following Heidegger we must push further than the usual conversations on divorce and assert that it reaches all the way to the ontological level. "As one man put it, his parents' divorce made him feel 'existentially well traveled.' As travelers, [children of divorce] learned to adapt, adjust, speak a new language, adopt customs according to different lifestyles."[49]

The changing of the homes, for instance, is not as much an issue of social capital and lost privilege as it is a strike on the child's being, for she *is* inside this location, acting with these very people.[50] When Dad no longer lives here, in a real way his being is different, for he lives in space and time in a different manner. If he were only a roommate, say, a cousin living in the basement who (finally) finds his own place to live, she would experience the cousin as different in his new space; this may be weird, but not ontologically significant. But when the one who moves to another place is her father, the one responsible for the origins of her own being, she experiences his very being differently, and this sends shockwaves back to her own being. Dad is only to *be* with her, for she comes from him and cannot know herself outside of his own being. And now his being is different in relation to her own.

The father no longer being the same means the child's being also must change (and here is where anxiety rushes in). She knew herself and her father as she encountered him in the safe place of the shared family space. When she now encounters him in a different place,

perhaps a small apartment, she experiences both him and herself differently. Neither is the same. Their *Dasein* has changed. Walking into his apartment and seeing him and his things here shakes not merely her sensibilities, but her *Dasein*. There is a break in social action, but because of the break in social action, there is a break in the continuity of her being. She must re-create her identity anew now that her home is no longer filled with the smell of his cologne or the sight of his dirty socks on the bathroom floor. She must now re-create her identity without the unity of biological family, for its division results in a new way of living that can no longer set the terms for her *Dasein*, since it is divided. We can see the ontological ramification when Jen Robinson says,

> [The divorce] wasn't supposed to affect me; my parents were having a "good" divorce—still on speaking terms with each other, each still wanting to actively parent. . . . Everything was just fine. Of course that wasn't quite true. Dad wasn't there tying his tie in the bathroom mirror when I was brushing my teeth. Mom wasn't there when my sister and I came home from school. And when my parents were around, I now worried about both of them [separately]. My sister and I saw Dad on Sundays; he picked us up after lunch and brought us home after dinner.[51]

In divorce, as opposed to, say, a family move, the social unit that provides ontological security in its community collapses. Mom and Dad's *Dasein* is changed in new space (whether it be physical, psychological, or emotional) after a divorce, and the child's being too is forced to change. But the child must change in a manner that experiences the being of Mom and Dad, in whose union of being she exists, as something now divided. We construct our being around things and actions like homes, rooms, etc., but these things are significant because they are the material of *Dasein* encountering *Dasein*, of persons encountering persons. It is painful to see her father's things in a new space, but they are only a tangible sign that *he* is in a new space and therefore is different (as she is without him at home, and here with him now). She must question who he is, and in so doing must ask who she is. Staal's reflection on her mom's departure, as she stands in an empty room remembering the location of the furniture,

the smells, and the hanging of her mother's clothes, hauntingly witnesses to Heidegger's point, powerfully revealing the ontological significance of divorce.

> Vanity tables. Dresses. Perfume. These are only symbols for a loss too painful to put into words. Because as soon as we lived apart, the mother I once watched, while dreaming of womanhood, was gone, and she was never coming back. In my mind now reside two mothers: The one I grew up with for my first thirteen years, the mom who helped me get ready for school, put my report card up on the fridge, and listened to the details of my day; and the one who replaced her, taking me out once a week for brunch and maybe some shopping afterward. They are separate and distinct, as is my relationship with each of them.[52]

3. I Care about Who I Am

But this point stretches even deeper, for Heidegger contends "that the most basic form of self-awareness is my awareness of *who I am to-be*."[53] This is the third trait of *Dasein*: the fact that our being is an issue for us, we care about being, we care about who we *are* and who we *will be*. Nonhuman creatures have being, but not *Dasein*. Their being is not an issue for them; they simply are. Because my dog does not (as far as I know) reflect on his being, he is unshaken *ontologically* if we move houses or even if he goes to live with another family. I may think it concerns him, but more than likely this is only my own being (my *Dasein*) projecting my feelings of his absence onto him. As hard as it is for me to believe, he does not care about me, only that I feed him and throw him the ball to fetch. Though he may undergo a period of adjustment, if he must live with another family, my dog doesn't stop and think, "Well, who am I and who will I be, now that I don't live with Andy?" But we humans do! We care about who we *are*, and our being seeks coherence. *Dasein* searches to know why and what it is, so identity formation itself is the operation of *Dasein*. Our being matters to us.

Divorce impacts *Dasein* because it throws identity up in the air. The child now must figure out who he or she will be in the future, and who he or she will be in the light of the broken union of those responsible for his or her *Dasein*. We have seen above how squarely

Giddens places identity as an issue in late modernity, and how on-tological security can be achieved only by finding some continuity in your biographical narrative. But here Heidegger pushes us to see that this need for identity is based not on cognitive or moral realities, but on practical ones. This means that even if we can think rightly about the divorce of our parents or accurately place blame ("It is my mom who destroyed our family"), we remain deeply shaken. What is at issue is how one practically lives, for *Dasein* is encompassed within agency, within acting in the world.

When the family is divided and now lives in separate worlds, as Elizabeth Marquardt has beautifully described it, the child must take on two distinct practical forms of action (agency). These two distinct forms of acting have the ramifications of forming two distinct, and at times inconsistent, ways of being. Jen Robinson, when discussing her transition between her parents' two worlds, even says "I was a different person." "At first, my mother would arrange not to be home when Dad picked us up and dropped us off, and I was glad. It was uncomfortable for me to be around them at the same time. *I was a different person with each of them*; each knew things about me the other didn't. . . . It was obvious that they would not have seen each other if they hadn't had to because of me."[54]

In a real way divorce seeks to do the impossible to the child: it seeks to divide *Dasein*, complicating the construction of an identity that includes the whole of your biographical narrative. This has the further ramification of pushing the child to wonder if *Dasein*, your being there, can be anything other than a shadow, for *Dasein* now lacks the ability to provide coherence in practical action in the world and cannot answer the child's question of who he or she will be in the future. Marquardt says about her own experience, "Over time we came to see each parent's home as a shadow of the other. Our divorced parents each lived in, and were aware of, only their own homes, but we were connected to both places."[55]

The power of this reality can be seen in the experience of Stephanie Staal. Now that her mother had moved out and her vanity and dresser were empty, her dad needed to rework their house. As he reworked their shared practical space, his being was upheld, as he was able to use the space to free his being from the pain of a failed marriage. But

as Staal articulates so poignantly, she experienced these transitions as the disappearance of her own being.

> Not that I blame him, then or now, for systematically dismantling the home I had always known. He needed to blast the slate clean, to remake the house as his and his alone; he certainly didn't need daily reminders of what no longer existed. We were, however, in two different places on this matter—while he was almost forty and eager to distance himself from the past, I was thirteen and felt every change as an irrevocable loss. I felt like I was fast disappearing into the distance, set loose as the ties to my past were cut one by one. I believed there was a safety in objects, that they represented concrete markers of my history, my identity, my place. Without them, the home that wrapped around me was at once familiar and foreign, and I wandered through the disconcerting patchwork of rooms, trying to figure out where I fit in.[56]

4. I Am Whether I Am Aware of It or Not

This leads us to Heidegger's final point about *Dasein*: "*Dasein* is delivered over to its being."[57] What this means is that *Dasein* is based on how we live and how we act, rather than what we know. In short, as Blattner says, "We cannot avoid the question by not thinking or talking about it."[58] We can be sure when a divorce occurs that a child is greatly impacted by it, whether it appears to be affecting the child or he or she refuses to discuss it. Because it strikes children at the most practical level of their existence, the level of their biological caregivers—their source of being—it strikes at the heart of their being, their *Dasein*. As eighteen-year-old Martin says, "No matter what anybody says, divorce will always affect you more than most people realize. Divorce is one of those things that'll affect you for better or for worse, even though I might not admit it fully to myself."[59] Marquardt and Norval Glenn's study concurs with Martin's words, highlighting nicely Heidegger's point. "Our study showed that children of divorce, even those who appear to be fine and successful later in life, are much more likely than their peers from intact families to share profound and moving stories of confusion, isolation, and suffering."[60]

Being That Is Being-With

Therefore, we must state directly what we have already insinuated above, that *Dasein* is *Mitsein*, that to "be there" is to "be with," for *Dasein* is embedded in the practical social world.[61] Heidegger states, "Our analysis has shown that Being-with is an existential constituent of Being-in-the-world."[62] Therefore, Heidegger reminds us that our *Dasein*, because it is practical in the social world, "is not independent of the selves of those around [us]."[63] This is what Heidegger commentator William Blattner calls "the immersion of the self in the social world." Heidegger calls this "solicitude," by which he means that in caring about who I am, I must also care about who others are. My being, as we have seen with the examples above, is contingent on the being of others.[64] Blattner states it more clearly when he says, "In confronting the question of my identity, I am also confronting the question of the identity of others. [Heidegger's] point is that I cannot disentangle who I am from who those around me are."[65] To be is to be with. This is not only a social theory or philosophical position, but also, as we will see in the next chapters, a theological assertion.

Conclusion

We have examined in this chapter how divorce is a reality of a future-oriented, detraditionalized late modernity. Throughout, we have seen that social life impacts us not just at the epistemological level by providing us structures (like the economy), but also at the level of ontology (who we are) by impacting how we act (agency). This has set the stage to argue, through Giddens's discussion of ontological security and Heidegger's *Dasein*, that divorce in this detraditionalized late modernity may have a deep ontological impact that is often overlooked. I've argued that divorce confronts the core of the young person's humanity, for it affects his or her being and acting in the social world (his or her *Dasein*).

Now, having made our way deeply into act and being (act as being), it is important that we allow more than social theory and philosophy to speak. We must turn to theology to see if it allows us ways of understanding the phenomenon of divorce in light of what it means to

be a human being (*imago Dei*) in relation to God's own being (Trinity) and acting (revelation), so that we might more richly understand the issues children of divorce face. Where we ended with Heidegger, *Mitsein* (being with), we will continue and push forward with a theological discussion on what it means to be human alongside not only neighbor but God.

4

Divorce and Theological Anthropology

Introduction

In the small church my friend pastors there are only three families with children. Their parents have attended the church since they were children themselves. Admirably, they desire for their children to have the same positive experience between the church building's four walls, even if the church's atrophy makes it no longer as lively a place as it once was. One of these three families has a particularly interesting story. The family consists of a mom and three children: a girl, and two boys. Of course it is not unusual for a single mother to be raising three children; what is unusual is that these three children do not have a father. Again, it is not unusual for children to describe themselves as not having a father, meaning that they do not see him or that he has not raised them. But in another sense they no doubt have a father, a person whose union with their mother led to their creation.

What makes these three children distinctive is that they quite literally have no father, for there was no union (even ever so brief) in which two people encountered each other to create another. As the story

goes, the mom, an attractive and successful corporate executive, got tired of waiting for the right man to finally cross her path. Yearning to be a mother, she took her destiny into her own hands and chose a sperm donor she (and now her children) have never met (and legally never will). She was then inseminated and became pregnant, once with her oldest son and then again with her twin boy and girl. This is clearly an action that can be taken only in late modernity, where tradition has thinned and we can resort to technology to manufacture a future that provides us with identity and intimacy.

There are no obvious signs that these three children have such an unusual story. They appear as normal as any other kids. In fact, many of their friends also lack interaction with and knowledge of their fathers. But it is clear that the nonexistence of a father leads to questions about their own existence, just as questions about one's parents' separation, I am arguing, leads to questions about one's ontological security.

On the bottom of an icebreaker worksheet one Sunday, the kids were asked to write something interesting about themselves. Most children wrote things like, "I can do a back flip," or "I have a Nintendo Wii." But Teddy, the twin brother, wrote something deeply ontological. He wrote, "I have no father." As this eight-year-old sought to answer a question about his own being ("What is unique about me?") he found himself up against negation, up against the reality that he is but is without, without something that is fundamental to his existence—the other responsible for his being.

In chapters 2 and 3 we considered the self as being (ontology) and acting (agency) in late modernity, drawing out this examination from the history we explored in chapter 1. But all this talk of ontology leads us into conversations beyond historical analysis and social or philosophical theory. Our deep examination of ontological realities within our humanity draws us into theological explication. So now our focus shifts to ourselves in light of God's being and acting, and how God's own being and acting makes us human as God created. One could read Teddy's answer, "I have no father," as a further question to the one asked ("What is unique about me?"). With Teddy's answer he is asking, "What does it mean to be me? To be human? And why with the reality of having no father do I feel I lack something within

me?" In this convergence of Teddy's deeply ontological questions, we will see if theology has some answers, some ways for those of us who have lived through the divorce of our parents to understand why it strikes us so deeply at the ontological level, feeling as though it cripples us or at least casts a shadow on our future.

Anthony Giddens has already taken us in this direction by constructing a rich social theory built not primarily on epistemology and structures but rather on ontology and agency. We have seen how social life is meant to provide people with ontological security, with a sense of being real. To examine how these deep streams of thought pour into theological contemplation, I turn to the work of the great Reformed theologian, Karl Barth. He stands as a giant on the horizon of twentieth-century theology, leading many to take shots at him as they seek space to do their own work. I will turn to Barth not because of his notorious reputation, but because, much like Giddens with his social theory, Barth is seeking to do theological construction (especially in his anthropology) through the categories of act and being. Barth moves past defining humanity in epistemological categories (knowledge) or structural realities (what theologians have called "the substantialistic faculties of humanity").[1] Rather, he seeks to articulate what makes humanity human through encounter as both act and being. Barth's whole theological project seeks to articulate God's being as act. We know God only because God has acted, revealing Godself (primarily in Jesus Christ). Therefore, revelation is central to Barth's thought: we know God because God has acted to make Godself known; we are (have our being) in and through God's act.

This attention to act and being has made Barth many theological enemies. For some, such attention to God's act ignores the larger epistemological categories of religious experience: Barth assumes too much independent action of God. For others, Barth's actualism too clearly takes priority over the written Scriptures, since for Barth the Bible is witness to God's act and being and is not a rigid determinative structure.[2] This is all relevant to us because it shows, from my perspective, that Barth's theology is important in helping us think of divorce and its consequences through the categories of being (ontology) and act (agency), and does so beyond the strictures of tradition. Barth is not concerned with recovering a lost structure from which

to speak of God, or a correct epistemological lens to discuss religious experience. Barth is concerned with the personal relational encounter of God with humanity. God, and therefore theology, is not tradition but the articulation of God's being through God's act of revelation. There is no doubt that Barth returns to traditional theological artifacts (like the Reformers and, most enthusiastically, the biblical witness), but he returns to them not as tradition, which Giddens has argued is waning, but as articulations of God's act and being. This return is not to fortify a lost foundational tradition, but rather to help us articulate the action and being of God that transcends and puts to judgment all perspectives (traditions) that seek to cage God's person. For Barth, theology is not recovery of a past tradition, but dynamic reflection on a living, relational God.

Relationship is central to Barth's theological project, for through relationship we see how act and being are fused. In relational encounter we come up against the very ontology of the other. We are as we are encountered. Therefore, much as we saw in chapter 3 with Giddens and Heidegger, Barth also contends that being is being-in-relation, being is being-with. He states, "Our corresponding being is a being in the encounter of [hu]man and fellow-[hu]man."[3] Following him, Douglas John Hall continues: "Simply in our being there we are being-in-relationship; our sheer existing points beyond itself. We are creatures whose being implies relatedness. . . . To be, to be-in-the-world, is to be with."[4]

This is true not only of human beings, but also of God. Or to state it in its correct priority, because the trinitarian God encounters God-self as a relational reality, humanity, as in the image of God (imago Dei), also finds its being through the act of relational encounter. We find ourselves in a state of ontological insecurity when we discover that we are alone. And this "aloneness," whether by choice or by circumstance, has the effect of melting the solidity of our humanity. It has a way of making us feel less than real. Psychologist Daniel Laing affirms exactly this when he asserts about ontological insecurity that "the individual in the ordinary circumstances of living may feel more unreal than real; in a literal sense, more dead than alive, precariously differentiated from the rest of the world so that his identity and autonomy are always in question."[5]

Barth's theological project, and his anthropology particularly, is not concerned with moral assertions or epistemological frameworks, but with the contrast between the real and the unreal.[6] To be human is to be real, for from the relational encounter of God's spoken word, being was formed from non-being. Therefore, to be human is to be real; it is to have ontological security by being-with and for others in relationship. Divorce, then, is for the child not an issue of right/ wrong or perspective, but an issue of being real. Divorce brings anxiety when one loses the most primary community of relationship that makes one real (in both its biological and relational capacities). It is the anxiety that you might slide into *nihilo* (nothingness), feeling yourself a shadow in a real world.

If ontological insecurity (the issue of divorce, as we argued in chapter 3) is the sense of being unreal, then Barth's anthropology, which seeks to articulate humanity in contrast to the real versus the unreal, is quite relevant for our argument. If we have our being as we are encountered by another, if we have our being as we find ourselves in relational communion, then from a theological perspective as well we might argue (as this chapter does) that divorce, as the dissolution of the primary relational community, strikes the child at the ontological level. It strikes the core of our humanity, making us question whether or not we are real.

So we will use Barth's theological anthropology as a jumping-off point, seeing what it might tell us about the phenomenon of divorce as it impinges on the child.[7] But we will look at more than just Barth's perspective. While we will focus on the contours of his anthropology by discussing the *analogia relationis* (in this chapter) and his unique articulation of the *imago Dei* (in the next chapter), we will also look at some thoughts of object relations psychology.[8]

Analogia Relationis—To Be Is to Be in Relationship

One of the most famous theological essays written in the twentieth century has one of the shortest and most captivating titles: *Nein!* [No!]. The title serves as both a condemnation and a proclamation. The essay is Karl Barth's response to his fellow Swiss theological giant,

Emil Brunner. Brunner had presented an essay in which he sought an analogy between God's being and humanity's being (an *analogia entis*, analogy of being, which stretches back all the way to Aquinas). Yet, in the shadow of the Nazification of Germany, Barth saw great dangers in this perspective. If we assume an analogy between God and humans at the level of ontology, then ironically we are released from attending to being as mystery, and agency as encounter with otherness. (Ultimately, if pushed to the extreme, this can be used to justify glorifying those who fit the analogy and killing those who do not.) When we see a direct analogy between God's being and our own, we can then control or possess God, deciding whom God can love and whom God cannot. Put differently, if there is an *analogia entis* between God's being and our own, then we find ourselves locked in the cul-de-sac of epistemology and structure. We become fixated on substantialistic structures within humanity and our knowledge of them. Alternatively, as Barth develops his theological anthropology, he seeks to start somewhere other than the *analogia entis*. Drawing from the work of the Lutheran martyr Dietrich Bonhoeffer, Barth seeks to articulate not an *analogia entis* (analogy of being), but an *analogia relationis*, an analogy of relationship between the being of humanity and the being of God.[9] Barth, then, contends that being is constituted not de facto, but in the relational encounter of actors. To be is to be in relationship.[10]

What this means is that humanity is not a copy of God's own being. God is God. But God in God's own being is in relationship. God as Trinity relates as Father, Son, and Holy Spirit to Godself. So too does humankind claim its humanity by being in relationship.[11] Thus, the analogy between God and humanity is not in substance, but in relationship. God has revealed Godself as a relational Being, and our being is also relational; we need to be connected to others in order to really be. We can assert this about God because of our focus on action (agency). We know God because God has chosen to make Godself known, not simply as a nondescript entity, but as a subject, as the covenant partner of Israel. We know God's being as relational because God has acted in relation to us, revealing God's very being through encounter, most fully in the incarnation. Therefore, our being also is upheld and made known through the action of being with and for others.

Barth seeks to work from the particular to the universal, rather than vice versa. Therefore, we experience the particularity of God's own being through God's action, and God's very action encounters us in the form of Father, Son, and Holy Spirit.[12] Barth states, "Even in His inner divine being there is relationship. To be sure, God is One in Himself. But He is not alone. There is in Him a co-existence, co-inherence and reciprocity. God in Himself is not just simple, but in the simplicity of His essence He is threefold—the Father, the Son and the Holy Ghost."[13] Because we know God in the relational, particular form of the Trinity, we can safely assume that in the universal reality of the eternal Godhead, God exists in the relational reality of Father, Son, and Holy Spirit. Therefore, the analogy stretches deep, so deep that relationship reveals the inner being of God: God in Godself is a relationship who acts to encounter us as Creator, Reconciler, and Redeemer.

Within the relational community of Father, Son, and Spirit, the real emerges out of nothingness (the unreal). Nothing exists outside this eternal relationship until the Godhead in communion chooses to create. This means relationship constitutes reality; it is relationship that leads to being (not the other way around). We find our being in being-with-others. Just as God is God in being three-in-one, so we *are* when we are in relational community.[14] In being in relationship with and for others, we are given the gift of our very being. Without another with whom to be in relationship, there can be no me. Paul Ricoeur says it this way: "Oneself as another suggests from the outset that the selfhood of oneself implies otherness to such an intimate degree that one cannot be thought of without the other."[15] Eberhard Jungel continues this thought when he states, "This means that we become whole not from within ourselves or from our own resources, but only from outside ourselves. . . . If we wish to experience ourselves as whole persons, we must experience more than ourselves."[16]

If we see humanity alone, we do not see humanity at all.[17] From this theological perspective the real is born out of the relational community of the Trinity; so by analogy we are real (and freed from the unreal) through relational community. Leron Shults asserts, "My sense of self [being real] is called into being and formed through

interaction with other persons within my particular set of overlapping communities."[18] God's very relational act for us as creator, reconciler, and redeemer frees us from the unreal.

This real versus unreal perspective may seem abstractly theological, but this is the very issue that Giddens picks up when he argues for the need for ontological security. Giddens follows object relations psychologists when speaking of ontological insecurity as feeling unreal, and he explains that the only way to feel real is to find ontological security in the dependability of relationship. The particularity of relationship within the Trinity itself is an analogy of how our humanity is upheld in relationship. Therefore, we might also argue that the family, as relational community, provides the child the dependability of connection, commitment, and companionship that in an actual way makes him or her real.

When the family is sunk, the relational unit that serves as both the origin and the environment for the child's being is lost. The thin line separating the real and the unreal becomes thinner, for in the brokenness of the marriage bond the relationality in which we are constituted collapses. We can hear this pointedly in the words of nineteen-year-old Robin: "I wonder about my sanity sometimes. I don't really remember things in the right order. Like if I remember things, I, remember them all messed up. I think I was trying to not be conscious, and I succeeded far too well, 'cause I don't remember a lot of stuff."[19] After the divorce she feels out of control, because she cannot seem to hold events together. She wonders about her sanity because she feels unreal; time itself seems to escape her being, and she finds herself clawing for time to be ordered in her memory now that she feels herself less than solidly real.

So it is through relationship that we are made real and saved from nothingness. According to Ann Belford Ulanov, this is the very assertion of object relations psychology, that to feel real (we can say from a theological perspective, to be real) we are in need of "non-me" objects to which to relate. We need to be in relationship with others; we must be in community to feel real.[20] From the very beginning parents constitute this "non-me" community that provides the environment to be real. In constant interaction with this community of mother and father, the child discovers himself and his world. When

this world collapses, the unreal floods his being, for even though he may be old enough to have other objects and communities in his life, he has lost the one that has been from the beginning the one that made him real, the one that is bone of his bone and flesh of his flesh. When this is taken away, the young person is lost. It is this very word, *lost* (we could just as easily say *unreal*), that Nicole uses in describing her state after her parents' separation and divorce. She also tells us how this loss of her family and this feeling of being lost or unreal have affected her. "That afternoon, after he left, she [her mother] sat us down on the couch and said he wasn't coming back. I can't even remember my reaction. I know I couldn't understand what was happening. *But I know exactly how I felt. Lost.* Now everything I see I have to know the cause, so I can explain the effect. Since I can't really understand why the divorce came about, I constantly struggle to make sense of my family."

To take one last example, we can hear the unreal powerfully in Martin's statement: "The divorce didn't change me, value-wise. Mostly it helped deaden me to the emotional impact of events. Like if the dog got run over, I probably wouldn't be as upset."[21]

But have I overstated this? To assert that divorce forces children into the unreal may seem drastic and overly dramatic. After all, it cannot be as bad as actually no longer being—as bad as actual death. A child may *feel* the tremors of non-being, the unreal, in divorce, but this cannot be assumed to be as devastating as the death of a parent (the actuality of negation and the unreal). By no means should we underestimate the suffering of losing a parent to disease, accident, or tragedy. To experience the funeral of a parent is deeply painful. But it raises its own issues. It does not, as I will argue, throw the young person's being into question, as divorce does.

The Difference between Divorce and Death

Sara McLanahan and Gary Sandefur in their book, *Growing Up with a Single Parent*, present a quantitative study of the effects of divorce on children. I wish not to examine thoroughly their study, but rather to use it to make my point about the ontological ramifications of

divorce. Thus, I will present only enough to enable us to compare the impact of parental death and of divorce.

These two sociologists from two renowned research universities, Princeton and the University of Wisconsin, show statistically that children living with both biological parents fare much better in the areas of educational achievement, avoidance of idleness in the workforce, and avoiding early procreation. They state boldly, "Children who grow up in a household with only one biological parent are worse off, on average, than children who grow up in a household with both their biological parents."[22] For example, they show that in the matter of dropping out of school, a child whose parents were never married and no longer live together has a 37 percent chance of not making it through high school; if a child's parents are divorced, there is a 31 percent chance. If there is no disturbance, the percentage is only 13 percent. In the area of teenage pregnancy, the children of unmarried parents face a 37 percent chance of early pregnancy. The chance for a child of divorce is 33 percent. It is only 11 percent for those living with both biological parents.

McLanahan and Sandefur believe there is such a gap because children who live with only one biological parent lose a wealth of social capital that keeps them focused on school and provides networks of job options, as well as oversight and modeling to avoid the traps of teenage pregnancy.

Yet there is an interesting anomaly in their statistical argument. Where the risk of high school dropout is 37 percent for nonmarital offspring, 31 percent for children of divorce, and 13 percent for children with no disturbance, it is only 15 percent for children who experience the death of one parent. This is only two percentage points higher than for children in undisturbed, two-parent families, and it represents less than half the number of children from divorced families. Children who experience the death of a parent are much less at risk to become pregnant (by twelve percentage points) than are children of divorce.[23] Why such a difference between divorce and death in child well-being? McLanahan and Sandefur believe this can be answered through social capital. Because of life insurance and less negative stigma, children are less likely after a death to lose as much social capital. This is logical and should not be dismissed. However,

for most middle-class people life insurance does not always keep families who experience the death of a parent stable (for instance, with all of the remaining members of the family living in the same home). And to assume that children do not feel stigmatized by friends who fear saying the wrong thing after the death of their parent may keep us from wondering whether social capital *alone* explains the statistical variation.

Rather, it seems that the difference between death and divorce has something to do with ontology. Death may shake a young person's being, as he witnesses the monster of negation take his mother, for example. But such a situation, though frightening, never throws his own being into question, as if making it only a shadow. It can suggest or reveal vulnerability: the death of a parent may witness to the reality that one day the child will also be overcome by death. But, again, it does not retroactively threaten his being as divorce does. Death looks to a future reality, an event that will happen as time unfolds for the young person. Divorce does not so much point forward as throw the foundational event of the child's very origins into regret and question. *Death promises the eventual end of his being; divorce questions if he ever should have been at all.* This no doubt is a much more haunting reality. Rather than wondering if you will be remembered at all after your death, divorce asks if you ever should have come into being, now that those who are responsible for your being have negated the relationship that created you.[24]

This also has a great amount to do with agency. As we have seen, we are given our being through action. Death (unless it is suicide, which opens up a whole other truckload of issues) rarely if ever occurs through the agency of the dying person. Disease, accident, and tragedy happen to the parent over and against their choice (action). But divorce is an action, not a fate; it may feel unavoidable, but from the child's perspective it will always come finally by the choice of one or both parents to end the union.[25] For instance, Natalie says, "There were days like that where I really, honestly wished she had died. Then there'd be only happy memories. I was scared of the idea of divorce when I was twelve, and I've never been scared of my parents dying. It never even occurred to me until the divorce."[26]

Because divorce is integrally connected to agency and because agency authors actions that create encounters that then form community, divorce weighs much heavier on the ontology of children. The child is the outgrowth of the community of Mom and Dad, of being-with. Death ends community person-to-person, but it does not negate the community of memory. The child in death must bear the reality that her dad is gone, but he remains a longed-for and missed agent in the still-existing community called family. He, even in his death, is part of the narratives and history of the community. But in divorce these narratives take on the residue of anger (or hatred), and the history is split. Now with Mom, Dad can never be spoken of, or only spoken of with frustration, suspicion, or indifference. In relation to the children, divorce then splinters a parent's being, while death does not. Staal articulates this ontological reality when she says, "Here's the thing, though: Time flirts with us, flashing what could have been, what should have been, what was. When a parent dies, children are at least given the pretense that they will travel through the five stages of grief in accepting the death. . . . But with divorce, there is no rubric detailing how we should act or feel, especially as we get older. Lacking the finality of death, divorce can start to mimic a film negative. We become hooked on what's missing, where blank spaces have replaced substance."[27]

My wife, Kara, and I experience this phenomenon in our own life in its various stages. It was one thing to grapple with our parents' divorces as we were newlyweds, but when we had children the impact hit us afresh. No longer would holidays be spent with Grandpa and Grandma; they were now to be spent with Grandma or Grandpa (and their new significant others). And Grandma's gifts could not be paraded in front of Grandpa, just as Grandpa's visits could not be shared with Grandma. Our own understanding of our new family and ourselves lacks a cohesive narrative even into the next generation. If, instead of divorcing, one of our parents had died, the memory and love would be preserved. The family narrative would include the missing grandparent. He or she would be part of the story even in absence, instead of someone awkwardly avoided or intentionally eliminated. Now we have to explain to our three-year-old again and again exactly how each of these four disconnected people is

connected to us and to him, instead of him sensing it, and knowing it, intrinsically.

While I do agree that McLanahan and Sandefur's statistical variations between children of divorced parents and children whose parents have died could be interpreted through the lens of social capital, and this does add needed texture to the issue, it seems to me that ontology is more fundamental. In ontological terms, divorce may be a heavier, or at least more existentially damaging, burden to bear than the death of a parent.

The Child's Being Begins in Love

But we need to push this argument for the *analogia relationis* a little further. The relational community of Father, Son, and Spirit is not simply an organization constructed around tasks. It is not a committee called together simply to do things (this, after all, would be to lose the oneness of the Godhead). Rather, the inner life of the Trinity is a unit, and the fabric of the unity of inner relation of Father, Son, and Spirit is love. Or to state it another way, the oneness, the unity of the Trinity, is constituted in the unity of love. The trinitarian God creates not out of need or want, but out of love, and the abundance of love shared in relationship propels the creation of another to share in it. The world is spoken into being out of nothingness as the very act of love of the Father to Son through the Spirit. God then chooses to act with and for this creation because God loves it, both as a whole and in its particularities. But God loves this creation because God is love; God's love for the creation is an outpouring of God's own love in the unity of Father, Son, and Spirit. It is relational love that leads to creation; love of Father to Son through Spirit leads to the real.

There is an analogy here when it comes to the family and children. Children are the creation of the relational love of mother and father. That is, they exist, they are real, because the parents' relational love spills over its boundaries and seeks others to embrace. The children, then, are a concrete sign of love, a sign that shows the power of love at such a level that the union of love can create another out of nothing. Love is so real that from the relational community of love, love

seeks to create from what was not. Children, at least theoretically, are the creation not primarily of genetics but of love. It is in love and for love that man and woman choose to create a child. The child is secure forever, for he, in his very being, is the mystery and monument of the creative power of love. The child possesses within himself his parents' own being, seen in the shared biological material, but at the same time in mystery is completely other than their beings. Therefore, the child in his otherness will have to bear his own burden of confronting the real and unreal. This, object relations psychology has told us, begins the minute the infant is born. The child will always need to return to the relational love of the parents as the ground of his own being, as the very power that pulled him from non-being to being, from the unreal to the real. And it is the very union and communion of mother and father over time that assures the child that he *is*.

It is no wonder that Teddy, the child born without a father, whom I mentioned in the introduction to this chapter, felt pains of the unreal deep in his being, for he *is* from the passionate love of his mother, but his being was not the product of relational love. Therefore, he cannot help but search for it; he cannot help but feel a question mark firmly wrapped around his being. Where is the other who makes me, me? And to whom do I belong? He *is* out of the desire of his mother, but not out of the love of one to another that chooses out of its own love to create an other. Or, as Ava Chin says, reflecting on her friends' and her own parents' divorce, "Most kids of divorce accepted their situations unquestioningly, but not without carrying with them the knowledge that love could be suddenly ripped apart. They cultivated a new belief in the impermanence of things, and the divorce became the lens through which they viewed themselves and the world."[28] Marquardt says, from her experience, "Perhaps nothing signals belonging more than physically resembling someone else. Yet, paradoxically [within our stepfamilies], we often found that resembling one of our parents marked us as an outsider, as someone who does not belong, rather than as an insider."[29]

When divorce strikes, love is lost, and when love is lost so too is the unity of community in which love is engendered.[30] Mom and Dad may individually still deeply love the child, but they are no longer a

unity; they no longer represent the community of love that created the child. Jen Robinson heartbreakingly articulates the experience of watching the community of love split. She has no doubt that each parent loves her. What hurts is watching dad pack his car as the tangible sign that the community of love is breaking apart. She says, "I sat in the front yard and watched my dad going back and forth between house and car with boxes. I don't remember now if he said goodbye, though I think he must have; what sticks in my mind is watching him start the car, pull out of the driveway, disappear down the road. I can feel the prickle of summer-hot grass on my legs, and the sadness, which would have been there whether he said goodbye or not."[31]

When divorce strikes and the unity of parental love is shattered, parents often redirect their loving attention from each other onto their children. The child will never regret this, but it cannot be assumed that this solves the problem of ontological security. For the child was created and made real not from the choice of one, but from the union of the love of a relational community. Therefore, often what children grieve is not the loss of love directed toward them, but the loss of the mysterious and powerful community of love that existed before them and elected to invite them into the world. For example, nine-year-old Anne yearns for this community of love even in its division: "If I had three wishes, the first would be my parents never got divorced. Two, my parents would get back together, and three, that I'd get my own bedroom."[32]

Between Two Worlds

Elizabeth Marquardt has written a moving, biographically laced piece called *Between Two Worlds: The Inner Lives of Children of Divorce*, to which I have referred throughout the previous chapters. In her book Marquardt, through rich articulations of her national study and her own story, asserts how divorce is the issue of living between two worlds. Marquardt has boldly argued that no matter how well divorce might be done, it always divides the world that the child must live in. Divorce forces the child, according to Marquardt, to live between two worlds.

Her thesis is profoundly simple. Marquardt argues that marriage itself is about the bringing together of two worlds. Marriage is the work of forming one world out of two. When children are born they are most often born into this reality. They are born into the single world called family. It is in this single world that they grow and have their life.[33]

Forming this single world no doubt is a process filled with tension, conflict, and compromise, but slowly one world is formed out of two. Children are born into this one world; they *are*, as I have argued above, following Barth's lead, the outgrowth of the love of this one world of two people. It is this very relational community of being that makes them real, both in actuality (they are born through its sexual union) and in its ongoing life (they *are* as they act within it). The child lives (has his or her being) in this family entity. He or she may be aware that his or her parents originally represented two worlds, they may even be cognizant of the continued work and conflict it takes for them to make their two worlds into one. But what is important to the child is that he or she has this union, this community called family.[34]

When divorce occurs, this one world splits into two. According to Marquardt, it is now the child's job to live between these two worlds. The parents in their divorce have asserted that it is impossible for them to maintain one world for themselves and for their children. But children, unlike the parents, are not free to escape the ramifications of the one world that is now unmade even as it was once made. The duty of making one world out of two does not end but is transferred from the parents to the children. It now becomes the child's job to do what his or her parents could not—bring these two distinct worlds together. She or he is now forced to live between them, moving in and out of their separate worlds, having no one place to be, moving back and forth between them, with only one parent while never (or very rarely) being with both.

These two worlds, postdivorce, become more and more separate as parents seek a new life distinct from the regrettable past. Marquardt states, "In our national survey, we found that almost two-thirds of children of divorce who stay in contact with both parents say they felt like they grew up in two families, not one. Many changes occur

in the wake of divorce. But from the child's point of view the essential change is this: The child suddenly inherits two distinct worlds in which to grow up."[35] The child must now negotiate different schedules, rules, perspectives, and expectations as she moves back and forth between the two worlds of her parents. It becomes her job to find some kind of unity between the distinct family backgrounds and ways of being-in-the-world her parents represent.[36]

Instead of the family being the place for her to have the belonging to be, it is her own being, cut off from their union, that holds her parents together at all. Their union created her, but now they are separate, wishing, were it not for her existence, to be strangers (or at best simply acquaintances) with each other. Their separateness, according to our ontological read of Marquardt, thrusts a division into the child's very being. The divorce, in separating those responsible for her being, forces her to live divided. We can hear this in the words of nine-year-old Jackie and twenty-one-year-old Loretta. Jackie says, "I wish there were two of me so each of us could live with Mom and with Dad. But I'd hate it if there were two of my sister!"[37] Loretta states:

> This wasn't just about my parents breaking up. This was about my family breaking. And they can't possibly know what this feels like. Their families are together. . . . You're divorcing a family, you're not divorcing just a person. I think even my dad had the wrong idea about that. He thought he was just divorcing a person, not breaking a family apart.[38]

This quote reveals how ontology is connected to community (being-with). The divorce is not just the end of marriage, but the end of the child's community of being, which forces her to live between two worlds. But now these two worlds are held together at all only through her person, which is disorientingly backward. She *is* through their person; she *is* through the union of their mutual action that elected her into existence (into the real), yet now it becomes her job, through her person, to hold these distinct worlds together. If it were not for her, these two distinct (indifferent or angry) people would have no relational connection at all, and yet she is "real" because of their intimate relational union. She cannot possibly bear this weight;

this is not about adaptation, but about ontology. Her very being is contingent on their unity, as she acts not just with them individually but as a unity. They have asked her to do their work, a work that undercuts her very being-in-the-world. We can see these ontological ramifications in Marquardt's own biographical words:

> Divorce is a problem for many reasons. . . . But the central, daunting task that was suddenly assigned to us following our parents' divorce was this: We, *and we alone*, had to try to make sense of our parents' increasingly different ways of living. The most important models for our own budding identities—our mother and our father—no longer had the job of rubbing the rough edges of their own worlds together in an attempt to hand us something reasonably whole.[39]

Without this wholeness in the union of those responsible for our being, together as a community of being for us to act with and for, as Marquardt says, "we are alone," and their division is borne into our being. Listen to the ontological recollections of Stephanie Staal as the division in her two worlds is announced:

> When I get home, my mother informs me she is leaving in a week and taking my sister with her, that it's easier that way. My father stands by the window holding Caroline, who sleeps peacefully against his shoulder, their faces iced by the early morning sunlight. I can't even contemplate the absence of not only my mother but my sister. The days of family are now numbered. The word "divorce" is never mentioned, but implicit is the understanding that this time, she is not coming back. I accept the news with a simple nod of the head. No protests, no angry words, no attempts at convincing them to change their minds. It is as if some tap has been tightened shut.[40]

This division reaches so deep, as we have noted, that for children of divorce, even their very appearance (hair color, way of talking, chin line) becomes a witness to the division in their worlds, as we have noted. Marquardt adds,

> When I talked with all kinds of young adults it became clear that in many families, whether married or divorced, it is apparently not uncommon for mothers to cry out in exasperation, "You're acting just

like your father!" Yet while young people from intact families recall their mothers uttering these words, the comparison never had much sting—even when their mother's frustration was clear—because these young people knew without question that their father was a full member of the family. They loved their fathers and almost all of them felt confident that their mothers loved their fathers too. How bad could it be, then, to be compared to him?[41]

But for those living between worlds, the very material of their being, their mannerisms, the shape of their eyes, their expressions, are no longer undeniable witnesses to their being as being-with these people. They become instead signs or reminders of division. The child's very person becomes a confusing reflection of inclusion and exclusion, for he is half of the present parent and half a reminder of a broken, regrettable bond. This is a division that weighs heavily, for it fractures his person. It is hard to feel real and whole between these two worlds, as Jen Abbas says powerfully: "Not only did the divorce break my home, but it broke my heart and shattered my sense of wholeness as well."[42]

Now standing between two worlds, and two worlds radically diversifying, the child's agency lacks coherence, leading him to wonder if his being has any coherence in itself. He must act one way in one world and another in the other world. His necessary duplicity witnesses to the confusion that stretches all the way to the ontological level. This is not to ignore that no matter whether his family is together or divided he will have to act within different worlds or roles (of work, recreation, family, commerce, and so forth). The specialization and compartmentalization of our lives into different worlds is a reality for all who live in modernity. But to have to act differently, even contradictorily, in relation to those who correlate and are responsible for your being is quite different. When there are two family worlds, the child is asked to do the impossible. To find his being in two opposed worlds, he is asked to be two people.

Conclusion

In summary, following Barth, we may assert that to be real is to be in a relationship. Ontology is constituted by relationality. From this

theological perspective we can assert that what is real is constituted by the relational reality of the Trinity, speaking what *is* out of what *is not*, out of nothingness. The Trinity does this *not* out of need, but out of the unity of the relational community of love. Therefore, just as God is God in relationship, in being Father, Son, and Spirit, so too is the human being human, real, by relationship. And as we saw, this theological assertion has a correlation with object relations psychology, which asserts that feeling real is constituted in relation to non-me objects. Therefore, to be is to be in relation with others, and there is no community more primary than that of mother and father, than those responsible for my being. When their community is not, my being is shaken.

Divorce and the Image of God

A Conversation between Theology and Object Relations Psychology

The moving truck appeared, to my surprise. The movers loaded a few boxes and some small furniture and then prepared to depart. The driver entered our foyer to request my dad's signature and, observing that the rest of the house was not in the transitional state of a move, asked him, as I sat hidden from him in the other room, "So, you sending this stuff to someone?"

"No," my dad responded, "I'm moving to Palm Springs."

"Oh," the driver said, putting two and two together. "I did a similar move six months ago. Best thing I ever did—the stupid bitch was driving me crazy." My dad laughed halfheartedly as the driver cackled with delight. Then, with a handshake and a "thanks," my dad's stuff was forever separated from my mom's, and part of my life became the negotiation of their separate worlds.

Three months prior, my dad began casually mentioning to us that he had decided to buy a condo in Palm Springs. We were told it would be a vacation house, a place for them (my parents) to rent out and to spend a few weeks away from the Minnesota winter. Yet this news

always came from my dad, and it was clear, mostly in my mom's silence, that she never was in on this desert getaway. Of course, that was because from the beginning, as would be confirmed with the moving truck, the condo was never a getaway from the cold Minnesota winter, but instead a getaway from a marriage turned cold.

I found it odd timing that my dad had chosen one of the few weeks that I was in town with Kara to have the moving truck come to announce his departure and therefore the end of their marriage. It was as if he allowed the truck to communicate what he could not. Oddly enough, their marriage ended that night *not* in a final round of screaming (I remember almost no screaming ever), but instead with them sitting together on the couch watching a movie, sharing popcorn as I had seen them do so many times before. They sat there as if the moving truck had never come, as if my dad's plane ticket wasn't one-way. It was a picture-perfect "good divorce." There was no explicitly expressed anger, the children were grown, and their final act as a couple was a friendly one.

Yet, for me, it was anything but "good." More accurately, the so-called goodness of it was disorienting. Their mutual popcorn-popping, video-watching marriage conclusion was a good moment as opposed to, I guess, murderous rage and violent threats. But watching them share this good moment was out of sync with the action of their split. It gave me no assurances that things would all be fine. Instead I became more and more aware that the road that lay ahead had now radically forked, causing me (making it my job) to find a way to travel both paths, while simultaneously finding my own road.

Kara and I wouldn't experience the complicated ramifications of this forked road in earnest until the birth of our son. As painful as witnessing the last act of my parents' marriage was, the problem with divorce, for children, is that its ending is never an ending. It instead becomes a more complicated way of being-in-the-world. Just weeks before our son was born, we found ourselves with a problem. All four of our parents were in relationships with others. Kara's mother had married her respective new mate, and it appeared that my parents might do the same soon. We realized that our son would have four biological grandparents, none of them living with his biological grandmother or grandfather. "What will we call these other people

in our parents' lives?" we wondered. We ourselves barely knew these new partners. We decided to write a letter explaining that we wanted to reserve the "grandparent" nomenclature for our son's biological grandparents. We explained that this was to help him understand where he came from, but, I suppose, it was also part of the struggle to articulate some sort of origins for ourselves as we birthed the next generation. For some, this letter was met with controversy. Since then we have watched these relative strangers take an interest in our son, an interest he affirms. Yet these relationships with him, and now with his little sister, continue to remind us that this is not how it should be. We are happy that these people care for our children and especially that they care for our parent. But their presence continues to be a reminder to us that the relationship that is responsible for our being is divided, that there are other children and other families in which our parents participate. And one day we will struggle to explain why in the stories of their childhood Meemaw and Beepaw are both with their mommy, and in photographs Grandma and Grandpa smile together with their daddy, when in our children's world, these people have never been in the same room, or same photo, with one another. And I can't help but resent my parents for the existential fear that my own children will feel as they struggle to make sense of what happened, that they may ever begin to wonder if Mommy and Daddy will one day live in different places and belong to other people, as their grandmas and grandpas do.

In the preceding chapters I made a bold assertion that divorce is primarily an issue not of social capital and simple psychology, but of ontology. Ontology, the loss of being, is the real issue of divorce and as such has the secondary effect of impacting a child's affect and psychological stability. We saw this by looking at the historical evolution of marriage, childhood, and divorce in the last five hundred to six hundred years, witnessing how divorce has moved from being about mergers to labor to love. We saw that divorce is a completely different animal in a world where marriages and families are constituted by love. To look more in depth at the love-based marriage/family, we followed Anthony Giddens's discussion of late modernity. Giddens's social theory revealed that social life should be thought about more deeply than at the levels of epistemology and structure; it should be

examined at the level of ontology and agency. This means that the construction of our social world changes how we formulate identity and intimacy; it changes how we *are* and *act* in the world. In late modernity identity and intimacy are no longer provided by tradition but become the work of individuals as they give their attention to colonizing the unknown future.

We saw that examining late modernity from the level of ontology and agency moves us to observe that our social world is to provide us with ontological security. Because of modernity's future orientation beyond tradition, ontological security becomes the small family's (mom, dad, and siblings) job. Therefore, when divorce strikes, it punctures ontological security, thrusting the young person into experiences of the unreal. To develop this further, in the last chapter, we turned to the theological anthropology of Karl Barth. Through his work we saw that being is being-with, for just as God is God in the relational community of Father, Son, and Spirit, so we have our being in relational community.

In this chapter we will push these thoughts deeper. Turning directly to Barth's perspective on the image of God (the *imago Dei*), we will see that what makes us human is not a collection of internal substances, but rather relationships. We have our being in acts of encounter; we are freed from the unreal through relationship. To drive this deeper, in this chapter we will place Barth's theological assertions about the image of God in conversation with object relations psychology. Through this conversation we will see that because we *are* from the act of encounter of biological mother and father, we are thrust into the unreal, into negation, when their union is torn asunder. For we are real and therefore have our being only through their union; when that union is regretted and negated, we no doubt feel our own being coming up against negation.[1]

Imago Dei (the Image of God)

Theological anthropology has many dimensions, but at its core rests the question, What does it mean to be made in the image of God? "In our image we made them" (Gen. 1:26). Understanding what this

image refers to has great ramifications. Certain interpretations of what the image refers to have been used to justify a number of evils in human history, such as domination of people groups and the exploitation of the earth itself. So what is meant by *image of God*? It often has been assumed that image is constituted in a common or shared substance between God and humanity. Just as a flu shot is a diluted form of the virus itself, so the image of God in the human person is a diluted form of God's own essence. Thus, humanity somehow shares an essence similar to God's; the substance that makes God, God is (at least in a diluted form) shared by us. This has led many theologians to articulate the image through categories such as intellect, will, or emotions. Humanity is made in the image of God because like God, and unlike other creatures, humanity possesses these composites. The human, it appears, is the only creature that possesses an ability to think, reason, and feel beyond instinct.[2] Because humanity uniquely possesses these attributes (in correlation to God's own essence), the *imago Dei* in humanity is the credential to have, in service to God, dominion (power, authority, and control) over the rest of creation. Put slightly differently, when thinking of the image of God as a substance, as a shared essence with God, the image of God in humanity becomes an individually possessed core essence. It is the bestowing of human dominion within (and over) creation. Freedom, liberty, and happiness are fundamental to this essence-based understanding of the image of God.

Yet Karl Barth presents a new interpretation of the image of God, which goes beyond essence and substance. Barth's interpretation may be more congruent with the biblical Hebraic understanding of *imago Dei*.[3] Rather than seeing the image of God reflected in these essential substances, what instead makes us human is not our capacities, but our relationships. Price puts it this way: "Barth proposes a major paradigm shift in theological anthropology: one from seeing the human being as an individual defined by innate faculties to seeing the person as a dynamic-interpersonal agent whose faculties arise only as they exist in relations to others."[4] Whereas all of creation is spoken into being out of nothingness by the act of God, only the human being can hear and speak to God. The image is not based in what humanity possesses, but in the fact that God acts to encounter

humanity, drawing humanity into relationship with God. Stanley Grenz helpfully states, "The relational understanding of the *imago Dei* moves the focus from noun to verb. This approach presupposes that a relationship exists between Creator and creature and views the image as what occurs as a consequence of the relationship—namely, the creature 'images' the Creator. Hence, *the imago Dei* is less a faculty humans possess than an act that humans do."[5] According to the biblical text, the human is the only creature that can hear God and respond to God. The human is in the image of God, because God has elected to be in a special kind of relationship with humanity, a special relationship of speaking and acting, a relationship of I to thou.[6] Therefore, what makes humanity an image or reflection of God is that we are fundamentally relational beings, bound to God (as we have pointed to) and to other humans (as is the direct focus of our argument) not by instinct or pattern, but by the election of love. We are (have our being) in acting with and for each other, just as God is God as Father, Son, and Holy Spirit.

When substantialistic categories such as intellect, will, and emotions are believed to constitute the image of God in us, then logically the image is in us (we possess it, like a pack of gum in our pocket or, better, a tumor attached to our liver). It is ultimately an individual possession. But when the image is seen as the reality of a relationship, then the individual is not only affirmed, but drawn beyond himself or herself to others (as well as to creation as a whole). To reflect the image of God is to be in community, it is to be with and for others, just as the Father is with and for the Son through the Spirit. To see the image as a substance injected into humanity that is lived out in the categories of intellect, will, and emotions is to assume that we are (have our being) outside of act (agency), that we do not need the other. Intellect, will, and emotions are individual structures that operate in epistemological categories; in themselves they are not bound in act (agency) and being (ontology). Intellect, will, and emotions are possible, after all, only in a relational environment of action. I am (have my being) not because I think, reason, or feel, but because I am bound to others who act with and for me.[7] This is the image of God. It is not something within us, but something that claims us. It is not something we individually possess, but something bestowed upon

us by a God who acts for us by giving us the community of male and female, giving us the other to be with and for. This connects again to Barth's understanding of the real. Reality itself is constituted not in substances and essences, but in relationships. We are real and freed from the unreal, not because we can think, reason, or feel, but because we are held in the community of others composed by the relational community of God. The *imago Dei* is that which is real, not because it is within us, but because it claims us and invites us into I–thou relationships with God, humanity, and creation.[8]

But what does this have to do with divorce and the children of divorce? While this theological anthropological perspective of the *imago Dei* has clearly *not* been directly cited in conversations about divorce, it has nevertheless been tacitly used. When the *imago Dei* is a substance that leads to the interpretation of dominion, then the human being possesses the authority and power to determine his or her individual life. Anything that seems to cage your freedom or self-fulfillment must be overcome. Divorce is justified because the marriage is destroying the liberty and happiness of an individual bestowed with the dominion of the image of God. But when the image of God is seen as a relational reality rather than as an individual substance, divorce cannot be carried out easily, for it is the end of community. It is the tragic loss of a community that once was filled with hope, love, and expectation, and that provides the child with his or her very being. When the image of God is seen as a relational reality, freedom is not understood as the freedom to do whatever is needed to make oneself happy and free. Rather, freedom is understood as the freedom to be for others.[9] In the logic of a relational *imago Dei* we find our freedom, not away from others, but in giving ourselves to others.[10] This is not to say that a relational understanding of the image of God makes divorce impossible (or impossibly sinful), but it does reveal a deeper conflict than is often spoken of. It asserts that we are ourselves not simply in self-directed freedom, but rather in being bound one to another. This is what "becoming one flesh" means.

Often when speaking of children in light of divorce, we assume the substantialistic perspective. We assume that divorce impacts them at the level of intellect, will, and emotions. Therefore, our actions for them seek to help them think correctly about the divorce

("It is not your fault"), reason realistically ("Mom and Dad are not getting back together"), and feel properly ("It is OK to be mad and sad, but soon you'll feel better and be better because Mom and Dad will be happier"). Most of the initiatives to help kids deal with divorce seem stuck in this substantialistic perspective. If a child seems to be coping well emotionally and intellectually with the divorce, we imagine that there is little or no issue. Yet it has been discovered of late (as children of the divorce culture have grown) that even those children who seem stable in the categories of intellect, will, and emotions, those who seem to have a handle on these inner substances, nevertheless cannot elude the deep tremors in their being because of the divorce of their parents. We can see this substantialistic perspective at work most clearly in the theory of the good divorce.

The Good Divorce

Sitting beside Katie Couric on the *Today Show*, Constance Ahrons made a case for her book *The Good Divorce*. She argued that 80 percent of the children she studied twenty years after their parents divorced now thought positively about the results of the experience. The other 20 percent, she argued, continued to hold to the belief that their parents' divorce was a negative and debilitating experience because of the extreme conflict they experienced even after the divorce. She stated that if parents could simply extract conflict from the experience, then divorce was really, in the end, not that big of a deal. Sitting beside her were three young adults whose parents divorced when they were children. They agreed with Ahrons: they felt solid in the categories of intellect, will, and emotions. They were proof, examples, according to Ahrons, that divorce could be good, or at least done well.

In her study Ahrons may rightly point to the resilience of young people. I agree that the human spirit is very resilient; after all, both Kara and I have found ways to cope and continue living full lives after our parents' divorces. We started a family, got (a number of) degrees, and bought a house. There are many who have not only survived

divorce but have grown to be well-balanced and whole adults in these substantialistic categories. They have college degrees, jobs, children, and mortgages. It may even be that a majority of children who lived through divorce could qualify for this label. But have they grown into such adults because of their parents' divorce or in spite of it? Does this, then, mean that divorce is not an issue, that divorce can be called good (at least 80 percent of the time)? The three young adults sitting beside Ahrons acknowledged that they had found ways to survive their parents' divorce, but I doubt that they would call it good! As Elizabeth Marquardt says, "Sure, a 'good divorce' is better than a bad divorce—but it isn't good."[11]

Judith Wallerstein has most forcefully spoken against the thesis of the "good" divorce that is bound, in my interpretation, to a tacit affirmation of a substantialistic understanding of the *imago Dei*. Wallerstein, doing a longitudinal study, has argued that divorce has ramifications that young people find very difficult to ever shake. They may find ways to succeed in society, but the marks of their parents' divorce remain lodged deeply within them.

Myth 1: Happy Parents Make Happy Children

Wallerstein explains that there are two myths about the "good" divorce—two myths that Ahrons peddles. The first myth is that happy parents make happy children. The idea is that if parents are not happy in the marriage and their own substance is tarnished, then their person is diminished, and as such they are both hindered in their parenting and therefore foster a less-than-happy home. The idea is that children need not communities of shared being, but zones of happiness, for their being is upheld not in community, but by having pure substance. We can see how this relates to Giddens's social theory. In the "good" divorce myth, what is seen as most important is that children and parents are able to seek self-fulfillment as they move into an unknown future.[12] The future is colonized individually, and it is occupied when the flag of happiness has been hoisted. In this scenario, the idea is simple: if children witness parents who are hindered from reaching for the future in a marriage because they lack happiness, then they themselves risk experiencing unhappiness

in the future. Wallerstein calls this the trickle-down myth. If parents can themselves be happy, then in turn so too will children.[13]

Wallerstein has shown that children who experience divorce rarely are ushered into a zone of happiness. Rather, she shows that statistically, children who live through their parents' divorce are often more at risk after the end of the marriage than in its less than blissful intactness.[14] This is not to say that happiness is not important, or that parents should tortuously toil in unions vacant of all joy. But we are not allowed to simply assume that a parent's happiness easily correlates to a child's. This, after all, is naive to begin with. Often divorce leaves neither parent equally happy; often one parent regrets the division or is painfully hurt by a revealed affair. Now the child must do the more difficult thing; he must be happy for a happy dad, but sad for a distraught mom. He is not free to acquire the surplus interest of their happiness. Instead he must live between the happiness and despair of each of his parents, negotiating their emotions, before he can even determine his own. Standing between their happiness and despair, he is not allowed to feel for himself, for his feelings may violate the happiness or despair of one parent. He is forced into the unreal; he is not allowed to *be with* them as he *is*, and his action must always be carefully chosen so as not to violate Mom or Dad's happiness or despair.

As I have argued throughout, what the child needs is not a zone of happiness, but a community of shared being, a community to be-with that is powerfully responsible for his or her being-in-the-world. This is more congruent with a relational understanding of the image of God. *The objective of the family is not to provide the child with happiness, but with ontological security*. The myth of transferable happiness is based solely in categories of epistemology, to wit: "If I know Mommy is happy, then I am happy." Children may altruistically believe this, and some may be relieved to be away from the chaos and tension of parental conflict. While having gained some serenity, they have lost something ontological; they have lost the community of their being, the union that is responsible for their being real.[15] This loss may be necessary, but it cannot be labeled good. A child may cognitively feel relieved that the intensity of fighting is diffused now that Mom and Dad no longer share a common space (or they may say this, being fed

the scripts of the myth of the good divorce), but now that the fighting has stopped between the walls of their home, it has crept inside their being.[16] Mom and Dad may not be fighting directly, but now the child is forced to fight with herself, seeking to find coherence in her being among brokenness and regret. If she is to find happiness in her mother's happiness, she will first have to come to grips with her ontological questions. She will have to find a place for her being. To be real, to be ontologically secure, to live in the fullness of the *imago Dei*, the child is not in search of happiness, but of belonging.

The good divorce is a myth because it has not considered the phenomenon from the perspective of ontology and agency. Elizabeth Marquardt relays an anecdote from a young man reflecting on the experience of his parents' separation. Listen for the ontological experiences of this young man at age twenty; listen for how the departure affects his very being in the world and his understanding of his own "realness."

> Several months later when I was up in my attic room I heard the back door close with a soft click. The sound was nothing out of the ordinary but something about it set me on edge. I crept down the stairs and found my mother sitting in the Kennedy rocker they had bought when my brother was born. Her face looked empty. "What happened?" I asked, dreading the answer. "Rob has left," she said. *The floor seemed to slide out from under me. My stomach twisted and my face was suddenly burning hot. I flung myself onto my mother's lap, sobbing uncontrollably. She held me tightly and slowly rocked. . . . All I felt was numb fear. . . . I was afraid for my mother to let go of me.*[17]

No knowledge, substances, or infusion of social capital will solve all this child's problems. He has lost ontological security; if his mother lets go of him, he fears that his very person will slide into the dark abyss of nothingness that has swallowed his community of being. If she lets go, he is alone, and alone he is no longer real.

Myth 2: Divorce Is a Temporary Crisis

Wallerstein explains that the "good" divorce has a second myth. "[It] is based on the premise that divorce is a temporary crisis that

exerts its most harmful effects on parents and child at the time of the breakup."[18] The idea is that divorce is like a haunted house. You walk through it knowing something is not right, ready to be startled as you turn the next corner, but after the shock occurs (the monster or ghost jumps out from around the corner) and you are through the house, the shock and fear are finished. It was terrifying in the haunted house, but once you are out, you are able to laugh with your friends and easily move on. The idea here is that what is hardest on children is the news of the breakup; once the news is broken (if done well), then the hardest part is over. Divorce can be "good" as long as you present the news correctly. The breaking of the news is assumed to be the most dangerous because it has the power, if not handled adeptly, to corrupt the young person's substance. Yet Wallerstein shows through her own research that divorce is "a life-transforming experience. After divorce, childhood is different. Adolescence is different. Adulthood—with the decision to marry or not and have children or not—is different. Whether the final outcome is good or bad, the whole trajectory of an individual's life is profoundly altered by the divorce experience."[19]

This second myth is tenable only if we understand divorce solely in epistemological substantialistic categories. That is, it's tenable only if we assume that knowledge (knowledge that Mom and Dad are getting separated) is the most painful reality of divorce, because it may corrupt the child's intellect, will, or emotions. But if ontology is more primary than these, if divorce is really an issue that impacts children at the ontological level, then the news of the breakup is just the beginning. For what is painful is not simply new knowledge, but the reality that your being-in-the-world is forever changing and what *is* will no longer be. The news of Mom and Dad breaking up is haunting, not because it forces transition and therefore threatens the child's substances, but because it shakes the child's being, forces him into the unreal. Remember hearing this ontological reality in the words of Nicole? "Now thirty-three, [she] still remembers the day when all her parents' hidden conflicts erupted with startling force. . . . 'I can't even remember my reaction. I know I couldn't understand what was happening. But I know exactly how I felt. *Lost.*'"[20]

Jen Robinson writes movingly about this experience of lostness. She discusses how she never knew (had knowledge of) the possible conflict that could end her parents' marriage. For her as a child, knowledge did not set the framework for her experience of her family; her being-with them did. This being-with was so deep that she could hardly imagine what it might mean for her to *not* be with them as a union. Robinson says,

> The divorce came out of the blue. I was aware of a troubling, myste-rious tension between my parents, and I had friends whose parents were divorced, so I wasn't living inside a bubble. But experience is often contradictory; one can be aware and innocent at the same time, especially in childhood. When I'd asked myself as I lay on the living room couch that day, *'What if Mom and Dad get divorced?' it was like asking, 'What if I'd been born in ancient Greece?' It wasn't any kind of reality.* As I grew older, that reality remained mysterious. Since I'd been too young during the years of their marriage to be aware of, or indeed interested in, my parents as separate individuals with their own relationship, I had no meaningful memories of their relationship with which to interpret the past. Knowledge appeared inaccessible. Why didn't I know it? Why couldn't I know it? As a teenager and young adult, there seemed to be something everyone else knew that was just out of my reach.[21]

The real issue, from an ontological perspective, is not the shock of new knowledge, but the reality that your community of being is disappearing. In the division of this community the child is forced into significant questions of identity and history. The moment of announcement is haunting, but it is haunting because of what it means for the being of the child. For it asks them to be in a way unimaginable, to be as if they were born in ancient Greece. The announcement is haunting because it is the announcement of the stripping of the community that made her real, that witnesses to her being in the image of God.

This (tacit) substantialistic understanding of the *imago Dei* has blinded our eyes to the real issue of divorce. Assuming this has led us to believe that by attending to a child's intellect and emotions divorce can be only a small disturbance to them. But if we believe

the *imago Dei* is a relational reality rather than a substance, the real issue of divorce is the destruction of the child's most primary community. He or she no doubt feels ontologically insecure and unreal, for not only do we have our being in relationship, but the image of God itself is a reality of the community of I to thou. This does not mean that divorce deletes the *imago Dei* in a child; the child still is capable of relational connection and therefore continues to be a creature made in the image of God. But divorce does strike at this most primary level, ushering the unreal into the core of our humanity, for this core *is* only through relationship. Accordingly, divorce does not threaten the image of God in us as though able to destroy it, but it does become a reality that stands in opposition to it, because it destroys that in which we are made real, the community of biological father and mother, the most basic community of I to thou. It is no surprise, then, that when divorce strikes us we feel like we are losing our realness, for our being has been pushed in opposition to our constitution in the image of God. Divorce cuts that deep.

The Biblical Text

What in the biblical text leads us to understand the *imago Dei* in such a relational way? Barth contends that theologically the creation accounts in Genesis provide a view both from above and from below. It can be read as a deeply theological and existential assertion when God states in Genesis 2 that "it is not good for the earth creature to be alone" (my translation). The adam (which simply translated means "the earth creature") is offered a number of different animal options to fulfill the need for companionship and community. Yet all these options fail, as the adam names the animals. They are unable to respond to the adam's naming as the adam responds to God and God to the adam. The failure to find another runs so deep that the adam must be put to death, for without community the adam is lost to the unreal. God's response ("it is not good for the earth creature to be alone") is a judgment that claims that the adam alone cannot be human, cannot exist in the real, that the earth creature without another is lost. There is no humanity without community. Even if

the potential human is created by God, in the singular the adam is not human and must be put to death, for the adam alone is an abstraction and cannot be real.[22]

But the adam is resurrected, now missing a rib, to meet the other that stands before the adam. From the despair of impossible communion (no animal is able), God acts to create possibility out of impossibility, providing for the adam another. Seeing this other, the adam proclaims, "This at last is bone of my bones and flesh of my flesh." Finally, there is community; finally, another makes the adam real. In the presence of this other the adam is not only given relational community, but given himself. Until this other is present there is no he or she; there is only a generic adam (earth creature). Now in the glow of this other, the adam is Adam, he (*ish*), and this other is Eve, she (*isha*). The adam has his person (can be he/his/him) only in the grace of her presence. Adam's "At last, bone of my bone and flesh of my flesh" asserts that this is an ontological reality; his being is given to him through her own (and vice versa). But this openness of mutual identification demands closed-ness as well. Eve is not simply a copy of Adam's being; she is other, she is mystery, she is female, and he is male. Their shared identification (as bone of my bone) demands the differentiation of male and female.[23] They find their being in the relation of one to another, I to thou.[24]

Barth believes that this passage in Genesis 2 is a commentary on Genesis 1:26–27 ("In the image of God he created them, male and female he created them."). Therefore, the social communal construct of male and female (a community of identification and differentiation) constitutes humanity. To be real is to be in relationship. Barth shows that without female there is no possibility for male; their mutuality runs as deep as ontology (unfortunately, Barth would tarnish this beautiful argument for gender equality in *Church Dogmatics*, III/4, with his labeling of the man as Creation A and the woman as Creation B). Barth also contends that Song of Songs is a commentary, or better, the response to Adam's assertion "At last bone of my bone and flesh of my flesh" by Eve, showing the deep love and mutuality that is present in shared community, which leads to being real.

This anthropological perspective on the *imago Dei* alerts us to the fact that the child has his or her being not in possession of certain

faculties (intellect, reason, feelings), but in relationship. When divorce strikes, it strikes at the level of relations, and this is what makes it so painful and haunting. Not only do these relations provide the young person with an environment of action to be, but this very relationship between biological mother and father is responsible for him or her being at all. As Staal says, "When children of divorce say 'I felt like my world was coming to an end,' they are usually not exaggerating. The announcement of divorce and a parent's departure can remain forever imprinted in our minds, with certain moments circling us back to the point of change and loss as we grow older."[25] From the view of this theological perspective, we must begin to understand divorce and its impact on young people not as a degradation of their faculties (though it may have this impact as well), but more deeply as tremors sent to their being through the break of the relations that make them real.

This is an interesting theological exposition on the biblical text, with significant ramifications for our understanding of divorce. But can this theological assertion that we *are* through relationship and therefore can fall into the unreal through its division be verified by other perspectives? We turn again to object relations psychology to see if that is the case.

Object Relations

In chapter 4 we drew object relations psychology into our inquiry, showing how Giddens was impacted by its perspectives for his social theory, as well as examining its correlations with Barth's discussions of the real versus the unreal. We saw that object relations psychologists, especially Daniel Laing, contend that our issue is the search to know ourselves as real, as ontologically secure. But how does this perspective connect to what we have articulated about the *imago Dei*? And how, then, does it help us understand the ontological significance of divorce on children?

Where Freudian psychoanalysis believed that the human being was at odds with his or her environment, having to cope with and control deep urges, object relations psychologists (heirs of Freud's

larger theory) saw the issue not so much as the need to control and confront individual urges, but rather as the need to come to grips with the need for an object (subject) to cling to.[26] Instead of looking solely at what made people sick, object relations theorists desired to examine what makes people, starting with the infant, whole or secure. Theresa Latini explains, "[The] object relations school of psychology . . . pushed beyond Freudian psychoanalytic theory by claiming that relationship is more fundamental to human being and doing than the powerful libidinal and food drives."[27]

Object relations could not ignore the significance of a good mother for security and the impact of a bad mother for dysfunction. Therefore, object relations psychologists moved beyond the individual-centric focus of a Freudian perspective and sought to examine the human as an agent in a social environment, most primarily and fundamentally the environment of mother and child. Much like Barth, then, object relations asserts that we have our being as we are with others. As Price says, "Barth has argued that we are as we act toward one another, and object relations has provided a tool to glimpse the material reality of this truth."[28] We have our being in relations not only when we are cognitively capable of acknowledging and participating in this community, but rather from our very first breath (or even before that, in the womb). As we have said above, to be, we need not-me objects to relate to. From the start we have our being through the acting of the mother. Just as we have identified the image of God in us as an acting verb of relational encounter, rather than as a predetermined substance, object relations psychology too asserts that we *are* through the action of others. John Macmurray, a philosophical forefather of object relations theory, explains that "the child can only be rescued from his despair by the grace of the mother; by a revelation of her continued love and care which convinces him that his fears are groundless."[29]

Where Barth has left this argument for relational ontology in the more general assertions of community and person meeting person, object relations has located this relational ontology primarily in the family, in the infant's caregiver. It has asserted that the family is the place of primary relational action that provides children with their being, with ontological security. When the mother fails the infant or,

I would add, the family is divided by divorce, the objective relational encounter in which the child has his being is lost, leading to feelings of being unreal. There are three major assertions of object relations psychology that address the phenomenon of divorce in connection to children. They fall into the categories of male/female, environment, and mirroring. We will take up each of these as they relate to Barth's *imago Dei* theology and shed light on the ontological ramification of divorce on children.

Male/Female

Just as male and female relationality is a key element of Barth's argument for a relational image of God, in object relations psychology male and female have a significant place.[30] While acknowledging that what is male and what is female is a social construction, it cannot be denied that there is such a thing as male and female, even if particular cultural definitions are socially constructed. For Barth, we saw that the image of God is constituted in the community of male and female, for male and female correspond to the identification and differentiation of God's own being for the world in I-and-thou relations. Barth states, "There is no being of man above the being of male and female. . . . [The hu]man is first and unquestionably and generally man and woman, and only then all kinds of other things, including perhaps father and mother."[31] So as male and female, we are with and for others in both identification and differentiation.[32] We are open to them as bone of our bone and flesh of our flesh, but at the same time closed; the other is other and must not become our pet, for in so doing the I–thou relation is destroyed. The categorical difference between male and female provides this closed-ness. We have our being as we act for others' beings in relationships of identification and differentiation.

Object relations theory helps us push this male-and-female perspective into the radius of the family and child. It argues, especially through Winnicott, that we are in need of both male and female interactions, or to say it even more boldly, it asserts that elements of male and female exist within us.[33] The community of male and

female becomes the location for the child to claim his being. In encounter with the care (the act) of the mother, the child encounters the necessary object or relationship to discover himself. In relating to the face of the mother, the child is freed from the unreal and made real through his own action to and for this face.[34] The ability to connect to others at the deep level of shared being becomes what Winnicott calls the feminine element within each of us. It is not that you must be a woman to have such a feminine side; rather, we all, whether male or female, need this to be. It is feminine because it originates from the motherly caregiver, from the face that becomes the needed other for the child to free it from the unreal. Ulanov states, "Through the female element of being in a mother or through a maternal identification in a man . . . being gets established. The mother's being at the core facilitates the child's coming into possession of that core. Being overflows as it offers itself, passing from one to another."[35]

But this female element of self-giving identification must be balanced by the male side. The child must be able to find herself not only through actions of identification, but also through acts of differentiation. The male side is the ability (which need not be represented by a man only) to be whole in oneself. It is the mother, or the female side, that pulls the child from the unreal to the real; it is the male side that pushes the child to claim her realness, her being, by seeing herself as an individuated or autonomous self, ready to encounter another in the communion of I and thou.[36] Ulanov states, "To feel real we need the female element of being, and we need it lifelong, lest we go mad by falling into too much objectivity. We also need the male element of being all our life, lest we go mad by falling into too much subjectivity."[37]

Object relations, like Barth's anthropology, sees the category of male and female as providing the ability for the needed identification and differentiation of relationship. Object relations pushes us further by arguing that these male and female elements exist *within* us. Because we are acted upon by mother and father, these male and female realities are burrowed into our being. To be healthy, according to Winnicott, we must have both the male and female elements within us.

The problem of divorce, then, and what makes it an ontological issue, is not simply that it affects the child's community of male and female.[38] This is true, but there is something more significant at play. The issue of divorce is that in the tragic division of the primary biological community of male and female (for there can be no existence without the union and action of male and female), the division is borne in the being of the child. Stephanie Staal testifies to this ontological reality of male and female in deeply painful words. "No matter how much my mother wanted to remain a part of my life after the divorce, I always come back to this: When she moved out, she didn't just leave my father, she left me too. I know this sentiment has become almost a cliché, but underneath all the rules and sensible measures lies a strong core of grief: Maybe my mother didn't love me quite enough."[39] When that relationship is put asunder and no longer exists, the child receives a tragic strike to her own being, for the male and female sides within her that seek coherence are struck by the division in the acting community of male-father and female-mother. It is not simply that she loses this community, but that she has been using this community to work out her needed male and female sides, working to make them a whole within her. When divorce occurs just as her mom and dad can no longer be together, and find strife between them, the male and female sides within her are themselves thrown into strife, or at least disequilibrium. With the male and female sides in strife, it becomes harder and harder for her to act for others in ways that uphold the needed balance of identification and differentiation. She may overidentify by too quickly entering sexual relations, deceived that such acts will bring union to her two sides (she is searching for a father figure).[40] Staal speaks powerfully of this:

What I do know is that I don't have to travel very far into myself to realize there is a part of me that, no matter what the circumstances, will always feel somehow deficient because my mother essentially missed out on those years when I was growing up. I feel there is a block between my mother and me, born not only out of her distance from my life but also because I, too, pushed her away. Sometimes I find myself today searching for the mother's love I lost, in the praise of a boss or

the arms of a boyfriend; the word and embraces of others, however, are usually inadequate approximations of a parent's love.[41]

Or a child may overdifferentiate, refusing to love anyone, providing the world with nothing but glares and sarcasm, blue hair, piercings, and tattoos. Observing young people over the last thirty years, Wallerstein speaks powerfully of this overdifferentiation:

> You were a little child when your parents broke up and it frightened you badly, more than you have ever acknowledged. When the family split, you felt as if you were splitting in two. When one parent left, you felt like there was nothing you could ever rely on. And you said to yourself that you would never open yourself to the same kinds of risks. You would stay away from loving. Or you only get involved with people you don't care about so you won't get hurt. . . . Your fears and your ways of responding to your fears, which were eminently sensible and logical at the time, became a part of your character and have stayed with you up to this day.[42]

In witnessing the division in the biological communion of male and female that is responsible for her being, the child finds it harder and harder to be real, to be an integrated, whole person, and therefore she finds it difficult to be appropriately open and closed to others. She needed both of her parents, as the unit that most powerfully correlated to her being, to balance her male and female sides of herself. A surrogate, such as a stepfather or aunt, may help mitigate risky behavior, but it will not completely end her search for this need to find balance between the male and female sides. For this needed balance is an issue of ontology. Her being yearns for identification and differentiation from those responsible for her being. She must be able to identify and differentiate herself not from generic others, but from the very others that created her. She must be able to identify her being with the union of their beings as she learns to differentiate herself from them. She needs them to be a unit, a whole community of male and female. Dealing with them in an ad hoc manner (e.g., her mom on the weekdays and her dad on the weekends) is not helpful, for she lacks the wholeness of the male and female encounter that she needs to bring together in her own being. Wallerstein states, "The

child in an intact family is free to turn alternately to each parent to meet her changing needs and wishes as she grows. Young adolescent girls typically turn to their mothers. Six-year-old boys want to be with their dads. But in the divorced family the child has to tailor her needs and wishes to the parent who happens to be scheduled in her life at any given moment. Many children complain that when they're with their moms they miss their dads and vice versa. Indeed they do."[43] Without their communion she is not allowed to work out her connection to and difference from them; in their divorce they have worked that out for her. And without the ability to work it out, her being is left searching and hiding.

Environment

The above discussion points to the importance of environment. It is not, as I have said, simple interaction with male and female people that is needed at the deep ontological level (this may provide needed social capital, but we are talking here of ontology). What is important for the infant is not only to have interactions with the mother, but to find himself in an environment that he can trust. This trusted environment needs to be maintained when the child grows. It is the trustworthiness of the environment that makes him feel real. When the infant awakens, he is helpless and must trust that his cry (his action) will be heard and responded to. If it is not, he will no longer be; without the reliability of the environment he cannot exist,[44] for he has his being as he encounters Mom and Dad in the distinction and unity of the environment.[45]

He encounters Mom and he encounters Dad. While it is important that he encounter their distinctness, it is just as important that he encounter the union as a family environment. He no doubt needs to learn, as he grows, to encounter his parents as individuals. But for his being, it is more important that he encounter a family, a unit of Mom and Dad that creates an environment beyond the husband and wife's individual wills.

This environment is constructed from the male and female, and the child is the result of male and female interaction. This is why

Barth states boldly that the *only* category within humanity is the distinction (not of race or nationality,[46] but) of male and female. The environment is formed through male and female, but the environment becomes a whole to the child. For it is the environment that he is taking into his being as male and female, and it is in the environment that he both belongs and is in the image of God. Seven-year-old Manolo heartbreakingly speaks of the division of this environment and his fear for his being as he exists without it: "Every night I pray over and over and over and over until I fall asleep that my dad will come back to the house. I know I see him a lot, but I feel scared when I think that he will never live here again. I feel like crying now to talk about it. I'm all done talking now."[47]

The child is the product of this environment, and by living in the environment he is given his being and discovers his uniqueness. The environment provides a spirit of ritual, which the individual parent cannot.[48] A routine is something chosen by the individual; a ritual is the cumulative practice and action of a group of people whether they cognitively or tacitly choose it. The individual may have routines, and these routines may impact another, but a ritual is a communal reality beyond the wills of individuals. Object relations has asserted that our being is in need of these rituals. In their power to order action and environment, rituals provide people with ontological security. The infant begins to trust and finds his being secure in the ritual of feeding and changing. The child finds security enough to feel real in the ritual environment of Christmas celebrations, Dad's morning slippers, and Mom's smell. But when these rituals are not provided, or divorce pulls them apart, making them not family rituals but individual parental routines and habits, the child is pushed into the unreal. The environment that is responsible for his being is divided and he finds himself pushed to and fro by routine, but communal ritual has slid into the dark, empty space between Mom and Dad. He is no longer given a prearranged and negotiated environment, but only disconnected zones of individual action. Marquardt points to this reality: "But the majority of those from divorced families say that as the years passed, our divorced parents did not have a lot of conflicts. Instead, we experienced something much deeper and more pernicious. The divorce left us with a permanent inner conflict between

our parents' worlds. This was a conflict for which we could imagine no resolution, a conflict for which many of us thought we had only ourselves to blame."[49] As we have observed in another context, the child must now do the very difficult: he must find a way to create an environment for himself out of the broken pieces of his now broken family, sporadic friendship groups, and consumer brands. Because this ritual environment is no longer provided by the cumulative action of kin, tribe, or village, the family (mom, dad, and children) must bear the full weight of this needed environment, making the dissolution of the family environment in divorce deeply (ontologically) painful. This environment of male and female is so important because it provides the child with mirroring.

Mirroring

In object relations theory the mother provides the child with ontological security, because, as Latini beautifully explains, "in face-to-face interaction between mother and child, the mother's countenance mirrors the infant's self. When the baby gazes into the mother's eyes, she sees herself. What she looks like is seen in her mother's countenance. . . . Such mirroring remains a need throughout one's life."[50] For good or for ill the family environment serves as mirror, which through its action reflects our being back to us, and in so doing determines it. We know we are (have being) because it is reflected back to us through others; this is Barth's very argument for *imago Dei*. This happens most primarily, according to object relations psychology, in the family. When the family environment is dysfunctionally abusive, the reflection is an ugly one, so ugly and dehumanizing that the environment may need to be put to death to keep it from destroying the being of the child. However, what happens most often in divorce, and what makes it so painful, is not that the mirror is providing a dehumanizing image, but rather that it is providing a needed true reflection and yet it is all of a sudden shattered. In the separation the mirror has broken apart; the child must now negotiate between multiple mirrors in multiple locales. Marquardt explains,

As children of divorce, we became insiders and outsiders in each of our parents' worlds. We were outsiders when we looked or acted like our other parent or when we shared experiences in one world that people in the other knew little or nothing about. . . . By contrast, we were marked as insiders by whatever traits we shared with the family members in one world—physical characteristics, personality, and name—as well as the experiences we shared with that family. . . . Yet because we grew up living in two worlds we never fully belonged in either place. At any moment, without warning, one of our distinguishing traits could mark us as an outsider.[51]

There is no longer a whole environment responsible for the child's existence. Now there are responsible individuals, living in different places with different mirrors that take no account of each other. The child of divorce, then, having lost the family environment, finds herself standing in a hall of mirrors. Standing between these multiple mirrors, *she* alone must find a way to orient herself to what is a true reflection of her being. Barth has told us that this is impossible outside of community, for the mirror is the result of a male and female environment of action in encounter. Therefore, the child's own action to find a true reflection of herself becomes a most complicated job. In a playhouse of disorienting mirrors she must search for her own being. She must admit that she is ontologically insecure (or hide it in other behaviors, whether risky or highly achieving).[52]

Divorce is an issue of ontology because it not only affects the male and female sides within us but undercuts our most primary communal environment and therefore shatters the mirror we need to know ourselves. It is not that young people do not have other mirrors in life for them to reflect who they are to them; such mirrors are ever present, in the form of the media, the school system, peer culture, and so on. But they do not have the direct line to the child's being that mother and father do.

Object relations psychology has helped us to see the significance of Barth's theological assertions. Through the lens of object relations theory, we can see that when divorce strikes the young person it shakes the *imago Dei* in them, throwing their being into question by dividing the community of male and female that provides an environment of mirroring. It does not destroy the image in them but

does have the power to deceive them into feeling themselves unreal. Divorce, then, is not primarily an issue of needed social capital and self-esteem (not an issue of epistemology and structure). It is an issue of ontological security. Divorce undercuts "(1) balancing of autonomy and belonging, (2) continued mirroring, (3) continuity of routine (often provided by social practices), and (4) bracketing out unbearable anxieties."[53] All four, Theresa Latini has argued, are needed to keep us from falling into ontological insecurity. As Ray Anderson has said, "To be human is to be concretely 'this person' belonging to 'these people.'"[54] Divorce is an ontological issue because inside the crater of the family's implosion the child remains a person, but now with no (especially in late modernity) "these people" to belong to de facto. Therefore, his "this person" is thrown into question. For the child, divorce is the breaking of our most primary cohumanity. From Barth's perspective as well as that of object relations theory, without cohumanity (without belonging to these people) the real gives way to the unreal.

Relationships of cohumanity form what Barth calls a "little history." Because our being is constituted in actions with and for others, we form a history, a history in which we know and understand ourselves. I know myself as belonging to these people because they have acted with and for me as I have acted with and for them. We have a history, an environment of rituals that mark who we are in time and space. Price explains Barth's perspective like this: "[A] being can transcend its own movement only as it is encountered by an other, engaging in a reciprocal relationship in which there is mutual change at the deepest level of being. Any such historical being, therefore, does not simply have a history, but is a history."[55]

The child is the product of the concrete historical action of mother and father encountering each other. Their most historically dynamic act (their most significant act as cohumanity) has been that which created the child. Therefore, the child, when born, enters the history of the family; the history of Mom and Dad's action with and for each other, and now together their action with and for the child. Their action with and for each other creates for the child "these people," who give him his being through their history. Obviously, "these people" as the unfolding of a history includes more than just a mom

and dad. For a number of children who have experienced the divorce of their parents, their grandparents, whom they often assume to be a rock of solid marriage, become "the pinnacle of romance" and dependable love.[56] But while witnessing a grandparent's marriage can have a positive impact, it cannot solve the ontological ramifications of the broken history caused by divorce. Staal states, "Nevertheless, my grandparents' relationship wasn't one that provided instruction in the everyday workings of a marriage; while their courtship is part of my history, it wasn't the union that directly produced me. With my parents' divorce, a link in my family chain was broken, creating a crucial distance between my grandparents' story and mine."[57]

In the reflective words of Jen Robinson, we can hear how the divorce of her parents both impacted her being and, in a weird way, blurred time and therefore history, forcing her to feel almost outside it or at least unable to order events in their unfolding.

> For many years I was unsure when exactly the divorce occurred. Though I know now that it was in 1978, the event retains a kind of haze in my memory. Was I ten? Eleven? It was early summer, but was it 1978 or 1979? I seem somehow to have lost a year. Paradoxically, while the exact year is slippery, the exact hour is sharply etched. In contrast to my parents, who both make a distinction between the time of palpable unhappiness, the time of separation, and the time of the final decree, for me there was a single epicenter in which their divorce occurred. This was the day my father left, the day they decided to divorce.[58]

The child has a history most fundamentally through the cohumanity of his mom and dad, for he is the product of their encounter. This encounter creates a history, and out of this history, it creates him. As he ages he no doubt has other histories, but he knows and enters them only through the primary history of the family, which stretches back to the history of mother to infant. When mother and father's cohumanity is split, so too is the child's history. Divorce dislocates the child from his most primary history, the history responsible for his being. Staal says pointedly, "Once we have lost the thread of common history that generally binds our families together, the past comes under scrutiny and is available for revision. In a shifting game of rancor and blame, our parents can offer up two different versions

of their marriage and divorce, fueled by their unresolved feelings toward their breakup."[59]

Marquardt's words are powerfully ontological as she witnesses, through an old videotape, the united history of her parents, a history of which she is the product. "That's where I come from!" she says. What is most haunting about seeing this tape is that before witnessing it, she had no memory at all of these two people together in such a way. "In one home movie from that brief era—I think my dad's younger brother was holding the camera—my parents give each other a long, deep kiss. They're hamming for the camera but there is unmistakable youthful passion there too. It's the only time I've ever seen them kiss, and I watch it a little embarrassed but also entranced. That's where I came from!"[60]

The video haunts Marquardt because she now stands in a divided history, a history that has become an antihistory, because it negates the encounter from which it emerged. With the divorce (the ending of relational encounter), the parents have said that they wish this history to no longer be, but the child still needs this history, for she is in the world only because of it. Now instead of being given a history to know herself, the child must work to construct her own history as she individually encounters each parent. But this becomes very complicated, for she will have to create a history of her own being from within an antihistory, from within the reality of parental strife and disconnection. History is created through cohumanity, but the child is without cohumanity of parents and therefore without history. No wonder she feels unreal.

It has too often been assumed that divorce is simply a moment, rather than a radical transformation of a young person's history. As we can hear in the voices of children, it is not the moment itself that is so hard to bear, but the fact that the moment of the announcement of the end of their community of being has a way of stretching both forward and back, dislodging the child from history. Divorce throws the past into question ("Why am I if they cannot be together?"), and it reaches forever into the future, for it strikes at the ontological level.

In the words of eighteen-year-old Jewel we can hear how it stretches backward: "Once I woke up in the middle of the night. Fortunately

my brother was still asleep, and I guess that was the first time I ever knew that anything was wrong with my parents. My dad said to my mom, 'I have not loved you in twenty years.' I was twelve, and so I was just like, 'So my dad didn't love my mom when I was created.' That alone repeats over and over in my head every time I see him. Every time I see him."[61] Jewel's words are not merely about adjusting to knowledge (of information she should not have heard). Rather, her issue is ontological. She cannot shake the fact that she was created in division. This division has come to rest within her; it has dislodged her from her little history by dividing the union of Mom and Dad. Her parents' divorce is not about a single, punctual, present moment, but rather it has the power to rewrite her past. Who is she, *is* she, if she was not the product of her parents' love? Even with the most amicable of breakups, such questions rush from the child's shaken being to the surface.

We can see in an interview of young adult Theresa, reported by Stephanie Staal, how divorce lives on and on after first knowledge of it, dislodging the child from history by throwing past action into question. And in so doing, the future blurs as well:

> It wasn't until they were outside the restaurant that her father finally crouched down, looked her in the eye, and told her he wasn't going to come home anymore. "I was in shock after that," Theresa says, and her voice still shakes almost twenty-five years later. "I remember having this sick feeling that my life was over. The rug was just yanked from under me and then it was never the same again. No safety zone replaced it. I was shell-shocked for years." She takes a breath, and adds evenly, "Everything I do in my life is to never let that happen to me again."[62]

Fearing the ontological terror that gripped her at that moment, Theresa's whole life now revolves around never again being caught at the vulnerable level of questioning her being. Remember the words of twenty-year-old Jody, who said, "It seems like it should be all over and done with after eight years, but it's really not. I guess I feel weird being like 'yeah, but . . .' because I'm twenty."[63] Or listen again to the ontological assertions of Amy as she reflects on this so-called temporary crisis:

Twenty years, three stepparents, and countless crying jags later, the story has no ending. I adapted, just as they say kids do. But divorce is more than a crisis to be worked through. No matter how well I weathered the storm when it was at its worst, I still emerged dripping with its effects, and feel a bit waterlogged to this day. Old doubts and questions linger, and mingle with fresh ones that arise as my parents and I get on with our lives. Married myself and seven months pregnant as I write this, I now fervently hope that my husband and I can give our children a life so solid they won't even think to question its foundation, like the one I knew until that afternoon.[64]

As Amy Conway notes, this is not to say that children of divorce cannot find some kind of wholeness in their lives, but it is to say that the division in the union responsible for their being leaves a mark that never disappears. Parents can assure the child repeatedly that they both (now individually) love her, but that is not her concern; she does not doubt this. Rather, she doubts who she is and whether she can be at all, now that there is no longer unity in the community of history responsible for her being.[65] Can she be, now that her action is toward two different people in two different milieus, who are connected only by a broken history of regret? "Can I be at all in this world?" is her question. If she is ready to abandon one parent, to never see him again for how he has abused her, then the division may be good news. But if she is not at this point (which most children are not[66]), then the announcement of divorce is not an end point for her, but a beginning. It is the beginning of her search for a place to be as she acts between their two worlds. She must find a way to be "this person" now that "these people" regret the union that created her. As Staal says so poignantly, "This is what I have left of the relationship that brought me into the world: I have photos, incomplete stories, and the bits and pieces of my own memory. . . . I can't pinpoint when their relationship crossed over some invisible trip wire, shutting their love down." She continues, "I will never truly understand the depth of the frustration, disappointment, and unhappiness they felt when they were together; by the same token, I doubt they will ever really understand my feelings when they divorced. The three of us stand on opposite sides of this divide of age and experience, although I want nothing more than to reach out and bring us all together."[67]

Barth has helped us to see that we have our being as we act with and for others. And this being is in the image of God who as Father, Son, and Spirit acts with and for humanity.[68] Object relations psychology has also argued that we have our being through the action of others and that this action not only determines our social location and therefore our outer life, but also impacts our perception of our inner psychological reality (we feel ourselves unreal). We might say, then, that divorce breaks the primary location of cohumanity, leaving us without a history, and is experienced as a death within us, for it throws our being into question. Just as the breaking of cohumanity in the Garden (Adam and Eve choose against God and then blame each other) meant "they shall surely die," so the breaking of the cohumanity of family is the concrete experience of negation. It was Kierkegaard who reminded us that just as we were created *ex nihilo* (out of nothing), this *ex nihilo*, or nothingness, still lives in us. While by God's word we were made real, our being is giving way to and returning to the unreal (until the final resurrection). We are aware, even in modernized society that tries to deny it, that we will one day be negated, that death will end us.[69] Barth and object relations psychology have pointed to the fact that because our being is being-with, when we are thrust into experiences of broken cohumanity we come up against negation; we feel in our being the threat of the void. My argument has been that this is what divorce does. By breaking our primary community of cohumanity, and stripping us of the history that created us, it has the power to awaken and feed the void that exists within us, pushing us to feel unreal.

The presence of the void within humanity and how divorce feeds it is the reason that theology needs to be an essential dialogue partner in our ontological framing of the phenomenon of divorce. Theology knows of communities of belonging that worship a God who has fully taken on the void (both in the world and in the self). It speaks of a God who negates negation, promising an eschatological (a final and complete) community where evil, sin, atrophy, or tragedy will never again end community, and will thus destroy the void forever. The church is this broken community of hopeful anticipation, which, in its own being, invites the broken beings of others to come and be real with and for one another, as Jesus Christ is with and for the church

and the world. As James Loder says, "Theologically, the church knows a power that runs even deeper than a mother love."[70] It will be these communities that know such a power that will be our focus in the final chapter. We will examine how they might, in their life, stand with and for young people facing divorce and its profound effects.

6

What Is to Be Done

The Church as a Community for the Broken

Just months after my parents' divorce was finalized, my mom moved out of our family home, a house my family had lived in since I was in kindergarten. She explained that she wanted to be closer to work. It seemed like a logical reason, and in her place I would have made the same decision. Yet I still felt at odds about it. I realized that this house, this place where I became me, would no longer be part of my life. I silently grieved that I would never be able to take my own children to this house, showing them the basement where I had played hours and hours of floor hockey, shooting a worn tennis ball into the back of a net, working out who I was as I contemplated the mysteries of the universe with stick in hand.

I suppose that even if my parents had stayed together, they more than likely would have moved to another house and eventually given some stranger the keys to the place where I became me. This felt different. It wasn't so much that the title of house was no longer in my family's name; it was that the family that once lived within its walls no longer existed. My parents were no longer a community of shared memory in which the life and history of that house would live on,

even if we would never enter its walls again. With my mom's move the family house I had known for twenty years seemed to disappear into the infinitely deep crack that now separated my parents. It felt like the house had not simply transferred ownership but had been negated; it had been eliminated from the universe, and my place in the world went with it.

This negation of family home for me came with none of the drama that it did for Kara. After the divorce of her parents, the suburban hobby farm where her family lived was sold to a developer, who, having no need for the house itself, allowed the local fire department to set it ablaze as a training exercise, literally reducing it to a heap of ashes. After the house burned to the ground, bulldozers showed up to radically transform the topography of these few acres, making them receptive to a new water treatment plant to serve the rapidly encroaching cul-de-sacs and suburban streets. Halfway through the destruction process, Kara's sixteen-year-old sister, Callie, visited the site. In the early evening air, all alone, Callie climbed into the tree house that still remained nestled in the broad branches of the large tree that stood next to where the house had been. Sitting there overlooking the ugly emptiness that had swallowed her home, she could only cry. This little tree house, which had fallen out of use as the children had become teenagers, was all that remained of the family that had lived in this place.

As she sat there, between her tears and breaths she could hear the faint sound of whining. Collecting herself, she climbed down to investigate. It was a cat, and not just any cat, but their family cat, "Momma Cat," who had lived both inside their home and outside in the small barn that had also been burnt to the ground. Standing there looking at Momma Cat, now surrounded by plowed dirt and vacant lots, she felt as lost and utterly abandoned as the cat. Without this place, without this farm, Momma Cat was simply an old stray, worthless to most. Without this place, without *home*, Callie—and Kara and I as well—wondered if in our parents' divorce we had ourselves become strays, people without a place, people without belonging.

In this final chapter we turn to a question more than likely on your mind throughout the last several chapters. That question, of course, is, in knowing all of this, what can be done? I fear even broaching

the question, let alone seeking to answer it. I fear to do so not only because I worry my answers may not be *right*, but more because I fear that in our search to solve problems, we might avoid the heaviness of the issue itself. We may think that somehow, if we do certain things, everything will be fixed. As the stories above testify, divorce for children is about much more than transition, it is about ontology; it is about having a place to belong and be, now that the union that created us has split. This is not something easily and simply mended. Yet, if anything can be done, it will have to be something that addresses this very issue. If the issue is only knowledge, then education should be our goal; if the issue with divorce is primarily social capital, then to policies and legislation is where we should direct our attention. But if divorce is an issue of lost being that is constituted in the community of biological father and mother, then the action we take for young people of divorce must place community at the center. So I contend that what children of divorce need most is *not* strategies for thinking correctly, but a place to belong, a community in which their humanity is upheld. If the home in which they had their being has been negated in divorce, a community beyond the family, which nevertheless embraces its actuality, is needed to ground their being somewhere. What kind of community must this be?

It must be a community that knows life and death, a community that seeks to be real in light of the unreal. It must be a community that proclaims that in its life, in its actions of being with and for one another, it participates in the fullness of God's love for the world. It must be a community that is not constituted in functions, but like the family is based in persons, and has the goal of loving and being with one another. It must be a community that, as Loder said at the end of the last chapter, asserts and witnesses in its life that it "knows a power that runs even deeper than a mother's love."

The Church as the Community of Being

It is the church *as community* that children of divorce need to solidify their shaken ontology. The church knows and participates in this power that is stronger than a mother's love. But it doesn't own

this power or control it; rather, a mother's love is a broken witness to it. It is the power of God made known in the suffering weakness of Jesus Christ, who acts to give up his own being that we might find ours. This new community cannot replace, and does not sublimate, the family, but it provides the members of a broken family a place to be-with and be-for as they suffer their ontological trauma. Nothing can replace the biological union of our parents. Nothing can erase the wounds and scars of our parents' divorces. But finding a communion that suffers with and for us can assure us that we are real, that our suffering is embraced concretely by these people called church, who witness to a God in Jesus Christ who bears our brokenness.[1]

It is the church community steeped in the suffering of the life and death of Jesus Christ that can bear the ontology shaken by divorce. It is the community that has witnessed (even ever so slightly) the promise of new life through the resurrection that can provide young people hope in the midst of their deep negations. The church community, then, is not a vehicle for help in its service. Rather, in its simple life together it becomes the context, the location, the field, that makes young people real—real if they can find and are invited to place their being within reach of these people who will stand with and for them as Jesus Christ stands with and for the church. The community of the church cannot eliminate the deep ontological fractures that occur when divorce strikes, but it can, in its communal life, stand with and for these children, bearing their brokenness. In this way it can hold them together, by whispering in words and deeds, "Your pain is beyond comprehension, and you suffer, but know that we share your suffering. You are not alone. You may have lost the union in the community that created you, but you are secure in this community that knows a power that brings life out of death, a power in which isolation gives way to belonging."

What can be done, then, is not a program to outlaw divorce or a recipe to produce magic pills that stabilize ontology. While the church and society must think long and hard about how to participate in strengthening families and marriages,[2] the church can offer its very life, its community of fellow sufferers, as the "these people" that children can be real with, therefore stabilizing their "this person." Unlike most other communities in our world, this intergenerational

community is bound together not by the pure relationship, but by the confession that we have our being as we act with and for one another through the power of the Spirit of Jesus Christ in suffering love. For young people struck ontologically by divorce, the congregation is a powerful location in which to find stability in their being, because the church as community is the place of being-in-encounter; it is to be a place where people *are* through its action of relational encounter.

But let's be honest, churches are governed more by the pure relationship of individual choice and taste than by the logic of the crucified God. Too many churches are too busy getting people to know things, or seeking jaw-dropping programmatic structures, to be aware of people's being and acting in the world (especially young people's),[3] not to mention too unaware to offer them the community's own being and acting as a place to stand. So how, practically, might a church move in this direction?

To get to these practical actions we will have to follow the very path this project has led us down, a path of placing experience, the social sciences, and theology in conversation. Therefore, to articulate these practical steps we must remember the four basic needs for an individual to feel ontologically secure, something that I argued is undercut by the divorce. These needs are:

- mirroring,
- the ability to balance autonomy and belonging,
- having routine,
- and bracketing out anxiety.

Karl Barth, our main theological dialogue partner, has presented four actions that constitute being-in-encounter, or to say it another way, actions that make us, and our neighbor, real. They are:

- seeing and being seen,
- speaking and listening,
- mutual assistance,
- and doing it all with gladness.[4]

These actions fit nicely with the four needs for ontological security that object relations psychology has presented us. Therefore, in the remainder of this chapter I lay out practices or dispositions that a church might take in relation to young people and divorce in each of these four areas:

- mirroring as seeing and being seen,
- the ability to balance autonomy and belonging as speaking and listening,
- having routine as mutual assistance,
- and bracketing out anxiety as doing the above with gladness.

These four areas provide a framework to examine practical actions that the congregation might take to be the community young people of divorce need to find themselves real (ontologically secure) within the church's very communal life.

Instead of painting my picture of practical action in broad strokes, I seek to get more precise by discussing these practices of the church in terms of three different kinds of people: the youth worker/children's minister, a parent, and a friend (which might include a grandparent, an aunt, or a neighbor to a young person going through the divorce of his or her parents). This picture of practical actions not only explores the broad movements of the church community but more intricately suggests what a few important people might do.

What Can Be Done?

1. Mirroring as Seeing and Being Seen

To be is to be-with others, as I have argued throughout this book. This being with others can have no more primary reality than that of biological father and mother. Being with others provides us our being because to be, to discover ourselves as real, we must experience ourselves through the gaze of others. We have our being as it is mirrored back to us in relationships; I know myself as others reveal who I am in relation to them.

What a congregation offers young people of divorce is a mirror, a mirror drastically different from consumer culture or a friendship group. For the congregation (at its best) is concerned not only with action (such as the actions to buy, wear, or conform to certain norms), but with being as it relates to action. The church through its praise, proclamation, and education seeks to mirror who we *are*—children of God, forgiven and loved, who then are called to go and do (act) likewise. The congregation *cannot* take away the fact that the young person's most fundamental mirror of biological union has cracked, but the congregation can, if it is brave enough, become a mirror that through its life can reflect back to young people who they are and where they belong.

To be together at this ontological level, the congregation must act in its encounter with young people's being; it serves as this needed mirror by seeing and being seen. It starts by seeing these young people. This entire book has sought to recast the experience of divorce, so that people, and communities, might better see what is actually happening with those experiencing separation and divorce. I fear that divorce has become so common in our culture that those of us who lead and participate in religious communities have stopped *seeing* it. Like violence on TV, we have seen so much of it that we no longer flinch at the sight of another case. Such a stance can only drive young people deeper into isolation, for our unwillingness to see due to overexposure communicates that the issue is not a big deal, that it is normal, that it is common to feel your very being stripped from within you. Of course, we often refuse to see the depth of the issue because we fear seeming harshly dogmatic or rigid, or making the divorced parent feel guilty. But "seeing" demands that we see not an issue, but a person, and as such we are able to affirm two things at once. We can affirm the pain of the young person without chastising the parent. Congregations then must find ways to convey that they see how painful this transition is for the child.

But there is another dimension to this. It is not only seeing that is important, but also being seen. To be a mirror the congregation is called to more than just seeing (this would make it a window), but in seeing to allow itself to also be seen.[5] Too often on our drives home or in our staff meetings, we church members say things like, "Poor Jessica, her

parents seemed so happy, she must be devastated." But then this is as far as it goes. We have seen but have not been willing to be seen, to allow young people to come close to us and see our feelings of compassion for them or, even more important, our own unique journeys of pain and suffering. This being seen not only is about reflecting compassion for the trauma that young people have faced but, even more basically, is about opening up the life of the congregation and its members for young people to see our common humanity. The congregation must take a disposition that communicates to all its young people that they are invited to come and see, come and see as their elders, parents, and friends seek to live faithfully for Jesus Christ.

In the invitation to come and see, a young person's being can be reflected back to her. As she sees the being-with of the community, she is given a place to stand. She is given others to belong to in the midst of the gripping pain of the loss of the union of familial community.

To become this community of mirroring by seeing and being seen, the congregation can focus on two overarching practices: accompaniment and sanctuary, both bound by empathy. *Accompaniment* is simply the practice of standing with another. It is quite amazing how unfamiliar it is for the church to accompany both children and parents in the storms of divorce. We tend either to violently attack an issue and a person who has failed to meet a standard or to ignore it altogether. Neither of these approaches is accompaniment. To accompany a young person living through the divorce of his parents is to not turn from the pain and confusion that he finds himself in; it is to stand with him in the midst of the pain, offering our presence as an act of care.

Often one of the most painful things for young people living with divorce (especially in their early years) is that the once functionally stable environment has now become anything but stable. Angry phone calls, lawyers' papers, new bedrooms, different schedules and routines, revealed secrets, and a different experience of their own parents leaves the once-safe place in stressful turmoil. What the congregation can offer, as it sees and is seen, is *sanctuary*. If it is willing to see and be seen, its life can become a safe place for young people to simply come and be. Coffee hour, the half an hour before youth group, the monthly potluck dinner, conversations in the parking lot, the familiar events and the rhythm of the community's life together become

sacred as young people are given sanctuary in a social environment that through empathetically acknowledging their situation (and its pain) provides a stable place to rest from chaos and upheaval.

With this as our backdrop, what might some key people do?

The Youth Worker/Children's Minister

- Be willing to approach tweens and teens to communicate your understanding of their situation. It may at first feel invasive to ask young people to speak about the event. But by simply saying, "Hey, I know this is a really hard time," we are communicating that we see. It need not be an overly drawn-out encounter (as a matter of fact, that may be counterproductive), but a simple word that says that you see how difficult this situation is can go a long way, by witnessing to the young person that he or she is not alone.

- Allow for multiple ways for kids to express their pain, whether through art, drama, or discussion. It would be powerful with tweens and teens to do a panel discussion, asking kids from divorced families to speak of their experience. You could also include adults who have been divorced and young adults that have lived decades with the divorce of their parents. When doing so, invite other members of the congregation to come and listen. Keep the conversation on the level of experience, but allow the safety for people to really speak of their experience. These shared stories of pain and questioning, when spoken, have the power to become a significant part of the narrative quilt of the community. And as their story is part of the narrative of the community, young people are given a history.

- Be willing to communicate with parents. Find ways to articulate how hard this is on their children without shaming the parents. Continue to offer help and support to parents.

- Don't over-program. Allow open space for young people to just *be*. All kids need this, and it provides the possibility for a community of mutual seeing.

- Find ways to move the center of gravity of the children's ministry or youth group from separate age-group cohorts to meaningful interactions between adults and kids.

Parent

- As hard as it is, invite your child to convey his or her disappointment, confusion, and pain about the divorce. Often your own ontological security is dependent on the belief that your children are (or will be) OK, that the divorce has not hurt them. You fear that you couldn't live with the fact that they are hurting so deeply. But this puts your child(ren) in a bind, because their own ontological security has been undercut, and they can find security only through facing the pain of the divorce directly. Yet they worry that to do so would hurt you. Give them permission to do it anyway, and while it will no doubt hurt, you face their pain as well.

- If you are in a congregation, do your best to not depart from your community of faith. It is very easy to feel ashamed or uncomfortable going to the same church after a divorce, but your kids need the community. They have more than likely built significant connections at this place and will need these relationships to feel real. After the divorce you will be tempted to change as many associations as possible, maybe choosing a new church. But allowing your child(ren) to stay connected to these people that know them through both parents is important (even if that feels painful to you).

- Allow something to be two things at once. It is possible that divorce is both a great relief to you and also a nightmare to your child. Allow it to be so. Don't try to fix things. It can make a child feel crazy if she knows the experience as deeply painful but is continually told by her father that it is good, that she should be happy because this is a good thing. It may be a good thing for Dad, but his good thing does not keep the same situation from being a hell for his daughter. *An event or experience can be two things at once.*

Friend

- If you are aware of it or were part of it, find ways to tell the young person the story of their parents' courtship and early marriage. Tell the young person stories of his or her birth and parents' shared reaction. We often shy away from doing this, acting as if these

people that created the child were never together, thinking that this keeps us from painful subjects—Why live in the past? we think. But this living in the past is essential for the ontological security of children. Hearing these stories may be painful and weird, but it does remind them that they are real, that although it is now broken, this history is their past. This history created them.

- Seek to convey that you are on the side of the child(ren) and not either parent. Therefore, allow the child(ren) to have whatever emotions they may, even if you think they misrepresent the situation. There may be a time to take sides, or situations that call for it, but in general the child(ren) must know that you have seen their situation, and this is primarily not a moral but an ontological reality.

- Make a commitment to be with the child(ren) on a regular schedule. The point will be to just be together.

2. Autonomy and Belonging as Speaking and Listening

The essence of healthy relational life is the balancing of identification and differentiation. To really belong is not to have your own will melted into the will of the community, as if you no longer have any opinions, thoughts, and feelings outside those of the group. Rather, to truly be-with, to have our being with others, we need to have our own individual beings, to recognize our distinct selves. But to discover this distinct self we need a place to identify with; we need a people to belong to, a community to serve as our mirror. For many children of divorce the balance between identification and differentiation gets off-kilter. In the midst of a split between their parents, children may overidentify, becoming their parent's soulmate, sounding board, or shoulder to cry on. It becomes the child's job to care for his or her parent. For other children, radical differentiation becomes the strategy. Heartbroken and shaken ontologically, they disconnect from everything and everyone, sliding deeper into the broken nothingness within themselves. Once talkative, outgoing kids can become detached, cynical, and cold.

What is interesting about both overidentification and overdifferentiation is that neither is built on reciprocated open dialogue and

discourse. When a child overidentifies he is often called into long processes of listening to his parent's experience but rarely allowed to speak of his own experience. He is there to help his mom. To share how he really feels would risk upsetting her and undercutting his role as her caregiver. He is open to hearing her, but she, in her pain, is not open to hearing him, to listening to him speak from the location of his suffering. In overdifferentiation communication is broken down as well. Hurt and angry, the child is unwilling to say anything or listen to anyone. He avoids all attempts at communication with sneers and sarcasm. His being is too raw to speak of it. It is too wounded to listen to others.

For children of divorce, congregations can become places able to speak and listen. It is not enough in the encounter of being, according to Barth, to only see and be seen, we must also enter into discourse. We must speak to and hear one another if we are truly to see and be seen.[6] What a difference a congregation could make if it could offer its life as a place where young people experiencing trauma, questions, fears, and doubts were allowed to speak them and be heard. Too often the church is perceived as thinking it has all the answers, believing that it can talk without listening, for it speaks for God. But hearing is the church's primary ministry, and in allowing those experiencing divorce to freely speak, the congregation offers ontological security to those doubting their own reality. By hearing and speaking in suffering humility, the church testifies that it knows a power that makes you real; by sharing in the church's life of speaking and hearing, we participate in the real. Barth says it this way:

> As I address another, whether in the form of exposition, question, petition or demand, but always with the request to be heard, I ask that he should not remain in isolation but be there for me; that he should not be concerned only with himself but with me too; in other words, that he should hear. Address is coming to another with one's being, and knocking and asking to be admitted.[7]

As I said in earlier chapters, one of the most painful aspects of divorce is that it punctures one's story. After the divorce, or as we age and come to grips with the divorce, it is ever harder to construct a clear narrative

of the relationships and events that brought us into the world. There persists a feeling of being disconnected, not only from ourselves, but from history itself. In the space between our parents, it is increasingly difficult to figure how it is that they, in some long-forgotten union, brought us into the world. By listening to and allowing young people to speak, the congregation, through its life, offers young people the chance to (re)construct their stories. It is often in speaking to others that we find connections and breakthroughs in understanding our place in the world. Therefore, it is through conversation with others that we often are able to embrace our being and to feel real, for speaking forces us to construct our history. And in a real sense too, by speaking this history inside the congregation, the congregation offers its own history and the history of its people as a place to stand for those feeling that their history has been lost. The congregation can do this powerfully, because it is representative of multiple generations. It bears in its life many histories across time. In the relation of broken person to broken person it provides young persons not only accompaniment and sanctuary, but also discovery of their story across time, as they are invited into the story of the multigenerational community. Martin Heidegger has asserted that language is the house of being, for in speaking and listening we are fully being-in-the-world, for we are being-with.[8] By speaking our story and hearing others' stories we grab hold of being; we are real. The congregation can help young people of divorce not just *through* things like programs and counseling, but *by* simply (but profoundly) making space to speak and listen.[9]

There are two interrelated practices the congregation might consider to become a place that sees and is seen as it speaks and listens. These two practical actions are *convening* and *connecting*, convening conversation and connecting people. This, of course, can happen in the fellowship hall, in weekly Bible study, or beyond, and often already happens in most congregations. But too often it is seen as a secondary function of the church. We see the care of souls happening in closed offices, and transformative worship happening in the pews of the sacred worship space. Yet it may be that the care of the souls and transformation happen most often in the convening and connecting of the people of God. What congregations then can do is convene spaces for intergenerational conversations to occur, make

places where personal stories can be spoken. Therefore, thinking must be done on how to connect these people. It must be done in a way that allows speaking and hearing to happen in organic ways, but we must not underestimate the power of simple convening as the way to connect them.

So, what might a few key people do?

The Youth Worker/Children's Minister

- Work to know the stories (even in their brokenness) of the young people with whom you work. It is amazing how often youth workers, children's ministers, and pastors know little of the story of the people they serve. Make it a major driving force of your ministry to know people's stories.

- Spend some of your programmatic energy convening places for adults in the congregation to listen to and speak with young people. Spend some of your educational energy informing adults of the importance of seeing and hearing young people as they allow young people to see and hear them. Use adult forums and even worship time to speak of this.

Parent

- Find the strength to hear your child, even if it feels like his or her articulation of the situation or past is hurtful to you—or even feels wrong. He or she wishes not to hurt you, but to have his or her feelings and perceptions understood. Work to listen without correcting, defending, or interpreting. Self-justification is a killer of mutual hearing and understanding.

- Try not to be threatened by your child's anger, fear, or sadness. Find someone else with whom to discuss how much his or her feelings hurt you.

Friend

- If you know his or her parents, keep telling the young person stories of when they were together.

- Tell the young person that his or her feelings are valid. Tell him or her how you have carried or dealt with regret, fear, or pain.

Sometimes just hearing the story of someone else confronting and dealing with deep suffering, even if it is unrelated to our own, can give us the strength to face ours. It gives us strength not only because it is inspiring, but more so because in hearing another person's story, we connect our person to his or her person, and as a result find our own humanity in this person-to-person connection.

3. Routine as Mutual Assistance

Maybe the most essential component needed for ontological security is the ability to have some kind of dependable routine whereby to organize our lives. In late modernity this routine is not given to people by tradition and instead must be individually negotiated. We already saw this above but also, more powerfully, saw how for young people routine and ritual are thrown into disorder by divorce. We have our being in time and space, which is organized by routine. Routine roots us into time and space and therefore makes us real, gives us our being. When divorce strikes, routine and ritual are changed. Christmas is different; Saturday mornings have changed; after-school habits, bedtime rituals, and many other activities shift dramatically.

The congregation offers the young person dependable, stable routines. These routines include such things as the fact that it meets every Sunday morning and Wednesday night and always has doughnuts and juice. They also include Lenten services, communion, special music, Advent, and Easter. We shouldn't convince ourselves that these routines in and of themselves are important to young people (or any people) on their own. No one comes to church simply for the routines and rituals as such. Yet what occurs (and of course this is why it is so hard for churches to change) is that our being becomes wrapped up within these rituals and routines. Within the routines of the congregation, people find a place to stand and be in time and space. We attach and then know ourselves in relation to these routines. This can be immensely frustrating when it is time for the church to change, and so it is that such rituals can actually be used to disempower young people (and others). It does witness to the power of routine that the

church can provide for young people feeling themselves unreal in the crater of lost routine and ritual due to divorce.

So, how do we walk this thin line between routine being the gift of grounding or the prison that makes adaptive change impossible? Routine and ritual can be a gift (and malleable to the needs of people) when they encompass *mutual assistance,* Barth's third area of being in encounter. To see and be seen, to hear and listen, demands that we not only see and communicate but also give assistance. This is not simply service, another program or initiative for the church to put in its bulletin. Rather than simple assistance, it is about *mutual* assistance.

It may be that the best way to help young people suffering the reality of divorce is not to do things for them, but to invite them into doing things for others. In giving assistance, young people discover their being alongside others. In serving with others through mission trips, service projects, and teaching, they discover the contours of their being in relation to action. When we allow young people to assist us, or see them as mutual partners in service, then they cannot help but be real. They may be living through the negation of the union that created them, but they *are,* for they are needed and valuable in relation to the congregation's service in the world. Barth says it this way,

> Assistance is actively standing by the other. It is standing so close by him that one's own action means help or support for his. It thus means not to leave him to his own being and action, but in and with one's own to take part in the question and anxiety and burden of his, accepting concern for his life, even though it must always be his and we cannot represent him. Assistance means to live with the other. As we see one another and speak and listen to one another, we call to one another for assistance.[10]

Two practices the congregation can take in inviting young people into mutual assistance are *persistence* and *prayer.* Persistence is the practice of continued invitation to serve, to take a risk, to discover your gifts, to see your life in the rituals of the congregation. Persistence, then, includes the congregation's continued reflection on its routines and rituals, seeking to make them open for all people.

There is nothing more mutual in the call for assistance than the continued ritual of communal prayer. Accordingly, in helping young

people deal with divorce we seek not to help them learn to pray aloud (though this may have its value), but to be prayed for and to pray for the congregation and world. Prayer is the primary location where routine and mutual assistance come together. Prayer has the power to take the shape of ritual and routine, but because it seeks communion with others and God, it also has the power to move us beyond dead, meaningless routine.[11] For in prayer we seek a new future in relation to God's continued action.

And what might a few key people do?

The Youth Worker/Children's Minister

- Assess your routines and rituals, helping young people take ownership of them and helping the congregation as a whole make sure they are hospitable to young people. Again, this points to the fact that open spaces may be just as meaningful as programs.

- Provide opportunities for young people to pray with and for adults in the congregation. But the key to this is not that this praying together becomes a religious, pious act, but that it becomes an act of seeing and hearing one another before God. This must be done with great care, and done in such a way that it possesses great significance.

- Recognize that weekly programs have their power not in their entertainment value, but in their ability to become routines and rituals that young people can build their lives around and therefore find ontological security in.

Parent

- Be aware that meaningful routines and rituals have died with the marriage. This may be liberating for you, but it is a great loss for your child. Children often feel like they know their parents through these routines and rituals and therefore know themselves in them as well. Allow your child to grieve the loss of these rituals. Allow him or her a place for happy memories. Just because a child longs for these lost routines does not mean he or she loves you less.

- Don't force a new family onto your child. Especially with an older child, allow him or her to see your new spouse as valuable to you, but not as someone who needs to be significant in your child's life. It can be quite painful and feel very odd to have to bear the pressure of entering a new family that you did not choose and which has no connection to your past routines and rituals.
- Persist in telling your child that you recognize how hard this is for him or her, and how weird it makes your child feel.

Friend

- Build in routines with young people. If you are a grandparent, an aunt or uncle, reflect with the young person on the routines and rituals that exist in the extended family. Discuss how Great-grandpa Hank used to decorate the Christmas tree or Aunt Jan would get up early to take her dogs out.
- Pray with these young people, or at the very least tell them that you are praying for them.

4. Bracketing out Anxiety by Acting in Gladness

All three of the above necessities for ontological security serve to bracket out paralyzing anxiety. We heard throughout this book, in the voices of those living through their parents' divorce, how divorce pushes young people into anxiety. This anxiety causes them to doubt the dependability of the universe or to wonder whether we are anything but a shadow within it. When a congregation opens its life to a young person, it provides a place secure in the universe, a dependable people to *be* alongside. The congregation's life, then, can assuage anxiety through its stability and dependability. But this stability and dependability must be built on something other than institutional footings. I suppose the Department of Motor Vehicles is dependable, but interaction with it is rarely life-giving and seems, at least for me, to cause more anxiety in my being. What allows the congregation to bracket out anxiety is its ability to *act in gladness*. This is Barth's fourth and final movement of the encounter of being.

At first read, this focus on gladness may appear trite. But it is of essential importance, because it means that the relationships of the

congregation will not be governed by rigid "oughts," but by the joy and desire of being with and for each other. For children of divorce, life seems filled with oughts and musts—you *must* spend the third weekend at your father's, you *must* share your room with your stepsister, you *ought* to care for your little brother while your mom is working late. By contrast, in the gladness of the community, people share in one another's life out of love for one another and God. In the midst of the community's gladness, young people are assured of their place within the community, assured that their being is secure here, that they are wanted. Though the family house has been sold or annihilated in a fire department drill, the community that sees, listens, assists, and does all in gladness places the young person on solid ground. It gives a place to belong that assures her that she is real, that there is at least one place in the universe that is dependable, and that its dependability is constituted not by court mandate but by joy, love, and the gladness of being together.

The practice congregations can participate in that can bracket out anxiety through gladness is *blessing*. A blessing is passed on to another out of joy and anticipation. In practicing blessing the congregation manifests its gladness that young people have a place in the congregation and are a blessing from the hand of God to the congregation. This blessing is the affirmation to be oneself. Barth says, "Humanity lives and moves and has its being in this freedom to be oneself with the other, and oneself to be with the other."[12]

The ontological insecurity caused by divorce forces young people to question whether they belong anywhere, now that the union that created them is divided. "The power to bless exists between people when they gather at the intersection of human and holy. Only a community can say, 'Bless you. Bless us. Yes. Yes.'"[13] When a congregation blesses another, it proclaims that this person not only has a place here but is a valued member. Gunderson explains strongly what blessing does: "Blessing is honest. It includes the damage, loss, death, and brokenness and still says that at any point the turn toward hope is rewarded by the possibility of participation in, and alignment with, the flow of life that is God's grace. Damage is not undone or erased. But neither is it permitted to have the last word, to establish an unpayable debt, to remain final."[14]

But blessing does more. It links past, present, and future. Through blessing we are given a story, a history and a future that are bound in the community that has blessed us. Barth states,

> The cure of souls understood in this special sense as the individual cure of souls means a concrete actualization of the participation of the one in the particular past, present and future of the other, in his particular burdens and afflictions, but above all in his particular promise and hope in the singularity of his existence as created and sustained by God. It means the active interest of the one in the divine calling and therefore in the being and nature of this specific other.[15]

Just as divorce frays our stories by dividing our histories, blessing becomes the fulcrum of a new story, bound in the history of a community.

So what might a few key people do?

The Youth Worker/Children's Minister

- Work with the congregation to find ways to bless young people. Make sure, however, that this is not simply an empty activity, but a ritual that truly invites the young person into the community's life.
- Celebrate the child's rites of passage (while acknowledging the tensions within the family), for example, honor the child's graduation or Boy Scout achievements; allow the congregation opportunities to attend basketball games or school plays.
- Give the child space and forums to share his or her gifts with the community and within worship—use the child's art for bulletin covers, put poetry in newsletters, display paintings or drawings in the church building, offer opportunities to perform musical pieces in worship or in special programs.
- Continue to provide young people ways to tell their stories. Allow these stories to be as painful as they are, but also remember to celebrate and care for one another in gladness and joy.

Parent

- Don't hide your suffering from your child, but also find ways to celebrate life with him or her.

- In the same way, allow your child to express his or her pain, but also allow your child to express joy and happiness—for instance, the joy of spending time with his or her mother—don't make your child feel ashamed or disloyal for being glad.

Friend

- Find ways to express how the young person brings joy to your life. There is great ontological power in mutual laughter.
- Give the young person sentimental gifts or tokens (such as a handwritten letter) that express your appreciation of him or her.

Conclusion

In the final chapter of this project we explored some ways to help young people living through divorce. These actions have been articulated in relation to the ontological issue of divorce: that it undercuts our being by tearing asunder those with whom we are most primarily being-with: the family of biological mother and father. To this end we place the congregation, and its relational life, as both the location and the activity that can provide young people with a place to belong, a place to be-with others in suffering and hope.

Yet, what might be needed most of all is for the church (universal) to recognize that divorce is much more than a societal problem that can be assuaged by psychology or better social services. These are all good things in themselves, but they do not address the heart of the issue. So the church might better serve the world and those millions of young people experiencing their parents' divorce if we could witness to the reality that divorce at its most primary level is an issue of ontology. It is an act that leaves us feeling unreal, lost, as though the world is unreliable. It is an experience that shakes us to the core, causing us to live forevermore with questions and scars. The church can alert the world to this reality and then suffer with those suffering. We can remind them that we know in the life of our communities a power that is stronger than a mother's love, a power able to hold their being securely.

Notes

Series Preface

1. James W. Fowler, *Faith Development and Pastoral Care* (Minneapolis: Fortress, 1987), 17.

2. Scott Cormode, "Constructing Faithful Action," *Journal of Religious Leadership* 3 (1/2), (Spring/Fall 2004): 267.

Introduction

1. The death of a parent does not create this same fracture ontologically in a child, because the union was never intentionally broken—it was severed by tragedy, and the community as a whole grieves and remembers the lost parent, upholding the community's wholeness even in its brokenness. This will be discussed further in chapter 1.

Chapter 1 A History of the Family, a History of the Self

1. What do I mean by "family"? While acknowledging that "family" is a particularly difficult thing to define, I will follow Degler's helpful definition. He states, "For our purposes here the family may be said to consist of five elements. The first is that a family begins with a ritual between a woman and a man, a ceremony that we call marriage, and which implies long duration, if not permanence, for the relationship. The second is that the partners have duties and rights of parenthood that are also socially recognized and defined. For the family has everywhere been the way in which the human being is socialized. . . . A third element is that husband, wife, and children live in a common place. This aspect, it needs to be said, is the least universal. Anthropologist George P. Murdock in his analysis of the literature on some five hundred different cultures points out that in about one-fourth of them the father lives apart from mother and children at least for a portion of the time. But in the great majority of even those cases the distance between the houses of father and mother is slight. A fourth element in the definition of a family is that there are reciprocal economic obligations between husband and wife—that is, they both work for the family, even though the amount and kind of labor or production may be far from equal. Fifth, the family also serves as a means of sexual satisfaction for the partners, though not necessarily as an exclusive one." Carl N. Degler, *At Odds: Women and the Family in America from the Revolution to the Present* (Oxford: Oxford University Press, 1980), 4.

2. Stephanie Coontz, *Marriage, a History: From Obedience to Intimacy or How Love Conquered Marriage* (New York: Viking, 2005).

3. Ibid., 31.

4. Ibid., 44.

5. "Probably the single most important function of marriage through most of history, although it is almost completely eclipsed today, was its role in establishing cooperative relationships between families and communities. In Anglo Saxon England, women were known as peace weavers because their marriages established ties of solidarity between potential enemies or feuding kin groups." Ibid., 31.

6. Yalom explains further: "In areas of Europe that held onto Germanic law, peasant marriage was primarily a contract between two families who came to an agreement about the size of the dowry and the wedding day. The wedding ceremony was essentially a legal transfer of the bride to the groom, presided over by her father or another elder within a circle of family members." Marilyn Yalom, *A History of the Wife* (New York: Perennial, 2001), 47. She continues, "At the other end of the social ladder, members of the nobility were guided by property concerns on a grand scale. Marriage was the means by which the powerful made alliances and transmitted inheritances. Fathers had the responsibility of finding the best partners for their sons and daughters so as to ensure proper unions and maintain their status into the next generation. Therefore, daughters were carefully supervised and allowed little opportunity to lose their precious virginity before they married, usually at an early age." Ibid., 49.

7. E. J. Graff, *What Is Marriage For? The Strange Social History of Our Most Intimate Institution* (Boston: Beacon, 1999), 5.

8. "Affection was most unlikely to be a basis of marriage if the families of origin of the young people held large amounts of property. For to permit a marriage to take place on the basis of personal or individual preference or whim, rather than by reference to family needs and prospects, threatened a family's holdings and perhaps its long-term future." Degler, *At Odds*, 9.

9. "People have always loved a love story. But for most of the past our ancestors did not try to live in one. They understood that marriage was an economic and political institution with rigid rules." Coontz, *Marriage, a History*, 10.

10. "The 'discovery' of childhood would have to await the fifteenth, sixteenth and seventeenth centuries. Only then would it be recognized that children needed special treatment, 'a sort of quarantine,' before they could join the world of adults." Colin Heywood, *A History of Childhood* (Cambridge, UK: Polity, 2001), 11.

11. Mintz and Kellogg articulate the importance of the kin unit: "Today spousal ties are emphasized, and obligations to kin are voluntary and selective. Three centuries ago the kin group was of great importance to the social, economic, and political life of the community. Kinship ties played a critical role in the development of commercial trading networks and the capitalizing of large-scale investments." Steven Mintz and Susan Kellogg, *Domestic Revolutions: A Social History of American Family Life* (New York: Free Press, 1988), 5.

12. "The Augustinian position 'brought down upon the child the great weight of Christian dogma.' The child was now seen as a willful creature and, in this respect, no different from an adult." Heywood, *History of Childhood*, 33.

13. "The general feeling was, and for a long time remained, that one had several children in order to keep just a few. As late as the seventeenth century, in *Le Caquet de l'accouchée*, we have a neighbour, standing at the bedside of a woman who has just given birth, the mother of five 'little brats,' and calming her fears with these words: 'Before they are old enough to bother you, you will have lost half of them, or perhaps all of them.' A strange consolation! People could not allow themselves to become too attached to something that

was regarded as a probable loss. This is the reason for certain remarks which shock our present-day sensibility, such as Montaigne's observation: 'I have lost two or three children in their infancy, not without regret, but without great sorrow', or Molière's comment on Louison in *Le Malade imaginaire:* 'The little girl doesn't count.'" Philippe Ariès, *Centuries of Childhood: A Social History of Family Life* (New York: Knopf, 1962), 39.

14. See Ariès, *Centuries of Childhood*, and Heywood, *History of Childhood*. They both sketch out this history.

15. "What is more controversial is the age at which children left home. It now seems that historians were rather too impressed with the very quotable Italian visitor. Some children undoubtedly left home to serve in another household about the age of 7. However, these must be seen as an unfortunate minority, drawn largely from the ranks of small peasants and agricultural labourers. Most young people waited until their teens or even their twenties before becoming apprentices or servants. An early census from 1422 for the French town of Reims showed female servants concentrated in the age-group 12 to 22, males that of 12 to 30. Ann Kussmaul calculated from evidence concerning early modern England that 13 to 14 was the most common age for moving into service in husbandry. Richard Wall in his turn drew attention to the village of Colyton, in Devon, during the 1840s. Here, 23 percent of boys in the age group 10–14 were absent from home, but a further quarter in the age-group 25–29 were still living with their parents. We are bound to follow him in concluding that leaving home was a protracted process, with no mass exodus at one particular age. A few very young children, under 10 years of age, were likely to be away from home, but otherwise the contrasts with the contemporary world were not striking." Heywood, *History of Childhood*, 116.

16. While from our location in the twenty-first century, this seems odd and maybe even cruel, it must be understood that marriage and family served many of the essential functions of human life that we have now given over to corporations and governments, such as retirement, health care, and life insurance. Coontz explains: "For centuries, marriage did much of the work that markets and governments do today. It organized the production and distribution of goods and people. It set up political, economic, and military alliances. It coordinated the division of labor by gender and age. It orchestrated people's personal rights and obligations in everything from sexual relations to the inheritance of property. Most societies had very specific rules about how people should arrange their marriages to accomplish these tasks." *Marriage, a History*, 9.

17. Mintz and Kellogg explain how belonging to a place included the community, providing a solid location of belonging. "For the Puritans, family ties and community ties tended to blur. In many communities, individual family members were related by birth or marriage to a large number of their neighbors." *Domestic Revolutions*, 5.

18. Yalom explains how divorce served this opportunity for reimagining. "Divorce was so common a feature in Roman life among members of the elite from the late republican period onward that few persons of any note seem to have been married to only one spouse. Men divorced not only to acquire a childbearing wife, but, more commonly, for social or political advancement. Major political players like the generals Pompey and Mark Anthony had no less than five wives apiece. However perfunctory these divorces, they often took an emotional toll on the family and particularly on the children—as in our own time. The great orator and statesman Cicero (106–43 B.C.E.) observed how 'astonishingly upset' his nephew Quintus was when he heard that his parents were contemplating divorce. The divorce did not take place, yet Quintus nonetheless became embroiled in the conflict between his parents, taking his mother's side, for the next five years." *History of the Wife*, 31.

19. Coontz provides a clear and helpful statement on why marriage changed in Europe, and did so much differently than in the rest of the world. The system of marrying for

political and economic advancement was practically universal across the globe for many millennia. But the heritage of Rome and Greece interacted with the evolution of the Christian church to create a unique version of political marriage in medieval Europe. As early as the sixteenth century the distinctive power struggles among parents, children, ruling authorities, and the church combined with changes in the economy to create more possibilities for marital companionship in Europe than in most other regions of the world." *Marriage, a History*, 7.

20. "Because a couple was expected to support the partner and their children, marriage had to wait until they had accumulated or inherited enough to sustain a separate household. Many guilds required journeymen and apprentices to remain single until they had passed the examination to become a master and could be assured of a steady livelihood." Ibid., 125.

21. Graff, *What Is Marriage For?* 15.

22. Graff adds some color to this assertion, "The skills you brought to the marriage could be just as important. For instance, vineyards and *vigneronnes* (women professionally designated as grape-growers and winemakers) were simply too valuable to let escape from the familiar circle—and so up to 50 percent of marriages were between cousins or even uncles and nieces. Meanwhile, having watched your cousins and neighbors grow up, you knew for yourself how reliable and well-honed were their work habits." Ibid., 14.

23. Stephanie Coontz, *The Way We Really Are: Coming to Terms with America's Changing Families* (New York: Basic Books, 1997), 54–55.

24. Degler, *At Odds*, 5.

25. "During the early colonial era, the family performed many functions that have since been relegated to nonfamilial institutions. The family was an integral part of the larger society. It was a 'little commonwealth,' governed by the same principles of hierarchy and deference as the larger society. During the seventeenth century, a sharp division between economics, religion, law, and politics and family life was unimaginable. All these aspects of life were part of a single, unitary, mutually reinforcing matrix." Mintz and Kellogg, *Domestic Revolutions*, xiv–xv.

26. "Puritan parents in Britain and colonial America have a reputation for remaining aloof from their young. Thomas Cobbett did after all assert in 1656 that wise parents would keep a 'due distance' between their children and themselves, on the grounds that 'fondness and familiarity breeds and causeth contempt and irreverence in children.'" Heywood, *History of Childhood*, 85.

27. Heywood states, "The age of 7 was an informal turning point when the offspring of peasants and craftsmen were generally expected to start helping their parents with little tasks around the home, the farm or the workshop. By their early teens they were likely to be working beside adults or established in an apprenticeship. They might well have left home by this stage, to become a servant or an apprentice of some sort." Ibid., 37.

28. "Children of all social classes and both sexes were frequently fostered out for long periods in order to learn a trade, to work as servants, or to attend a school. Since the family was a place of work and its labor needs and its financial resources often failed to match its size and composition, servants or apprentices might temporarily be taken in or children bound out." Mintz and Kellogg, *Domestic Revolutions*, 15.

29. Neil Postman explains, "What all of this led to was a remarkable change in the social status of the young. Because the school was designed for the preparation of a literate adult, the young came to be perceived not as miniature adults but as something quite different altogether—unformed adults. School learning became identified with the special nature of childhood." *The Disappearance of Childhood* (New York: Vintage Books, 1994), 41.

30. Mintz and Kellogg, *Domestic Revolutions*, 20.

31. "During the early modern period, the majority of families sought work for their children as a matter of routine. Indeed, the authorities worried more about the sins of 'sloth and idleness' among the young than about excessive work." Heywood, *History of Childhood*, 121. Heywood continues, "In sum, children were perhaps the most flexible workers within the family economy, ranging from full-time employment outside the home to helping their parents with a wide range of light jobs. As such, although it is difficult to measure their precise contribution, they were valued members of a team." Ibid., 128.

32. The Enlightenment gave birth to two new concepts of children. They would not become commonplace until the nineteenth century, but they were born as the self became an object of reflection. Postman explains, "We might call them the Lockean, or the Protestant, conception of childhood, and the Rousseauian, or the Romantic, conception. In the Protestant view the child is an unformed person who through literacy, education, reason, self-control, and shame may be made into a civilized adult. In the Romantic view it is not the unformed child but the deformed adult who is the problem. The child possesses as his or her birthright capacities for candor, understanding, curiosity, and spontaneity that are deadened by literacy, education, reason, self-control, and shame." *Disappearance of Childhood*, 59.

33. "The freedoms afforded by the market economy had their parallel in new political and philosophical ideas. Starting in the mid-seventeenth century, some political theorists began to challenge the ideas of absolutism. Such ideas gained more adherents during the eighteenth-century Enlightenment, when influential thinkers across Europe championed individual rights and insisted that social relationships, including those between men and women, be organized on the basis of reason and justice rather than force. Believing the pursuit of happiness to be a legitimate goal, they advocated marrying for love rather than wealth or status." Coontz, *Marriage, a History*, 146.

34. Arlie Russell Hochschild explains, "In the eighteenth century, young parents . . . might have been faced with a bad crop of corn in their field, a fire in the barn, a child's colic. And one might have suffered a 'nervous disorder,' said to be caused by diet and damp weather. Each might have found it hard to communicate. Each might have felt alone. But they wouldn't have dreamed of divorce." *The Second Shift* (New York: Penguin Books, 1989), 176.

35. Coontz continues, "The measure of a successful marriage was no longer how big a financial settlement was involved, how many useful in-laws were acquired, or how many children were produced, but how well a family met the emotional needs of its individual members. Where once marriage had been seen as the fundamental unit of work and politics, it was now viewed as a place of refuge from work, politics, and community obligations." *Marriage, a History*, 146.

36. Degler, *At Odds*, 14.

37. Mintz and Kellogg, *Domestic Revolutions*, xv.

38. "By the late nineteenth century, during the sentimentalizing Victorian era, young people chose their mates for themselves, falling in love with another's unique inner spirit, then joining their hearts and souls and bodies in a romantic fusion." Graff, *What Is Marriage For?* 171.

39. Coontz, *Marriage, a History*, 156.

40. This was not only a middle-class phenomenon, according to Degler. "Even in slum districts few married women were employed outside the home. A study made in 1893 in New York, Baltimore, Chicago, and Philadelphia showed that only 5 per cent of the New York wives were employed, and that was the highest proportion among the four cities." *At Odds*, 385.

41. Ibid., 81.

42. Yalom states women's responsibilities more directly: "What, then, were the responsibilities of middle-class wives supported by their husbands? These fell into three major categories: 1) obeying and satisfying one's husband, 2) keeping one's children physically and morally sound, and 3) maintaining the household (cleaning, washing, preparing food, etc.)." *History of the Wife*, 181.

43. I am following Coontz's argument. She states powerfully, "As I continued my research, however, I became convinced that the 1950s Ozzie and Harriet family was not just a postwar aberration. Instead it was the culmination of a new marriage system that had been evolving for more than 150 years. I now think that there was a basic continuity in the development of marriage ideals and behaviors from the late eighteenth century through the 1950s and 1960s. In the eighteenth century, people began to adopt the radical new idea that love should be the most fundamental reason for marriage and that young people should be free to choose their marriage partners on the basis of love." *Marriage, a History*, 5.

44. Even in the early moments of the rise of the love-based marriage, some worried about where it would lead, Coontz explains. "As soon as the idea that love should be the central reason for marriage, and companionship its basic goal, was first raised, observers of the day warned that the same values that increased people's satisfaction with marriage as a relationship had an inherent tendency to undermine the stability of marriage as an institution. The very features that promised to make marriage such a unique and treasured personal relationship opened the way for it to become an optional and fragile one." Ibid., 5.

45. "Since the sixteenth and seventeenth centuries, the 'middle-class' desire has been to isolate children, and later adolescents, from the world of adults. Young people have been increasingly 'infantilized' by efforts to keep them out of the workplace, to repress their sexuality and to prolong their education in schools and colleges. The child, as a weak and vulnerable being, was to be constantly supervised, detached from the temptations of the world and subject to rigorous discipline." Heywood, *History of Childhood*, 38.

46. Mintz and Kellogg, *Domestic Revolutions*, 44.

47. "The primary reason, of course, why married women, even those who were poor, did not hold an outside job was that women were the child rearers." Degler, *At Odds*, 385.

48. "The domestic role of women, which we have been calling the separation of the spheres, went hand in hand with the new conception of children as precious, and different from adults. In ideal and in practice the mother was responsible for carrying out the novel and special view of children. . . . Women, it is true, had always reared children, but in the 19th century it was increasingly recognized as primarily, and, more important, properly the woman's task." Ibid., 73.

49. Graff, *What Is Marriage For?* 114.

50. "There is no question that over the last two hundred years the family has been shedding, one by one, virtually all the functions it fulfilled in previous centuries. No longer is the family the principal place of learning for the child; it has long since ceased to provide either medical or psychological care, except of the most trivial kinds. Members of the family who need such help usually seek it elsewhere. It has been a century or more at least since religious life was centered at the family hearth or dinner table. Almost as many years have passed since the family ceased to be an economic unit in which members worked together to earn a collective living. The principal function of the modern family, at least over the last century and a half, has been to rear children and provide a haven, a place of rest, refreshment, and spiritual replenishment for its members." Degler, *At Odds*, 451–52.

51. Ibid., 71. Degler adds, "A further sign that children were gaining new recognition as individuals and as special beings was that celebration of birthdays began only in the 19th century." Ibid.

52. "The family's role in education, in health care, and in care of the aged, poor, and the mentally ill had increasingly been assumed by specialists and institutions outside the family. At the same time, however, the family had acquired new burdens and expectations. The middle-class family was assigned primary responsibilities for fulfilling the emotional and psychological needs of its members. Along with providing economic security and a stable environment for children, family life was now expected to provide romance, sexual fulfillment, companionship, and emotional satisfaction." Mintz and Kellogg, *Domestic Revolutions*, 107–8.

53. "In the end, though, perhaps the most significant point to make about kinship ties in the 19th century is that they were weak relative to the intensity of feeling and cohesion within the family of origin. Closeness of the nuclear family was particularly apparent in the strain produced when marriage broke a woman's connection with her family of origin." Degler, *At Odds*, 106.

54. In the nineteenth and into the mid-twentieth century to be granted a divorce, fault had to be found. At first glace this may seem contradictory to the love-based marriage. Yet a deeper look reveals that the fault divorce seems to heighten the ideology of love-based marriage. If love is broken, being that it is so precious and wonderful, there must be fault; broken love must have a reason. Therefore, fault divorce isn't the effect of love-based marriage but of a hyperindividualism of a consumer society linked together with a love-based marriage. Coontz explains this period's culture of fault divorce: "Right up through the 1950s, judges routinely ruled that individuals seeking to end a marriage could get a divorce only if they were free from any 'suspicion' that they had 'contributed' to the problems they were complaining about. In 1935, for instance, the Supreme Court of Oregon reviewed the divorce suit of Louise and Louis Maurer. The judge acknowledged that the husband was 'domineering and overbearing' and given to sudden bursts of temper that 'caused his wife and children to fear him.' But he noted that the wife had also engaged in behavior that 'can not be condoned' and therefore denied the divorce. Because neither party came to court 'with clean hands' the court found, neither of them deserved relief from the marriage, even though their quarreling 'would drive happiness out of any home.'" *Marriage, a History*, 214.

55. "Conservatives had long claimed that rising expectations about finding happiness in marriage would lead to an increase in divorce. They were now proved right. Increasingly, people filed for divorce because their marriages did not provide love, companionship, and emotional intimacy, rather than because their partners were cruel or had failed to perform their marital roles as housekeeper or provider." Ibid., 202.

56. "When unhappy nineteenth-century couples lacked the legal grounds or the financial means or the moral or religious support to seek a divorce, many separated. In doing so, they entered a complex legal netherworld, one framed by uncertainties of legal jurisdiction and authority as well as of moral identity and responsibility." Nancy Cott, *Public Vows: A History of Marriage and the Nation* (Cambridge, MA: Harvard University Press, 2000), 29.

57. Ibid., 107.

58. Coontz, *Marriage, a History*, 149.

59. See ibid., 307–8.

60. "The seeming stability of marriage in the 1950s was due in part to the thrill of exploring the new possibilities of married life and the size of the rewards that men and women received for playing by the rules of the postwar economic boom. But it was also due to the incomplete development of the 'fun morality' and the consumer revolution.

There were still many ways of penalizing nonconformity, tamping down aspirations, and containing discontent in the 1950s." Ibid., 238.

61. Ibid., 8.

62. "Fantasies are not the best basis on which to construct family relationships and personal ties. Western individualism has always fed daydreams about escaping external constraints and family obligations, but prior to the era of mass consumption, most people had no doubt that the real world imposed limits on self-aggrandizement. They knew that the only sure source of self-identity and security lay in relationships with others. Consumer society has increasingly broken down our sense that we depend on others, that we have to live with tradeoffs or accept a package deal in order to maintain social networks." Stephanie Coontz, *The Way We Never Were: American Families and the Nostalgia Trap* (New York: Basic Books, 1992), 176.

63. Coontz, *Marriage, a History*, 250.

64. Of course the argument is that this isn't the end of the family (maybe the marriage, but not the family). Rather, it is the evolution of a new kind of family, a single-parent or blended family. While there is no reason to degrade the importance of these new family forms, voices from within them, as we will see in chapters 3 through 6, have begun to articulate deep questions about them.

65. Barbara Dafoe Whitehead, *The Divorce Culture: Rethinking Our Commitments to Marriage and Family* (New York: Vintage Books, 1996), 57.

66. "However, the notion of divorce as the working out of an inner life experience cast it in far more individualistic terms than in the past. Because divorce originated in an inner sense of dissatisfaction, it acknowledged no other stakeholders. Leaving a marriage was a personal decision, prompted by a set of needs and feelings that were not subject to external interests or claims. Expressive divorce reduced the number of legitimate stakeholders in divorce to one, the individual adult." Ibid., 67.

67. "The historical transformation in marriage over the ages has created a similar paradox for society as a whole. Marriage has become more joyful, more loving, and more satisfying for many couples than ever before in history. At the same time it has become optional and more brittle. These two strands of change cannot be disentangled." Coontz, *Marriage, a History*, 306.

68. Mintz and Kellogg touch on the loss of communal structures for young people in this period. "Transience and isolation were characteristics common to suburban family life. Population turnover in the new suburbs was extremely high, as families relocated as they climbed the corporate ladder, resulting in a lack of stability." *Domestic Revolutions*, 185.

69. Mintz and Kellogg hit on the pain of divorce from the child's perspective and point in the direction we are headed in this project. "On the other hand, it is clear that divorce is severely disruptive, at least initially, for a majority of children, and a significant minority of children continue to suffer from the psychological and economic repercussions of divorce for many years after the breakup of their parents' marriage. It is also apparent that children respond very differently to a divorce and to a parent's death. When a father dies children are often moody and despairing. During a divorce, many children, and especially sons, exhibit anger, hostility, and conflicting loyalties." Ibid., 226.

Chapter 2 Marriage and Divorce in Late Modernity

1. "Whereas marriage was earlier first and foremost an institution sui generis raised above the individual, today it is becoming more and more a product and construct of the individuals forming it." Ulrich Beck and Elisabeth Beck-Gernsheim, "Individualism and 'Precarious Freedoms': Perspectives and Controversies of a Subject-Oriented Sociology,"

in *Detraditionalization*, ed. Paul Heelas, Scott Lash, and Paul Morris (London: Blackwell, 1996), 33.

2. "What is modernity? As a first approximation, let us simply say the following: 'modernity' refers to modes of social life or organization which emerged in Europe from about the seventeenth century onwards and which subsequently became more or less worldwide in their influence." Anthony Giddens, *The Consequences of Modernity* (Stanford, CA: Stanford University Press, 1990), 1.

3. It is not that tradition has completely disappeared; it is rather that it has radically been transformed by our changing conceptions of time and space. Giddens states, "In modern times some forms of traditional authority continue to exist, including, of course, religion. Indeed, for reasons that are to do precisely with the connections between modernity and doubt, religion not only refuses to disappear but undergoes a resurgence. . . . Forms of traditional authority become only 'authorities' among others, part of an indefinite pluralism of expertise. The expert, or the specialist, is quite different from the 'authority,' where this term is understood in the traditional sense. Except where authority is sanctioned by the use of force (the 'authorities' of the state and legal authority), it becomes essentially equivalent to specialist advice." Anthony Giddens, *Modernity and Self-Identity: Self and Society in the Late Modern Age* (Stanford, CA: Stanford University Press, 1991), 195.

4. Giddens means the following by *tradition*: "Traditions involve the following qualities: (1) they depend upon ritual, which often, although not always, takes the form of collective ceremonial; (2) they involve repetition and therefore a certain classicism; (3) they imply a notion of 'ritual truth.' The truth of tradition is given by the codes of practice which it enshrines. . . . (4) Tradition is always collective: individuals can have their own rituals, but traditions as such are group properties. (5) The reason for this, as the French sociologist Maurice Halbwachs pointed out, is that tradition is a form of collective memory. It transmits experiences through ritual." Anthony Giddens and Christopher Pierson, *Conversations with Anthony Giddens: Making Sense of Modernity* (Stanford, CA: Stanford University Press, 1998), 128.

5. Kenneth Tucker, *Anthony Giddens and Modern Social Theory* (London: Sage, 1998), 127.

6. "Modernity, almost by definition, always stood in opposition to tradition; hasn't modern society long been 'post-traditional'? It has not, at least in the way in which I propose to speak of the 'post-traditional society' here. For most of its history, modernity has rebuilt tradition as it has dissolved it. Within Western societies, the persistence and recreation of tradition was central to the legitimation of power, to the sense in which the state was able to impose itself upon relatively passive 'subjects.' For tradition placed in stasis some core aspects of social life—not least the family and sexual identity—which were left largely untouched so far as 'radicalizing Enlightenment' was concerned." Ulrich Beck, Anthony Giddens, and Scott Lash, *Reflexive Modernization: Politics, Tradition and Aesthetics in the Modern Social Order* (Stanford, CA: Stanford University Press, 1994), 56.

7. "Modernity destroys tradition. However (and this is very important) a collaboration between modernity and tradition was crucial to the earlier phases of modern social development." Ibid., 91. A response to doubted tradition is fundamentalism. "Fundamentalism for me is tradition waging a bitter battle against a cosmopolitan, reflexive world which asks for reasons." Giddens and Pierson, *Conversations*, 130. For Giddens, fundamentalism is a uniquely modern invention that occurs only because modernity forces tradition to justify itself in the glare of doubt.

8. Giddens, *Consequences of Modernity*, 49. Giddens explains further: "In conditions of high modernity, in many areas of social life—including the domain of the self—there are no determinant authorities. There exist plenty of claimants to authority—far more than was true of pre-modern cultures. Tradition was itself a prime source of authority,

not located within any particular institution, but pervading many aspects of social life. Diffuse though it may have been, tradition was in an important sense a single authority. Although in the larger pre-modern cultures there may quite often have been clashes between rival traditions, for the most part traditional outlooks and ways of doing things precluded other alternatives. Even where there were vying traditions, involvement in a traditional framework was normally quite exclusive: the others were thereby rejected." *Modernity and Self-Identity*, 194.

9. Anthony Giddens, *The Transformation of Intimacy: Sexuality, Love and Eroticism in Modern Societies* (Stanford, CA: Stanford University Press, 1992), 41.

10. John Thompson, "Tradition and Self in a Mediated World," in *Detraditionalization*, ed. Heelas, Lash, and Morris, 90.

11. Our risk, as Kaspersen explains, is manufactured. "We live in a manufactured uncertainty; that is, an uncertainty which does not derive from nature, but which is inherent in the humanly created world." Lars Bo Kaspersen, *Anthony Giddens: An Introduction to a Social Theorist* (Oxford: Blackwell, 2000), 153.

12. Giddens and Pierson, *Conversations*, 210.

13. "To analyse what risk society is, one must make a series of distinctions. First of all, we must separate risk from hazard or danger. Risk is not, as such, the same as hazard or danger. A risk society is not intrinsically more dangerous or hazardous than pre-existing forms of social order. It is instructive in this context to trace out the origins of the term 'risk.' Life in the Middle Ages was hazardous; but there was no notion of risk and there doesn't seem in fact to be a notion of risk in any traditional culture. The reason for this is that dangers are experienced as given. Either they come from God, or they come simply from a world which one takes for granted. The idea of risk is bound up with the aspiration to control and particularly with the idea of controlling the future." Giddens and Pierson, *Conversations*, 208–9. Giddens continues, "The idea of 'risk society' might suggest a world which has become more hazardous, but this is not necessarily so. Rather, it is a society increasingly preoccupied with the future (and also with safety), which generates the notion of risk. . . . The word refers to a world which we are both exploring, and seeking to normalize and control. Essentially, 'risk' always has a negative connotation, since it refers to the chance of avoiding an unwanted outcome. But it can quite often be seen in a positive light, in terms of the taking of bold initiatives in the face of a problematic future. Successful risk-takers, whether in exploration, in business or in mountaineering, are widely admired." Ibid., 209.

14. "What distinguishes the premodern from the modern is not the emergence of risks, for social action has always been connected with risks. Rather, the difference between the two types of societies is a different risk profile. Whereas the earlier societies were primarily subjected to the vagaries of nature in the form of natural disasters, bad harvests, or epidemics, the situation is different in modern society. The problems caused by nature are essentially reduced, and instead conditions made by humanity create the greatest dangers. The risk profile of modernity entails that certain types of risks are globalized and intensified." Kaspersen, *Anthony Giddens*, 100.

15. Giddens and Pierson, *Conversations*, 105. Giddens explains further: "Manufactured risk isn't associated only with human intervention in nature, but also with social change in an information society based upon high reflexivity. Consider marriage and the family, for example. Up to even a generation ago, marriage was structured by established traditions. When people got married, they knew, as it were, what they were doing. Marriage was formed to a large degree in terms of traditional expectations of gender, sexuality and so forth." Ibid.

16. Elizabeth Marquardt, *Between Two Worlds: The Inner Lives of Children of Divorce* (New York: Crown, 2005), 4. Marquardt continues, "The children of low-conflict couples

fare *worse* after divorce because the divorce marks their first exposure to a serious problem. One day, without much warning, their world just falls apart." Ibid. Sara McLanahan and Gary Sandefur add, "From the child's point of view, these two types of conflict (abuse versus weak commitment) are very different matters. In the latter case, the child would probably be better off if the parents resolved their differences and the family remained together, even if the long-term relationship between the parents was less than perfect." *Growing Up with a Single Parent: What Hurts, What Helps* (Cambridge, MA: Harvard University Press, 1994), 31.

17. David Royko, *Voices of Children of Divorce* (New York: Golden Books, 1999), 19.

18. See Ava Chin's *Split: Stories from a Generation Raised on Divorce* (Chicago: Contemporary Books, 2002).

19. Stephanie Staal, *The Love They Lost: Living with the Legacy of Our Parents' Divorce* (New York: Delacorte, 2000), 16.

20. Giddens, *Consequences of Modernity*, 34.

21. "Giddens claims that one characteristic of the post-traditional society is a process of individuation, which implies that individuals now actively have to work for trust in their social relations. Increasingly, social reflexivity involves the interrogation and undermining of tradition, and consequently tradition can no longer provide a firm set of norms and beliefs, which used to create trust. Now we have to negotiate about the conditions of all social relations; we negotiate about the norms and ethics which should form the basis of relations between man and woman, between friends, and between parents and children." Kaspersen, *Anthony Giddens*, 98.

22. "To understand how divorce affects children over the long haul, we need to explore the fact that the divorced family is not just a cut-off version of the two-parent family. The postdivorce family is a new family form that makes very different demands on each parent, each child, and each of the many new adults who enter the family orbit. For millions of children the experience of growing up—of simply being a child—has changed. For millions of adults, the experience of being a parent has been radically transformed." Judith Wallerstein, *The Unexpected Legacy of Divorce* (New York: Hyperion, 2000), 10.

23. Royko, *Voices of Children of Divorce*, 174.

24. Giddens is skeptical of the argument of a plural self. Like those who make this argument, he agrees that identity is flexible, but he still contends that the objective is to find a singular identity (though that may change often). "Naturally, individuals adjust both appearance and demeanour somewhat according to the perceived demands of the particular setting. That this is so has led some authors to suppose that the self essentially becomes broken up—that individuals tend to develop multiple selves in which there is no inner core of self-identity. Yet surely, as an abundance of studies of self-identity show, this is plainly not the case. The maintaining of constants of demeanour across varying settings of interaction is one of the prime means whereby coherence of self-identity is ordinarily preserved." *Modernity and Self-Identity*, 100.

25. Beck, Giddens, and Lash, *Reflexive Modernization*, 80.

26. Giddens and Pierson, *Conversations*, 19.

27. "The reflexivity of modernity extends into the core of the self. Put in another way, in the context of a post-traditional order, the self becomes a reflexive project. Transitions in individuals' lives have always demanded psychic reorganisation, something which was often ritualised in traditional cultures in the shape of rites de passage. But in such cultures, where things stayed more or less the same from generation to generation on the level of the collectivity, the changed identity was clearly staked out—as when an individual moved from adolescence into adulthood. In the settings of modernity, by contrast, the altered self has to be explored and constructed as part of a reflexive process of connecting personal and social change." Giddens, *Modernity and Self-Identity*, 33.

28. Loyal explains Giddens's position of reflexivity further: "In contrast, reflexivity in modern social orders has little or no intrinsic connections with the past, so that 'social practices become routinely altered in the light of incoming information.' In such a situation, social practices can no longer be defended by simply appealing to tradition. Thus, although traditions may continue, they can only do so in recognition of incoming information and not merely for the sake of tradition. Giddens calls this 'wholesale reflexivity.' Here, in contrast to the Enlightenment, reason subverts reason in terms of establishing foundational knowledge. Knowledge in modernity is continually revisable, such that it holds 'until further notice.' The result is 'futurology,' whereby the future constantly remains open to possible alternatives. These social circumstances should not be characterised as postmodernity, but rather as a radicalising of modernity, or as 'late modernity.'" Steven Loyal, *The Sociology of Anthony Giddens* (London: Pluto, 2003), 122.

29. Giddens, *Modernity and Self-Identity*, 5.

30. Kaspersen explains further, "Rather, the identity is found in the ability to maintain a unique narrative about oneself. This narrative, which constitutes the person's biography, cannot be a purely fictive narrative, however. It must constantly incorporate events which take place in the external world and simultaneously filter these, so that they can enter into the continuous narrative of the self. Besides the ability to keep this self-narrative going, a stable self-identity also requires other aspects of ontological security, above all knowledge and recognition of external reality, with objects and persons. The feeling of self-identity is simultaneously fragile and robust. Fragile because the biography with which the individual reflexively is working is only one narrative out of many possible narratives that can be told about the development of the person's self. Robust because it is linked to the strong ability of the self to prevent the conflicts, tensions and changes which the self encounters in the constant change of environments from undermining the feeling of identity." *Anthony Giddens*, 104.

31. "Each of us not only 'has,' but *lives* a biography reflexively organised in terms of flows of social and psychological information about possible ways of life. Modernity is a post-traditional order, in which the question, 'How shall I live?' has to be answered in day-to-day decisions about how to behave, what to wear and what to eat—and many other things—as well as interpreted within the temporal unfolding of self-identity." Giddens, *Modernity and Self-Identity*, 14.

32. "However, regardless of gender, social status, and the like, Giddens claims that in the era of modernity one is forced to choose a lifestyle as part of one's self-identity. Lifestyle contains a special set of practices which create the routines necessary for maintaining ontological security. A person with a given lifestyle finds it easier to choose, as certain options and certain types of choices lie beyond the lifestyle." Kaspersen, *Anthony Giddens*, 105.

33. Giddens, *Modernity and Self-Identity*, 97.

34. Giddens believes the rise of therapy in late modernity is a sign of the loss of tradition to determine being and agency in the world. When some are confronted with this freedom, they become overwhelmed and need to find help and accompaniment in the reflexive project of the self in late modernity. "Therapy is not simply a means of coping with novel anxieties, but an expression of the reflexivity of the self—a phenomenon which, on the level of the individual, like the broader institutions of modernity, balances opportunity and potential catastrophe in equal measure." Ibid., 34.

35. This is what Heidegger means by being-with-others. In the next chapter we will pick up his thought and its relevance for our topic.

36. "A pure relationship is one in which external criteria have become dissolved: the relationship exists solely for whatever rewards that relationship as such can deliver. In the context of the pure relationship, trust can be mobilised only by a process of mutual

disclosure. Trust, in other words, can by definition no longer be anchored in criteria outside the relationship itself—such as criteria of kinship, social duty or traditional obligation. Like self-identity, with which it is closely intertwined, the pure relationship has to be reflexively controlled over the long term, against the backdrop of external transitions and transformations." Giddens, *Modernity and Self-Identity*, 6.

37. Giddens, *Transformation of Intimacy*, 63.

38. "The changes involved here signal not just the transformation of intimacy but in a way the creation of intimacy. The rhetoric of intimacy is relatively new; it reflects a post-traditional world where emotional communication becomes crucial to the sustaining of relationships inside and outside of marriage. The patriarchal family of course reflected men's economic dominance, but its emotional inequalities seem to me equally important. It allocated a central role to male sexuality, linking virtuous women to marriage, separating them from the various categories of fallen women—prostitutes, courtesans and harlots. That schismatic view of women still persists, among both sexes, but it is manifestly incompatible with relationships formed through equal communication. Where achievable, 'intimacy' implies equality, in (what are now called) relationships, a word that is also relatively new, as used in this cluster of intimacy-type notions and actions." Giddens and Pierson, *Conversations*, 119.

39. Giddens makes this very assertion, "Modes of behaviour and feeling associated with sexual and marital life have become mobile, unsettled and 'open.' There is much to be gained; but there is unexplored territory to be charted, and new dangers to be courted." *Modernity and Self-Identity*, 12–13.

40. Don Browning, no conservative family-values type (quite the opposite), nevertheless has argued through evolutionary biology and psychology the importance of biological parents for children. For instance, he states, "Evolutionary psychology tells us why both biological parents and members of the extended family are so important to a child's well-being. It is kin who are most likely to contribute to the flourishing and defense of children. It is not just mother and father who are important to children but the whole crowd: grandparents, siblings, aunts and uncles, and so on. They all tend to be concerned, at least more than other people, about the children to whom they are related. This explains, even today, why the great bulk of childcare not done by parents is done by members of the extended family." Don Browning, Bonnie Miller-McLemore, Pamela Couture, K. Brynolf Lyon, and Robert Franklin, *From Culture Wars to Common Ground* (Louisville: Westminster John Knox, 1997), 109. Browning has used evolutionary biology as his starting point in his argument. I am agreeing with the importance of biology, but rather than grounding it in kin altruism, for example, I see it in direct relation to our being, with biology as the intrinsic bond that allows for rich community and gives us our being.

41. Sara McLanahan and Gary Sandefur in their groundbreaking study *Growing Up with a Single Parent* make a very significant argument for the need for biological families. "Children who live with both parents do better, on average, than children who live with only one parent or with neither parent. If we compare the high school graduation rates of the children in one of our samples, for example, we find that 87 percent of children from two-parent families receive a high school degree by age twenty, as compared with 68 percent of children from families with only one biological parent. Most reasonable people would agree that a gap of 19 percentage points is a large and important difference" (9).

42. Jen Abbas, *Generation Ex: Adult Children of Divorce and the Healing of Our Pain* (Colorado Springs: Waterbrook, 2004), 17.

43. Royko, *Voices of Children of Divorce*, 137.

44. Wallerstein articulates this very challenge of having a society where marriages are built on the pure relationship, but pure relationship cannot provide a firm foundation for families with children. "The sobering truth is that we have created a new kind of society

that offers greater freedom and more opportunities for many adults, but this welcome change carries a serious hidden cost. Many people, adults and children alike, are in fact not better off. We have created new kinds of families in which relationships are fragile and often unreliable. Children today receive far less nurturance, protection, and parenting than was their lot a few decades ago. Long-term marriages come apart at still surprising rates, and many in the older generation who started the divorce revolution find themselves estranged from their adult children. Is this the price we must pay for needed change? Can't we do better?" *Unexpected Legacy of Divorce*, 297.

45. Giddens concurs with this when he states, "Where a person becomes a step-parent of an older child, the connections established from the beginning take on the characteristics of the pure relationship." *Modernity and Self-Identity*, 98.

46. Jen Robinson, "Normal Abnormal," in Chin, *Split*, 20.

47. Michelle Patient,"Rootless," in Chin, *Split*, 209.

48. "The divorced family is not a truncated version of the two-parent family. It is a different kind of family in which children feel less protected and less certain about their future than children in reasonably good intact families." Wallerstein, *Unexpected Legacy of Divorce*, xxxv.

49. Matt Briggs, "Floating Bridge," in Chin, *Split*, 84.

50. Staal, *Love They Lost*, 21. Wallerstein adds, "Divorce is a life-transforming experience. After divorce, childhood is different. Adolescence is different. Adulthood—with the decision to marry or not and have children or not—is different. Whether the final outcome is good or bad, the whole trajectory of an individual's life is profoundly altered by the divorce experience." *Unexpected Legacy of Divorce*, xxxiii.

Chapter 3 Divorce as an Issue of Being

1. *One Divided by Two: Kids and Divorce*, directed by Joyce Borenstein (Montreal: The National Film Board of Canada, 1997).

2. McLanahan and Sandefur provide a nice definition of social capital. "We view the lack of parental and community resources as a deficit in what the sociologist James Coleman calls *social capital*. Social capital is an asset that is created and maintained by relationships of commitment and trust. It functions as a conduit of information as well as a source of emotional and economic support, and it can be just as important as financial capital in promoting children's future success. The decision of parents to live apart—whether as a result of divorce or an initial decision not to marry—damages, and sometimes destroys, the social capital that might have been available to the child had the parents lived together." *Growing Up with a Single Parent*, 3.

3. Royko, *Voices of Children of Divorce*, 196. "For instance, her [Wallerstein's] most recent book shows that experiencing parental divorce during childhood has a 'sleeper effect': its worst symptoms often appear when children of divorce leave home and attempt to form intimate relationships and families of their own, but do so with much less ability to trust and little idea of what a lasting marriage looks like." Marquardt, *Between Two Worlds*, 10. This is because the divorce is an ontological issue primarily, something we have failed to recognize.

4. Royko, *Voices of Children of Divorce*, 195.

5. Giddens, *Consequences of Modernity*, 92.

6. "For Giddens, trust is closely connected to 'ontological security.' The foundation of ontological security evolves in the infant in relation to the mother and father. The child possesses a strong ontological security system if there are many strong, positive routines in relation to the mother. The trust that evolves between the child and the mother is a kind of vaccine which prevents the child from being exposed to unnecessary dangers and threats. Trust is thus the protective shield of the self, enabling it to handle the many new

situations of choice which constantly appear. Consequently, trust becomes a necessary precondition and foundation for interaction with the abstract systems." Kaspersen, *Anthony Giddens*, 102.

7. "How is such faith achieved in terms of the psychological development of the human being? What creates a sense of ontological security that will carry the individual through transitions, crises and circumstances of high risk? Trust in the existential anchorings of reality in an emotional, and to some degree in a cognitive, sense rests on confidence in the reliability of persons." Giddens, *Modernity and Self-Identity*, 38.

8. Staal, *Love They Lost*, 59.

9. Giddens, *Modernity and Self-Identity*, 66.

10. Robert Kegan, *The Evolving Self: Problem and Process in Human Development* (Cambridge, MA: Harvard University Press, 1982), 47.

11. See Ernst Becker, *The Denial of Death* (New York: Free Press, 1973).

12. Being-toward-death is Heidegger's way of articulating that our being is bound in the world and as such cannot escape its non-being. This tacit awareness of our being giving way to non-being impacts how we are in the world.

13. "Over a third of us from divorced families, twice as many as our peers, disagreed with the statement 'My parents protected me from their worries.' As we'll see, being a little adult also means doing special things for your parents with little help from other adults." Marquardt, *Between Two Worlds*, 44.

14. "What Penfield observed here, although he did not spell it out, was the dual nature of self-relatedness as packed into a single symbol, 'I.' The self both is a body and it has a body; to the extent that it says 'I,' it is embodied, but to the extent that it creates new or unprogrammed meaning or when it declares 'You did that; I didn't,' it has a body and uses it to express transcendent purposes." James Loder, *The Transforming Moment* (Colorado Springs: Helmers & Howard, 1989), 77.

15. Staal, *Love They Lost*, 171.

16. "These first two dimensions, the self in its relation to the lived world, are properly the subject matter of psychology (and the other anthropological disciplines). . . . Theology is primarily concerned with these last two dimensions of human existence, although it is concerned with them in order to understand how they bring transformation to the first two dimensions." Leron Shults, *Reforming Theological Anthropology* (Grand Rapids: Eerdmans, 2003), 66.

17. Loder explains, "I prefer to speak of void with the implication that nothingness, or negation of being, is not beyond experience; indeed, it is part of the uniqueness of human being that negation is meaningfully included in the composition of our 'lived worlds' and in our sense of 'self.'" *Transforming Moment*, 81. Loder continues, "We always have difficulty composing out or covering over the nothingness because it is not merely 'out there,' it is embodied in the very heart of the transformed self." Ibid.

18. "However, both these dimensions of human being are weak with respect to the third: the possibility of annihilation, the potential and eventually the inevitable absence of one's being. I will discuss this dimension under the rubric of the 'void,' because this is the end result of each human being, implicit in existence from birth and explicit in death. The 'void' is understood as the ultimate telos toward which all experiences of nothingness point; 'nothingness' refers to the 'faces of the void' taken collectively." Ibid., 70.

19. Barth too has a place for negation of the void. "The man who fears death, even though he contrives to put a somewhat better face on it, is at least nearer to the truth than the man who does not fear it, or rather pretends that there is no reason why he should do so." *Church Dogmatics*, III/2, ed. G. W. Bromiley and T. F. Torrance, trans. G. W. Bromiley (Edinburgh: T&T Clark), 598.

20. Below we see how Loder is drawing on perspectives from object relations but placing them in his theological anthropological perspective. "Repression is not all that occurs. There is a cosmic sense of loneliness that persists because the ego is a functional solution to an existential problem. The underlying loneliness repeatedly and indirectly signals to the conscious ego that it is built on negation and nothing-hence our longing for a face that will not go away, for a face that will do for the maturing ego what it did for the child at three months. It is important to remember that the ego as defense system works mightily to maximize survival and satisfaction, and it tries not to allow the sense of negation and abyss to break into awareness." James Loder, *The Logic of the Spirit: Human Development in Theological Perspective* (San Francisco: Jossey-Bass, 1998), 135.

21. Ibid., ix.

22. "This I would say is precisely where we must begin to discuss the 'Holy.' The reason we do not cease to live is the deep sense that we are not merely three-dimensional creatures." Loder, *Transforming Moment*, 85.

23. Amy Conway, "Looking Back, Moving Forward," in Chin, *Split*, 187.

24. Staal, *Love They Lost*, 25.

25. Kegan touches on some of these very points: "The classic failure of the culture in the third function at this age is, of course, the dissolution of the parental unit—death, divorce, or separation. While divorce is a crisis for every member of a family at every stage of development, it is particularly risky for a child . . . because it represents a blow to the very heart of the culture which holds the child—a culture which earlier focused on a single parent and will later extend beyond the parents. But right at this moment the essence of the culture is the couple itself." Robert Kegan, *The Evolving Self: Problem and Process in Human Development* (Cambridge, MA: Harvard University Press, 1982), 158.

26. This may be why divorce is often the hardest (and its effects the longest lasting or everlasting) on the majority who were, upon the announcement of the marriage's end, living in a functional (dependable) family unit, like many of the voices we heard from above. And why for others, divorce may be welcomed when abuse and chaos is so prevalent that the actual division of the family provides more dependability and therefore more ontological security than its continued existence would have. For those who have witnessed or experienced the one who shares their eyes, nose, and hair color as a monster, it is a great relief to their very being to escape him or her. For in experiencing the one who shares his or her being acting so horrifically, tremors are sent to one's own being about its own goodness.

27. Quoted in Giddens, *Modernity and Self-Identity*, 66.

28. Staal, *Love They Lost*, 97.

29. Ibid., 9.

30. Marquardt, *Between Two Worlds*, 8. "I think I can. The key phrase they all use is, 'I am a child of divorce.' I hear it repeatedly when I talk to people in their thirties, forties, or even sixties. What exactly does it mean? Divorce in childhood creates an enduring identity. Because it typically occurs when a child is young and impressionable and the effects last throughout her growing up years, divorce leaves a permanent stamp. That identity is made up of the childhood fears that you can't shake despite all the successes and achievements you've made as an adult." Wallerstein, *Unexpected Legacy of Divorce*, 62.

31. "Heidegger provocatively labels this inability to exist 'death.'" William Blattner, *Heidegger's Being and Time* (New York: Continuum, 2006), 140.

32. Ibid., 141.

33. Royko, *Voices of Children of Divorce*, 63.

34. "Harry Stack Sullivan, noted psychoanalyst, said he could bring patients to relive almost any experience from anxiety to violent trauma, but he could not bring them to relive loneliness." Loder, *Transforming Moment*, 83.

35. Marquardt, *Between Two Worlds*, 48.

36. Loder, *Transforming Moment*, 81.

37. Staal, *Love They Lost*, 103.

38. Ibid., 62.

39. "In pre-modern contexts, tradition has a key role in articulating action and ontological frameworks; tradition offers an organising medium of social life specifically geared to ontological precepts. In the first place, tradition orders time in a manner which restricts the openness of counterfactual futures." Giddens, *Modernity and Self-Identity*, 48.

40. Giddens, *Consequences of Modernity*, 92.

41. William Barrett, *Irrational Man: A Study of Existential Philosophy* (New York: Doubleday, 1962), 217.

42. These four traits are taken from William Blattner's *Heidegger's Being and Time*, 33–41.

43. Ibid., 33.

44. "Dasein is always in a world, and Heidegger talks of 'Being-in-the-world' as the basic constitutive state of Dasein. Thus the Dasein is considered in concrete, embodied existence, and not as a bare thinking subject." John Macquarrie, *Martin Heidegger* (Richmond: John Knox, 1968), 14.

45. Blattner, *Martin Heidegger's Time and Being*, 35.

46. Ibid.

47. Ibid., 12.

48. "Heidegger's phenomenological approach to the self focuses first on a basic form of self-disclosure: I am what matters to me. Seen thus, I cannot disentangle myself from those around me and the world in which I live. In a phrase, we are being in-the-world." Ibid., 41. Mulhall: "Heidegger's use of the term 'Dasein', with its literal meaning of 'there-being' or 'being-there', to denote the human way of being emphasizes that human existence is essentially Being-in-the-world; in effect, it affirms an internal relation between 'human being' and 'world.'" Stephen Mulhall, *Heidegger and Being and Time* (London: Routledge, 1996), 40.

49. Staal, *Love They Lost*, 243.

50. Jen Abbas articulates the significance of home that we are interpreting through Heidegger. "Many referred to home in either the past tense or as a future hope. While home is a place to our friends, it is often a memory to us. One woman looking at home in the rear view mirror replied, 'I've been told that home is where your heart is, but then I can never go home because now it's someone else's house. My happy memories are still trapped there.'" *Generation Ex*, 88.

51. Robinson, "Normal Abnormal," 15.

52. Staal, *Love They Lost*, 123.

53. Mulhall, *Heidegger and Being and Time*, 36.

54. Robinson, "Normal Abnormal," 16 (italics mine).

55. Marquardt, *Between Two Worlds*, 70. Marquardt continues this thought powerfully: "A vacation spot, a hotel, a prison, hell—the degree of tension varies, but the common theme is of being a visitor, an outsider, or an unwilling captive when staying with our fathers. Still, more than half of us who stayed in touch with both parents agree, 'I felt like I had two homes.' And that too is problematic. When people speak of home they always use the singular. They say, 'There's no place like home,' 'You can't go home again,' 'Home is where the heart is.' We, on the other hand, had two places that were, at least potentially, home." Ibid., 69.

56. Staal, *Love They Lost*, 99.

57. Mulhall, *Heidegger and Being and Time*, 39.

58. Ibid.

59. Royko, *Voices of Children of Divorce*, 198.

60. Marquardt, *Between Two Worlds*, 32.

61. "Just as he did not waste time trying to prove the existence of an external world, Heidegger does not trouble to prove that there are other selves. On the contrary, he holds that community or 'Being-with' is a basic existentiale of the Dasein. Just as there is no existence apart from a world, so there is no existence apart from other existents. But the other existent is not seen as an object within the world but as a co-Dasein." Macquarrie, *Martin Heidegger*, 27.

62. Martin Heidegger, *Being and Time* (San Francisco: HarperSanFrancisco, 1962), 163. Mulhall explains further, "For if Dasein's Being is Being-with, an essential facet of that which is an issue for Dasein is its relations to Others; the idea is that, at least in part, Dasein establishes and maintains its relation to itself in and through its relations with Others, and *vice versa*. The two issues are ontologically inseparable; to determine the one is to determine the other." *Heidegger and Being and Time*, 67.

63. Blattner, *Martin Heidegger's Time and Being*, 39.

64. Blattner drives this point deeper, "Heidegger responds, 'Being-with is an existential characteristic of Dasein even when factically no other is present-at-hand or perceived' (156/120). Even when we are alone, we are still acting for the sake of some self-understanding that is interwoven with the self-understandings of others. To be with others is not to be in their presence, but rather for what they are pursuing and how they lead their lives to make a difference to me. Even, therefore, if one is a hermit or recluse, having retreated to a cabin in the hills of Idaho to get away from everyone, others matter to one, in this case, as being despicable or to be avoided. Being a recluse is an anti-social way of understanding oneself and one's relations to others. Being anti-social is a 'privative' way of being social; it is a stance on the significance of what others pursue." Ibid., 67.

65. Ibid., 39.

Chapter 4 Divorce and Theological Anthropology

1. We will discuss this in detail below.

2. George Hunsinger explains Barth's actualism: "At the most general level it means that he thinks primarily in terms of events and relationships rather than monadic or self-contained substances. So pervasive is this motif that Barth's whole theology might well be described as a theology of active relations. God and humanity are both defined in fundamentally actualistic terms." *How to Read Karl Barth: The Shape of His Theology* (Oxford: Oxford University Press, 1991), 30.

3. Barth, *Church Dogmatics*, III/ 2, 320.

4. Douglas John Hall, *Imaging God: Dominion as Stewardship* (Grand Rapids: Eerdmans, 1986), 119.

5. Quoted in Theresa Latini, "From Community to Communio" (Dissertation, Princeton Theological Seminary, 2005), 249.

6. "Barth characteristically did not think in terms of the 'real,' and the 'ideal,' but rather in terms of the 'real' and the 'unreal.'" Hunsinger, *How to Read Karl Barth*, 38.

7. It is often wrongly assumed that Barth was a theological bully who had no room for other fields of study to intervene in the work of theology. "As such, the exact science of man cannot be the enemy of the Christian confession. It becomes this only when it dogmatises on the basis of its formulae and hypotheses, becoming the exponent of a philosophy and world-view, and thus ceasing to be exact science. As long as it maintains restraint and openness in face of the reality of man, it belongs, like eating, drinking, sleeping and all other human activities, techniques and achievements, to the range of human actions which in themselves do not prejudice in any way the hearing or non-hearing of the Word of God." Barth, *Church Dogmatics*, III/2, 24. While this quote reveals that Barth seeks to keep distinct boundaries between disciplines, Price asserts convincingly that at least

the late Barth was more than open to cross-disciplinary conversations, especially in the area of anthropology. "Barth allows for the possibility that scientific studies of humanity can be helpful for theology, as long as they describe human behavior as symptoms of the human phenomena and avoid encroaching on the domain of theology by asserting that their findings are 'axiomatic, dogmatic and speculative.' Theology is prepared to welcome the general knowledge of humankind presented by natural science—provided that natural science describes human beings in their relation to the natural order, not in relation to God or ultimate reality." Daniel Price, *Karl Barth's Anthropology in Light of Modern Thought* (Grand Rapids: Eerdmans, 2002), 108. What this points to is the need to think through how one is relating disciplines. It is beyond this project for me to take the space to spell this out here, but if the reader desires, he or she may find my method, which is implicit here, in "Youth Ministry as an Integrative Theological Task: Toward a Representative Method of Interdisciplinarity," *Journal of Youth Ministry* 5, no. 2 (Spring 2007).

8. Daniel Price has written an invaluable book on Barth's anthropology in conversation with object relations psychology. He states, "The most important parallel between Barth and object relations psychology is that both give due attention to the relational matrix of human personhood—both develop a 'dynamic' view of the person." Price, *Karl Barth's Anthropology*, 9.

9. Bonhoeffer states directly, "The likeness, the analogia, of humankind to God is not analogia entis but *analogia relationis.*" *Bonhoeffer Works, Creation and Fall* (Minneapolis: Fortress, 1997), 65. In footnote 22 of *Creation and Fall* the editor explains how Barth drew from Bonhoeffer: "'Analogy of relationship.' Karl Barth in his doctrine of creation, which he began to set forth in the summer semester of 1942, took over from Bonhoeffer the idea of the *analogia relationis* as the key to understanding the image of God in humankind . . . and made it into a basic foundation stone of his anthropology." Ibid.

10. "[The analogia relationis] grounds being in personal action, rather than grounding act in the prior condition of being, which has been the case with most of Western philosophy since Plato." Price, *Karl Barth's Anthropology*, 137.

11. "One thing becomes apparent in our study of Barth's usage of analogy: he does not deny the usefulness of analogy. He merely denies an analogy of "being" that assumes an ontic connection between God and humanity that may serve as a noetic bridge for us to reach out to God apart from his prior reaching out to us." Ibid., 135.

12. Price offers helpful remarks to those that find it strange to focus our theological conversation on the doctrine of the Trinity. "It may seem odd to the non theologian that someone like Barth would construct his theology on belief in the triune God, as if it provided the bedrock of unshakeable certainty. Belief in the Trinitarian God of traditional Christianity might seem idiosyncratic, if not obscurantist in light of modern thought—and even in light of many modern theologies. It will seem less odd, however, if we allow ourselves to see that the exact sciences proceed with a number of implicit 'fundamental beliefs' that can neither be refuted nor proved, but that nonetheless function as the foundation for the scientific enterprise itself." Ibid., 111.

13. Barth, *Church Dogmatics*, III/2, 218.

14. Stanley Grenz fleshes this out: "The trajectory of thought that includes philosophical voices such as Buber, Polanyi, and Macmurray has given rise to a new social personalism, to an understanding of personhood that sees the self as socially determined. Social personalism might be described as the realization that the self is not ultimately merely a 'what,' an essence, but a 'who.' Moreover, this 'who' emerges communally rather than in isolation; that is, it emerges together with other 'whos' and from within a conversation of persons-in-communion, but ultimately from a conversation with Another, who thereby constitutes the identity of the 'who' as a person-in-relationships." *The Social God and*

the Relational Self: A Trinitarian Theology of the Imago Dei (London: Westminster John Knox, 2001), 12.

15. Paul Ricoeur, *Oneself as Another* (Chicago: University of Chicago Press, 1992), 3.

16. Eberhard Jungel, *Theological Essays* (Edinburgh: T&T Clark, 1989), 127.

17. "No, at the very root of my being and from the very first I am in encounter with the being of the Thou, under his claim and with my own being constituting a claim upon him. And the humanity of human being is this total determination as being in encounter with the being of the Thou, as being with the fellow-man, as fellow-humanity. . . . We cannot accept any compromise or admixture with the opposite conception which would have it that at bottom—in the far depths of that abyss of an empty subject—man can be a man without the fellow-man, an I without the Thou." Barth, *Church Dogmatics*, III/2, 247.

18. Shults, *Reforming Theological Anthropology*, 2. Hall drives this point deeper: "I attempted to characterize what I believe is the first principle of the ontology of the tradition of Jerusalem, namely, that it is an ontology of communion: that being as such, within the parameters of this tradition, must always be understood to mean 'being-with.' Our human being implies within itself a movement toward 'the other.' The correlate and counterpart of our human being, the 'other' to whom the essential self is open, is not in any simple sense God only; for God, whom we image, is also in this tradition being-with (Emmanuel). It is, therefore, impossible for us to be in a relationship with God without in that same movement toward the Other called God being turned toward the others called neighbors (Mitmenschen) and toward the inarticulate creation." *Imaging God*, 142.

19. Royko, *Voices of Children of Divorce*, 184.

20. "More startling is Winnicott's notion that to feel real, the self must begin and return to merger states with not-me objects." Ann Belford Ulanov, *Finding Space: Winnicott, God, and Psychic Reality* (Louisville: Westminster John Knox, 2001), 72.

21. Royko, *Voices of Children of Divorce*, 194.

22. McLanahan and Sandefur, *Growing Up with a Single Parent*, 1.

23. "Children born to an unmarried mother are 6 percentage points more likely to drop out of high school than children whose parents divorce. The difference is statistically significant but not very large. Children who lose a parent through death, however, have a *much* lower dropout rate than other children from disrupted families. The risk of dropping out of high school is the same for children who live with a widowed parent as for children who live with both their parents—15 and 13 percent, respectively, a difference that is not statistically significant." Ibid., 67. They continue, "A similar pattern appears when we look at teenage motherhood. Young women who were born out of wedlock have a slightly higher chance of becoming a teen mother as young women whose parents divorced (the 4 percentage point difference is not statistically significant), whereas young women who experience the loss of a parent through death are much less likely to become teen mothers than young women who experience a divorce—21 percent for the former as compared with 33 percent for the latter. In this case, the difference between girls of widowed mothers and girls in two-parent families is statistically significant." Ibid., 68.

24. "Nineteen-year-old Natalie says, 'Sometimes, I honestly wish my dad had died [instead of getting a divorce]. . . . People would have sympathy for us. People would have understood. They wouldn't have judged.' As sad as that may be, it illustrates the parallel between the two major categories of loss for a child: death and divorce. Children often describe being more terrified of divorce than of parental death." Royko, *Voices of Children of Divorce*, 6.

25. "But children of divorce have one more strike against them. Unlike children who lose a parent due to illness, accident, or war, children of divorce lose the template they need because of their parents' failure. Parents who divorce may think of their decision to end the marriage as wise, courageous, and the best remedy for their unhappiness—indeed,

it may have failed at one of the central tasks of adulthood. Together and separately, they failed to maintain the marriage. . . . This failure in turn shapes the child's inner template of self and family. If they failed, I can fail, too. And if, as happens so frequently, the child observes more failed relationships in the years after divorce, the conclusion is simple." Wallerstein, *Unexpected Legacy of Divorce*, 34.

26. Royko, *Voices of Children of Divorce*, 198.

27. Staal, *Love They Lost*, 17.

28. Chin, *Split*, 6.

29. Marquardt, *Between Two Worlds*, 101.

30. "*Parents* is plural, but in common usage it refers to the singular unit of a mother and father. A child knows that his married parents are two separate people, of course, but quite often he thinks of them as a unit, especially when he is young." Ibid., 22.

31. Robinson, "Normal Abnormal," 14.

32. Royko, *Voices of Children of Divorce*, 204.

33. Wallerstein concurs, "But over and beyond the child's view of mother and father as individuals is the child's view of the relationship between them—the nature of the relationship as a couple. Our scholarly literature is full of mother–child and, more recently, father–child experiments, but as every child could tell the professor, the child sees her parents as a twosome. She is intensely and passionately aware of their interaction. What could be more important or more enthralling? These complex images of parental interaction are central to the family theater and are of lasting importance to intact families." *Unexpected Legacy of Divorce*, 32–33.

34. Jen Abbas adds beautiful color to this argument. "Our parents may have worked hard to give us a sense of home in both of their dwellings—two rooms of our own, two sets of toys and clothes and things. And yet, we still felt unsettled because although we were members of two households, we didn't share in the complete history of either. We simply could not be in two places at once, so no matter where we were, we were missing out on something at our other home. We could not create a comfortable familiarity with someone we saw only every other weekend and on special occasions. Home is the comfort of one shared last name under one shared roof. Home is not made from the extraordinary, but from the ordinary. Home is made of countless seemingly meaningless moments of monotony: Sunday mornings reading the paper (comics first), Saturday morning chores (bathrooms last), endless patterns and traditions undefined until they disappear." *Generation Ex*, 90.

35. Marquardt, *Between Two Worlds*, 21. Marquardt continues, "There is still another reason why our parents' divorce made them seem like polar opposites to us. Divorce, like marriage, can be seen as an institution. Our parents were related to one another not through a structure that emphasized their unity—marriage—but rather through one that emphasized their difference and opposition: divorce. Unlike the banner of marriage announcing their unity to the world, the banner of divorce announced to everyone, including us, that the differences between them were larger than anything they might share in common. Even if they did not feel starkly opposed to one another the structure of divorce nevertheless made them seem that way to us." Ibid., 109.

36. "The divorce process further reinforces the parents' separateness. Litigation and conflict over possessions and children encourage them to define themselves in opposition to each other and to break all lingering ties, except those to the children." Ibid., 27.

37. Royko, *Voices of Children of Divorce*, 74.

38. Ibid., 196.

39. Marquardt, *Between Two Worlds*, 29 (italics mine).

40. Staal, *Love They Lost*, 50.

41. Marquardt, *Between Two Worlds*, 102.

42. Abbas, *Generation Ex*, 102.

Chapter 5 Divorce and the Image of God

1. It has to be stated, though we lack the space to delve into it, that Barth's anthropology is Christocentric. It is through the humanity of the particular person Jesus Christ that we know what it means to be human. Barth's theology works from an interesting dialectic, which at first glance seems contradictory. Barth seeks to construct his theology around the Triune God, but only to discuss what can be known of God's being through God's revealed action. Barth seeks to do theology in the location of revealed mystery. But how can he do this? How can he focus on the Trinity (which is unknown to the human agent) and yet only discuss that which God has revealed? This seeming paradox finds coherence in Barth's dogged Christocentrism. He can focus on the triune nature of God (God's being) by focusing on the fullness of God's revelation (God's act) in the concrete humanity of Jesus Christ. Jesus stands simultaneously in the mystery of being God in the second person of the Trinity and human being. Therefore, when Barth turns to anthropology, he finds nowhere else to look for what it means to be human other than in the revealed humanity of God in Jesus Christ. What it means to be human, as the Triune God constitutes humanity, can be discovered fully by giving attention to Jesus Christ, who through incarnation is in communion with both the Trinity and humanity simultaneously.

If humanity is given its being only in relationship (both relationship to God as God's creation and also through communion with human others), then, Barth contends, we must look no further than Jesus Christ for our understanding of what it means to be human. Only Jesus Christ as human being lives directly from the relational life of God and therefore is free from the distortion of sin. But in so doing Jesus lives completely for others to reconcile humanity back into relationship with God and therefore overcome sin. According to Barth, sin is the present reality of the unreal; it is that which is antithetical to the real, to being, and if being is being-with, then sin is that which destroys relationship. "The medium through which sin passes is one of broken interpersonal relations." Price, *Karl Barth's Anthropology*, 283. Sin is the actuality of broken community. If we are created to be in community, if that is what is real, then sin serves the unreal by destroying relationship.

Jesus Christ, as fully human and yet the Son of God, bears the sin of the unreal on the cross. The cross is no doubt our justification, but as such it reveals a God who bears the unreal of broken relationship so that sin as the unreal might be forever broken and so that relationship between God and humanity, and humanity to humanity, might be possible. Therefore, as Ray Anderson says, "The effects of sin are not overcome through a more rigorous form of spirituality but through a renewed . . . sociality." *The Shape of Practical Theology* (Downers Grove, IL: InterVarsity, 2001), 168. We could say that the effects of divorce on the child are not overcome primarily through epistemological perspectives, thinking rightly, or even through injections of social capital, but must be dealt with on the ontological level of relational communion.

According to Barth, Jesus Christ is the real; he is real because he has overcome the unreality of broken communion with resurrection. Thus, resurrection promises eternal community between God and God's creation as well as between human being and human being. Therefore, Jesus Christ as real is ontologically for others. As Barth states directly, "He [Jesus] cannot be at all, and therefore for God, without being for men." *Church Dogmatics*, III/2, 217. In the humanity of Jesus we see the true form of humanity as being and acting with and for others. Price states, "Because Jesus is a man for others, the human being who is abstractly considered—apart from coexistence with his or her fellow humans—is not fully human. This means that for authentic humanity, relationship to others is actual, not potential or optional. It is in relationships that the human being is essentially formed. We might say that for Barth the real self is formed only as it finds itself in others." *Karl Barth's Anthropology*, 138. And this is justified for Barth because of who Jesus Christ is.

He is (in his very being) the man for us. Therefore, Jesus shares deeply in our existence, sharing our place in the suffering of brokenness and the joy of union.

A painful result of divorce is that the primary community of mother and father can no longer share in the fullness of the child's life. There are now zones in which they seemingly cannot tread. This is not the same as respecting a child's boundaries, which exist with or without the divorce. Rather, there are places that the child invites (needs) the parent to be, but the parent cannot go, for their community as family is no longer present. The child yearns for her dad to be present at graduation, but her dad cannot attend because her mom and stepdad have already claimed this zone. This keeps Dad from being with and for his daughter as he might wish, and as she needs. The constant process of presence and withdrawal, withdrawal and then presence, is painful. This, according to Barth, is not the way of our humanity, for it is not the way of Jesus Christ. Barth states, "If the humanity of Jesus is originally and totally and genuinely fellow-humanity this means that He is man for other men in the most comprehensive and radical sense. He does not merely help His fellows from without, standing alongside, making a contribution and then withdrawing again and leaving them to themselves until further help is perhaps required." *Church Dogmatics*, III/2, 212. Rather, "Jesus helps others not from without, or even beside, but from within, taking their place." Price, *Karl Barth's Anthropology*, 130. If Jesus Christ is ontologically for others, then we as human beings are called in our humanity to be with and for others. The problem with divorce is not that it divides parents' feelings and desires to love and care for their children. The problem is that it keeps them from being with and for them, which whole and "real" community demands.

Therefore, Barth's Christocentric anthropology pushes us forward in our discussion. Through Jesus Christ we see that the *analogia relationis* rests deeply within our humanity, and that our humanity, from the view of this trinitarian/Christocentric perspective, is fundamentally act and being. We are as we act in community and, as such, are real. Divorce, as we will see below, impacts the child at the level of act and being. In the dissolution of the fundamental community, the child comes up against the unreal, for his being and acting in the world is divided. This short christological excursion has been important to set the stage and clear the way for an examination of Barth's understanding of the image of God (the *imago Dei*). This will have great implications for further understanding the phenomenon of divorce.

2. "There is no need to reject outright Aristotle's definition of anthropos as 'a rational animal,' or to repudiate those who marvel at human capacities for deeding, determining, planning, judging, changing, and so forth. However, what the equation 'being = being-with' does require of us is that we view all such capacities and endowments according to their function as attributes enabling us to become what we are intended to be: serving and representative creatures, stewards whose complicity of mental, spiritual, and volitional powers makes it possible for us, within the creation, to image the holy and suffering love of the Creator." Hall, *Imaging God*, 141.

3. "In the long history of the development of the concept of 'image of God,' the idea that it refers to a specific form of relationality is relatively new. Barth traces this development in CD, III/1 (183ff.), and builds his own proposal by supplementing the theses of Wilhelm Vischer and Dietrich Bonhoeffer, viz., that the imago Dei involves the idea of human relatedness. He explicitly argues that 'I-Thou' relationality is constitutive for divine and human being: 'the *tertium comparationis*, the analogy between God and man, is simply the existence of the I and the Thou in confrontation. This is first constitutive for God, and then for man created by God' (185)." Shults, *Reforming Theological Anthropology*, 124.

4. Price, *Karl Barth's Anthropology*, 117.

5. Grenz, *Social God and Relational Self*, 162.

6. Hall says it this way: "The image of God is something that 'happens' as a consequence of this relationship. The human creature images (used as verb) its Creator because and insofar as it is 'turned toward' God. To be imago Dei does not mean to have something but to be and do something: to image God." *Imaging God*, 98.

7. This is the very argument John Macmurray makes in *Persons in Relation* (London: Faber and Faber Limited, 1961) against the Cartesian *cogito, ergo sum* ("I think, therefore I am").

8. Jungel follows this assertion. "Humanity comes into existence as a social reality and in this corresponds to God the creator. In terms of the *concept of God*, this must mean that the God to whom humanity corresponds is no solitary God. Rather, God is himself concerned with community; his being is such that he wishes others to participate. Moreover, the consequence for our relation to God of the fact that humanity is created in the image of God as a societary being, is that our God must always be seen as also the God of others. As *my* God he is at the same time *your* God, and so is defined as *Deus pro te*, as 'God for you.'" *Theological Essays*, 136.

9. "Barth develops this view from his understanding of human freedom. Just as God's freedom expresses itself in his love, so human encounter is truly human only when it is a free reciprocal relationship. Therefore, 'Humanity lives and moves and has its being in this freedom to be oneself with the other, and oneself to be with the other.'" Price, *Karl Barth's Anthropology*, 153.

10. Bonhoeffer says this very powerfully. "To say that in humankind God creates the image of God on earth means that humankind is like the Creator in that it is free. To be sure, it is free only through God's creation, through the word of God; it is free for the worship of the Creator. For in the language of the Bible freedom is not something that people have for themselves but something they have for others. No one is free 'in herself' or 'in himself'—free as it were in a vacuum or free in the same way that a person may be musical, intelligent, or blind in herself or in himself. Freedom is not a quality a human being has; it is not an ability, a capacity, an attribute of being that may be deeply hidden in a person but can somehow be uncovered. Anyone who scrutinizes human beings in order to find freedom finds nothing of it. Why? Because freedom is not a quality that can be uncovered; it is not a possession, something to hand, an object; nor is it a form of something to hand; instead it is a relation and nothing else. To be more precise, freedom is a relation between two persons. Being free means 'being-free-for-the-other,' because I am bound to the other. Only by being in relation with the other am I free." *Creation and Fall*, 163.

11. Marquardt, *Between Two Worlds*, 173. "Aiming for a 'good divorce' might help adults feel better about their decision to divorce, or about the divorce that has been thrust upon them, but the stories of children of divorce show that it is wrong and misleading to describe our experience as 'good.'" Ibid., 171.

12. "However, when one looks at the thousands of children that my colleagues and I have interviewed at our center since 1980, most of whom were from moderately unhappy marriages that ended in divorce, one message is clear: the children do not say they are happier. Rather, they say flatly, 'The day my parents divorced is the day my childhood ended.'" Wallerstein, *Unexpected Legacy of Divorce*, 26.

13. "This 'trickle down' myth is built on the enduring fact that most adults cannot fathom the child's world view and how children think." Ibid., xxix.

14. "Children in postdivorce families do not, on the whole, look happier, healthier, or more well adjusted even if one or both parents are happier. National studies show that children from divorced and remarried families are more aggressive toward their parents and teachers. They experience more depression, have more learning difficulties, and suffer from more problems with peers than children from intact families. Children from divorced and remarried families are two to three times more likely to be referred for psychological

help at school than their peers from intact families. More of them end up in clinics and hospital settings. There is earlier sexual activity, more children born out of wedlock, less marriage, and more divorce. Numerous studies show that adult children of divorce have more psychological problems than those raised in intact marriages." Ibid., xxix. Marquardt and Glenn's findings are similar: "When Dr. Norval Glenn and I compared young adult children of divorce with their peers from intact families, we found that for children in a 'good divorce' often compares poorly even to an unhappy marriage, so long as that marriage is low-conflict (as approximately two-thirds of marriages that end in divorce are)." Marquardt, *Between Two Worlds*, 16.

15. Throughout this work I have made bold statements about the importance of biological families for their ontological correlation to children. This assertion is not made in a philosophical/theological vacuum but is supported by University of Princeton sociologist Sara McLanahan and University of Wisconsin sociologist Gary Sandefur. They state, "Children who grow up in a household with only one biological parent are worse off, on average, than children who grow up in a household with both of their biological parents, regardless of the parents' race or educational background, regardless of whether the parents are married when the child is born, and regardless of whether the resident parent remarries." *Growing Up with a Single Parent*, 1.

16. "This is nonsense. The 'happy talk' she describes, which bears no relationship to the child's actual experience, serves only to convince the child that she dare not confess to feeling pain, because the grown-ups don't want to hear of any negative feelings about their divorce or that they lack understanding. It only makes things harder for the child, who learns very quickly to keep her true feelings well concealed and to follow the program." Wallerstein, from foreword of Marquardt's *Between Two Worlds*, xvi.

17. Ibid., 117 (italics mine).

18. Wallerstein, *Unexpected Legacy of Divorce*, xxx.

19. Ibid., xxxiii.

20. Staal, *Love They Lost*, 63 (italics mine).

21. Robinson, "Normal Abnormal," 24 (italics mine).

22. Anderson provides helpful commentary: "The first human was not deficient because he lacked a wife but because he lacked a human counterpart necessary to his existence. The divine image is not grounded in a social or cultural pattern but in a core social relation." *Shape of Practical Theology*, 259.

23. Jungel also follows Barth in this assertion. "But this existence in which humanity corresponds to God is one of *co-humanity*. Without any doubt the text emphasizes the duality of human existence; hence the change between the singular and the plural in the object: God created *humanity* by creating *human persons* as male and female." *Theological Essays*, 135.

24. "The void in Adam was of a kind that none of the animals could fill. Westermann sees in this feature of the story another indication of the social character of human existence: 'Gen 2 acknowledges that people do not find the true meaning of human life in the mere fact of existence; if this were the case, then community with the animals would be enough. But people find the meaning of life only in human community; it is only this that makes true humanity.' Anticipating the end of the story, Westermann then adds, 'the human community is centered around the community of man and woman.'" Grenz, *Social God and the Relational Self*, 275–76.

25. Staal, *Love They Lost*, 51.

26. Price provides a helpful note. "The choice of the term 'object relations' seems unfortunate, since the 'object' referred to is usually a person. The American term for 'object relations' seems a bit more suited to what it describes: 'interpersonal relations theory.' But I shall stay with the British term since it is mostly British psychologists I

cite, and it serves its purpose with suitable economy of expression. 'Object' has a more technical ring to it, and since the external object can be internalized, it is perhaps best to stay with this technical-sounding term, in spite of its impersonal intonations." *Karl Barth's Anthropology*, 25n52.

27. Latini, "From Community to Communio," 249. Price: "When this is done, we arrive at the conclusion that the human psyche strives not merely for libidinal pleasure, but for object relations. In common parlance, the human soul contains an irreducible hunger for human love." *Karl Barth's Anthropology*, 226.

28. Price, *Karl Barth's Anthropology*, 227.

29. Macmurray, *Person in Relation*, 90.

30. Price provides a helpful disclaimer: "In describing male and female as our most basic form, Barth is not implying that there can be no relationships between male and male, or female and female. He means that all relationships are subsumed under the original relationship of male and female. Even in the relations of male to male and female to female, male and female is the basic structural distinction; by this Barth means that we cannot exist other than as a male or a female. But he also is pointing to a less obvious fact that in the differentiation of male and female we find a clue to the meaning of our existence: we are made to be in relation to 'the other.'" *Karl Barth's Anthropology*, 159.

31. Barth, *Church Dogmatics*, III/2, 289, 293.

32. We can see the identification and differentiation of relationship in Barth's following statement: "If I speak to him and not about him, he is neither It, He nor She, but Thou. . . . For when I say 'I' and therefore 'Thou' to someone else, I empower and invite and summon him to say 'Thou' to me in return. The declaration 'I' in what I say is the declaration of my expectation that the other being to which I declare myself in this way will respond and treat and describe and distinguish me as something like himself. When he accepts my 'I'—and in turning to him I count on it that he is able to do so—he cannot possibly regard me as an It or a mere He or She, but I am distinguished from all other objects for him as he is for me, and distinguished from and connected to me as I am from and to him." Ibid., 244–45.

33. This position is no doubt open to fierce feminist critique (or at least uneasiness), yet Ann Belford Ulanov is not ready to give it up as she states, "We must remember that Winnicott's idea of a female element of being is something that belongs to all of us. We must resist the cultural conditioning that identifies this element with maternity. It is an element of being, a feminine mode of being. It concerns being, not motherhood. We receive its establishment of being with our mothers, but that does not prescribe motherhood as the only way to live it." *Finding Space*, 81.

34. "We learn through the female element of being that being communicates itself through giving itself, sharing itself, passing itself on to us in our ordinary devotion to the humble body tasks of life." Ibid., 71–72.

35. Ibid., 73.

36. Ulanov explains that "the male element accents the separateness of I and other. The object exists more independently of us, in spite of our projections, not because of them. We may identify with the other, but we do not become the other. An I and a You exist, and we do things to and with each other and know about each other. If thwarted, this male element of being issues in frustration, even anger, which enhances the objectivity of the object." Ibid., 70.

37. Ibid., 73.

38. McLanahan and Sandefur, from their perspective as sociologists, see this very problem. "In addition to altering the relationship between fathers and children, family disruption affects the mother–child relationship. Most single mothers are forced to fill two roles simultaneously, without adequate support. . . . This can lead to inconsistent

parenting, which makes it difficult to provide the kind of discipline coupled with affection that children need." *Growing Up with a Single Parent*, 28.

39. Staal, *Love They Lost*, 72.

40. "Early sex was very common among girls in the divorced families and has been described in several national studies. In our study, one in five had her first sexual experience before the age of fourteen. Over half were sexually active with multiple partners during their high school years. In the comparison group, the great majority of girls postponed sex until the last year of high school or their early years in college. Those who engaged in sexual activity did so as part of an ongoing relationship that lasted an average of a year." Wallerstein, *Unexpected Legacy of Divorce*, 188.

41. Staal, *Love They Lost*, 147.

42. Wallerstein, *Unexpected Legacy of Divorce*, 62.

43. Ibid., 136.

44. Ulanov discusses the power of the environment and the painful scars it can leave when it fails. "Failure of environmental support at this level of being results in maiming. Clinically, I have found that communication from this level of hurt takes a long time to arrive at and then announces itself as unspeakable." *Finding Space*, 69.

45. Macmurray discusses the significance of this environment. "He is born into a love relationship which is inherently personal. Not merely his personal development, but his very survival depends upon the maintaining of this relation; he depends for his existence, that is to say, upon intelligent understanding, upon rational foresight. He cannot think for himself, yet he cannot do without thinking; so someone else must think for him. He cannot foresee his own needs and provide for them; so he must be provided for by another's foresight. He cannot do himself what is necessary to his own survival and development. It must be done for him by another who can, or he will die." Macmurray, *Persons in Relation*, 48.

46. See *Church Dogmatics*, III/2, 286.

47. Royko, *Voices of Children of Divorce*, 203.

48. Barth articulates this environment by discussing the shape of person to person interactions, discussing person to person rituals as actions. "We must see and be seen, speak and listen, because to be human we must be prepared to be there for the other, to be at his disposal. . . . There is indeed a necessary connexion at this point. If I and Thou really see each other and speak with one another and listen to one another, inevitably they mutually summon each other to action." *Church Dogmatics*, III/2, 260–61.

49. Marquardt, *Between Two Worlds*, 17.

50. Latini, "From Community to Communio," 252.

51. Marquardt, *Between Two Worlds*, 22.

52. "To outside observers, the children of divorced parents may look no different than the children of intact parents. We ran on the playground, went to school, argued with our siblings, played with blocks, drew pictures in our bedrooms. But we were also vigilant. When Mom came home we gauged her mood. When we stayed at Dad's we were often quiet and on good behavior. We paid close attention to the different rules at each parent's home and the conflicts in their expectations of us. We wondered if we looked or acted too much like our father and if that made our mother mad at us. We struggled to remember what we were not supposed to say, what secrets or information about one parent, we should not share with the other. We adjusted ourselves to each of our parents, shaping our habits and beliefs to mimic theirs when we were around them. We often felt like a different person with each of our parents." Ibid., 31.

53. Latini, "From Community to Communio," 265.

54. Anderson, *Shape of Practical Theology*, 167. Barth says, "I am not a true I and do not genuinely exist without him. I am only an empty subject if I do not escape that difficulty in relation to him." *Church Dogmatics*, III/2, 255.

55. Price, *Karl Barth's Anthropology*, 120. Price explains further: "As human beings encounter one another they create a history, not in a primary sense—only God is the Creator of history in the primary sense (Heilsgeschichte)—but in a secondary sense, what Barth calls a 'little history' (kleine Geschichte)." Ibid., 142.

56. "I thought [my grandparents'] union was the pinnacle of romantic drama, a way of embracing life in the face of death. But more than that, their story gave me a sense of my own place within the family, a small link in an unbroken chain that extended from the past into the present and beyond." Staal, *Love They Lost*, 28.

57. Ibid.

58. Robinson, "Normal Abnormal," 13.

59. Staal, *Love They Lost*, 33.

60. Marquardt, *Between Two Worlds*, 8.

61. Royko, *Voices of Children of Divorce*, 14.

62. Staal, *Love They Lost*, 60.

63. Royko, *Voices of Children of Divorce*, 196.

64. Conway, "Looking Back, Moving Forward," 187.

65. Marquardt moves in this ontological direction when she says, "While a 'good divorce' is better than a bad divorce, it is still not good. For no matter how amicable divorced parents might be and how much they each love and care for the child, their willingness to do these things does absolutely nothing to diminish the radical restructuring of the child's universe." *Between Two Worlds*, 16.

66. McLanahan and Sandefur add; "From the child's point of view, these two types of conflict (abuse versus weak commitment) are very different matters. In the latter case, the child would probably be better off if the parents resolved their differences and the family remained together, even if the long-term relationship between the parents was less than perfect." *Growing Up with a Single Parent*, 31

67. Staal, *Love They Lost*, 20.

68. Wolf Krötke puts this nicely back within God's own action and being. "Therefore, relatedness to others marks out the human creature as belonging to God. It reminds the human person that he or she is determined to be God's covenant partner. It makes the enactment of a life of co-humanity into the task of a lifetime which does not take place at some distance from God, but which, on the contrary, is itself intrinsic to our relation to God. And so, a 'humanity without the fellow-man' (CD III/2, p. 229) is a possibility ruled out by the knowledge of God." "The Humanity of the Human Person in Karl Barth's Anthropology," in *The Cambridge Companion to Karl Barth*, ed. John Webster (Cambridge, UK: Cambridge University Press), 168.

69. Krötke explains this in Barth. "What is more problematic, however, seems to be the fact that we must die. For between our birth and our death lies our life in sin by which we make death into the 'radical negation of life': 'Death means that our existence as human beings is really and finally a negation' (CD III/2, p. 625). For us death becomes 'the final evil [malum]', the 'sign of God's judgment' (CD III/2, p. 626) because it finally confirms that by our actions and omissions we have made space for the destruction of the earthly relationships in which we exist." Ibid., 171–72.

70. Loder, *Logic of the Spirit*, 224.

Chapter 6 What Is to Be Done

1. Ray Anderson explains further: "Because Christ emptied himself and thus presented himself to the world in this 'kenotic' sense, the ministry of the cure of souls also has a kenotic aspect. In taking our weaknesses on himself and in solidarity and identity with sinful humanity, Christ himself created the mandate for a kenotic presence and ministry in the world. This led Bonhoeffer to say 'it is implicit in the NT statement concerning

the incarnation of God in Christ that all men are taken up, enclosed and borne within the body of Christ and that this is just what the congregation of the faithful are to make known to the world by their words and by their lives.'" *On Being Human* (Pasadena, CA: Fuller Seminary Press, 1982), 201.

2. For instance, Don Browning et al. say the following about the church's action to strengthen families. "We recommend four strategies that local churches can use to address the reality of divorce. First, prevention is the best cure. The best prevention is extensive marital preparation. . . . The second strategy would have church-based marriage counseling begin with a humane bias toward preserving marriages as, indeed, much of secular marriage counseling is starting to do. . . . The third strategy calls for churches to love, minister to, and sustain the divorced. In spite of what churches do to discourage them, divorces will occur, although we hope they will become increasingly less common. . . . Churches should do more to address what we have called 'the male problematic.'" *From Culture Wars to Common Ground*, 318–20. By "the male problematic," Browning et al. mean the fact that many men in society seem not to be as invested, psychologically and emotionally, in raising their children.

3. Anderson drives this point deeper: "In this way, the primal act of salvation history, the incarnation and atonement, achieves the ontological foundation for all renewal and healing of persons. We do not first of all become 'believers' and then 'members of the community of Christ.' Rather, in Polanyi's words, 'our believing is conditioned at its source by our belonging.' When one asks 'who am I?' the theological significance of the question may be expressed as 'where is my place of belonging?' where is the place which promises my healing and which affirms my health as a person? Where is the 'feet of Jesus,' where I may be found, in my right mind?" *On Being Human*, 175.

4. See Barth's *Church Dogmatics*, III/2.

5. "To see the other thus means directly to let oneself be seen by him. If I do not do this, I do not see him. Conversely, as I do it, as I let him look me in the eye, I see him. . . . All seeing is inhuman in which the one who sees hides himself, refusing to be seen by the fellow-man whom he sees. The point is not unimportant that it is always two men, and therefore a real I and Thou, who look themselves in the eye and can thus see one another and be seen by one another." Barth, *Church Dogmatics*, III/2, 250.

6. "The isolation in which we try to persist, the lack of participation which we show in relation to others and thus thrust upon others in relation to ourselves, is inhumanity. The expression: 'That is no concern of mine,' or: 'That is no concern of yours,' is almost always wrong, because it almost always means that the being of this or that man is nothing to me and my being nothing to him; that I will neither see him nor let myself be seen by him; that my eyes are too good for him and that I am too good for his eyes; that my openness reaches its limit in him." Ibid., 251.

7. Ibid., 256.

8. Barth holds to something similar when he states, "Humanity as encounter must become the event of speech." Ibid., 253.

9. Hunsinger relates this nicely to the discussion of empathy in seeing and being seen, "The theological significance of mutual empathy lies in its commitment to know and be known. One cannot be known apart from one's willingness to make oneself known, apart from revealing oneself through speech. . . . Mutual self-disclosure lies at the heart of mutual empathic relationship, as each person opens up her world of meaning for the other to know. In the church, such mutual willingness depends upon the trust that each member of the body of Christ is indispensable to the whole. Each member needs the others as hand, ear, eye, or foot so that the whole body might function together as one organic whole." Deborah van Deusen Hunsinger, *Pray without Ceasing: Revitalizing Pastoral Care* (Grand Rapids: Eerdmans, 2007), 58.

10. Barth, *Church Dogmatics*, III/2, 262. "My humanity depends upon the fact that I am always aware, and my action is determined by the awareness, that I need the assistance of others as a fish needs water. It depends upon my not being content with what I can do for myself, but calling for the Thou to give me the benefit of his action as well." Ibid., 263.

11. "As is perhaps fitting, we begin with prayer. The community works, but it also prays. More precisely, it prays as it works. And in praying, it works. Prayer is not just an occasional breathing of the soul, nor is it merely an individual elevation of the heart. It is movement in which Christians jointly and persistently engage. It is absolutely indispensable in the accomplishment of the action required of the community. It cannot possibly be separated from this action." Karl Barth, *Church Dogmatics*, IV/2, 3, ed. G. W. Bromiley and T. F. Torrance, trans. G. W. Bromiley (Edinburgh: T&T Clark, 1962), 3.2, 882.

12. Barth, *Church Dogmatics*, III/2, 272.

13. Gary Gunderson, *Deeply Woven Roots: Improving the Quality of Life in Your Community* (Minneapolis: Fortress, 1997), 94.

14. Ibid., 96.

15. Barth, *Church Dogmatics*, IV/3.2, 886.

Index

95010